UNDERSTANDING ADHD

A Practical Guide for Teachers and Parents

WILLIAM N. BENDER
University of Georgia

Merrill, an imprint of
Prentice Hall
Upper Saddle River, New Jersey *Columbus, Ohio*

Library of Congress Cataloging-in-Publication Data
Understanding ADHD : a practical guide for teachers and parents/
[edited by] William N. Bender.
p. cm.
Includes bibliographical references and index.
ISBN 0-13-348731-8
1. Attention-deficit-disordered children—Education—United States.
2. Education—Parent participation—United States. I. Bender, William N.
LC4713.4.U53 1997
371.91—dc20 96-23914
CIP

Cover art: © 1994 Akeia McCamey/Columbus, Ohio/Franklin County Board of Mental Retardation and Developmental Disability
Editor: Ann Castel Davis
Production Editor: Christine M. Harrington
Photo Coordinator: Angela Jenkins
Design Coordinator: Karrie M. Converse
Text and Cover Designer: Anne Flanagan
Production Manager: Patricia A. Tonneman
Electronic Text Management: Marilyn Wilson Phelps, Matthew Williams,
Karen L. Bretz, Tracey Ward
Director of Marketing: Kevin Flanagan
Advertising/Marketing Coordinator: Julie Shough

This book was set in Zapf Calligraphic by Prentice Hall and was printed and bound by R.R. Donnelley & Sons Company. The cover was printed by Phoenix Color Corp.

Simon & Schuster/A Viacom Company
Upper Saddle River, New Jersey 07458

Photo credits: Scott Cunningham/Merrill, pp. 81, 107, 149, 183, and 227; Barbara Schwartz/Merrill, p. 1; and Anne Vega/Merrill, pp. 23, 45, and 123.

Printed in the United States of America

10 9 8 7 6 5 4 3 2

ISBN: 0-13-348731-8

Prentice-Hall International (UK) Limited, *London*
Prentice-Hall of Australia Pty. Limited, *Sydney*
Prentice-Hall of Canada, Inc., *Toronto*
Prentice-Hall Hispanoamericana, S. A., *Mexico*
Prentice-Hall of India Private Limited, *New Delhi*
Prentice-Hall of Japan, Inc., *Tokyo*
Simon & Schuster Asia Pte. Ltd., *Singapore*
Editora Prentice-Hall do Brasil, Ltda., *Rio de Janeiro*

Preface

HOW TO USE THIS BOOK

Students with attention-deficit hyperactive disorder (ADHD) can present an array of personal and academic problems, but they can also be a joy, a challenge, and a pleasure to teach. Numerous parents and teachers today seem to be at wit's end dealing with the vast array of problem behaviors that many of these students demonstrate. However, if the impulsivity and attention span problems associated with this disability can be managed effectively, these students can become an asset to the classroom and home environment.

There is a silver lining within the cloud of ADHD. Both at home and in the classroom, students with ADHD will often present novel and quite unusual solutions to problems and issues. These solutions may not always be effective, but they will usually be highly creative and, invariably, interesting. Personally, I have met numerous highly creative persons with ADHD, including students who have also been served in programs for the gifted. Of course, attention problems, impulsivity, and sometimes conduct disorders must be managed for students with this disability to succeed, but students with ADHD will represent an important addition to your class or household.

This book is intended as a practical guide to assist you in managing children or students with ADHD and facilitating their success to discover their uniqueness and creative potential. Specific strategies and techniques in a wide number of areas are presented that will facilitate learning for individuals with ADHD in both the home and the school environment. Specifically, we present lists of suggestions for dealing with particular problems—

suggestions such as behavioral contracts for the home or classroom, self-monitoring strategies, and homework checklists. Some strategies are presented in several chapters to demonstrate applications in classrooms at various ages, as well as in the home. You should feel free to modify these strategies and adapt them for your situation, as needed. This set of specific techniques, and the detailed instructions and examples associated with each, should prepare you to deal with even the most complicated manifestations of ADHD.

Chapters 1, 2, 3, 4, and 5 present background information and management approaches for students with ADHD, with a particular emphasis on the most current available knowledge. Chapter 1 presents an overview of ADHD and a personal example of how one student with ADHD felt as he progressed through school. This experiential perspective provides important insights for every parent and teacher. Chapter 2 includes a fairly involved medical emphasis and may be somewhat difficult for the nonmedical practitioner to follow. However, all the chapters in this text may be read independently of the others, and the reader is encouraged to skip around to the topics of his or her choice.

Chapter 3 summarizes our current understandings related to the emotional and social aspects of this disorder. This is important information for both the parent and the teacher in dealing with students with ADHD. Chapter 4 delineates the assessment procedures typically used for students with ADHD across the age span. Parents and teachers should become fluent in their understanding of these assessment issues. Chapter 5 describes the issues associated with medical interventions that must be team managed. Team management by parents, teachers, medical practitioners, and, if possible, students, offers the best chance for effective medical management.

Chapters 6, 7, 8, and 9 present specific instructions for teaching the child or adolescent with ADHD in the home and/or school environment. These chapters concentrate on detailed instructional techniques beginning in the preschool years and continuing across the age span. Chapter 6 describes the interplay between the parents of preschool children with ADHD and the preschool programs. Chapter 7 describes in detail an array of strategies that would be appropriate for elementary settings and middle school, and Chapter 8 delineates strategies for the secondary school level. Of course, teachers and parents are encouraged to utilize these strategies wherever they can do some good; teachers, regardless of their grade placement, are encouraged to read these chapters together to acquire a number of effective strategy ideas. Chapter 9 deals with a host of issues concerning the adult with ADHD. Perhaps more than any other chapter, this section of the text must be viewed as tentative, since study of adults with ADHD began only recently. However, various effective strategies are described, as well as areas of special concern for the adult with ADHD. Understanding these issues can help both the caregiver and the person with ADHD.

I sincerely hope that this practically focused book will be a treasure of ideas for parents and teachers. While many of the approaches discussed are not particularly new or novel, each strategy recommended in this text has been used with students with ADHD with some degree of success, and I have tried to provide enough detail so that you can implement these ideas in your own situation.

I would also like to invite parents and teachers to send additional suggestions to me and communicate with me directly about other ideas. Without promising a written response, I do try to respond to as many of these letters as I can, and I am always looking for good strategy ideas for this group of kids. Best of luck in the challenging endeavor of teaching children with ADHD.

William N. Bender
Department of Special Education
University of Georgia
Athens, Georgia 30602

ACKNOWLEDGMENTS

I would like to thank the following reviewers for their helpful comments and suggestions: David W. Anderson, Bethel College; Sandra Cohen, University of Virginia; John Dodd, Montana State University, Billings; Mary Jensen, Western Illinois University; Kathleen Tomaino Knops, College of DuPage; and Martha Meyer, Butler University.

Contents

CHAPTER 1

ADHD at Home and in the Classroom

William N. Bender, Ph.D.
University of Georgia

In the field of education there is probably no single construct as misunderstood as that of attention-deficit/hyperactive disorder (ADHD). For the last decade, this relatively new concern has generated confusion among educators, as well as the public, and constant modification of the definition of *ADHD* simply adds to this confusion. Practical information on ADHD is in demand. Teachers, parents, and children all have good reason to be highly motivated to learn about the disorder.

School psychologists receive very little training on assessment of ADHD, and even less training on the classroom-based interventions for it. Teachers view this new term with relative discomfort, fully aware that they heard it first from a TV news show and not in their recertification courses. Frequently, parents know more about this disorder than do teachers. Perhaps the most motivated of any group to learn about this phenomenon, parents find that the disorder, if present in one of their children, may disrupt the entire social family structure (Baker, 1994). Further, new information that parents receive is often confusing, and sometimes directly conflicting, with other information.

Finally, the affected children themselves seem to be the most confused of all. They realize that they are trying in both their home and in their academic endeavors, and yet they feel that they never seem to get the rewards associated with that effort. However, one simple focus can assist in understanding ADHD; the children must be the single focus for educators and parents wading through the morass of information on ADHD. In any new field, one is wise to stay focused on the issue at hand, and in this area, the primary focus must be how to assist children and youth with this disorder.

THE EXPERIENCE OF ADHD

Perhaps the most effective way to remain focused on students with ADHD is to try to understand this phenomenon through the eyes of a child. This chapter includes the personal story of Alan Brown, a young man who was diagnosed with ADHD as a child. Alan's story is a good example of what it's like to be a child with ADHD. (Alan's insights were originally published in *Attention,* a magazine published by an advocacy group called CH.A.D.D., Children and Adults with Attention Deficit Disorders; for membership opportunities, contact CH.A.D.D., 499 NW 70th Avenue, Plantation, FL, 33317, 305-587-3700.)

Alan's Early Years in School

I often wondered why I wasn't in group time in kindergarten. The teacher sent me in the corner to play with a toy by myself. I was singled out but I didn't know why or what it was. Toward the middle half of first grade, the teacher called my mom in for a conference. She was telling my mom, "I'm always having to call on Alan: 'Alan, be still, please. Yes, you can sharpen your pencil for the third time. You have to go to the bathroom, again?'"

That evening, my teacher educated my mom. She told my mom about Attention Deficit Disorder. My teacher suggested taking me to the doctor and letting him run some tests. Mom and I went to see the doctor. After some testing, the doctor put me on Ritalin. Within about two weeks the teacher said I was completing my homework, making good grades and feeling good about myself. Although we (my Mom and I) thought our battle was won, we had no idea what adventures were waiting for us.

Second grade went by. I was doing O.K. in school. My teacher would usually write on my report card, "Alan worked hard this six weeks. Encourage him to read at home." I hated to read; it was so hard to understand what I had read. I loved to play outside, run in the field, and ride on my bicycle. A free spirit.

By the time I got to third grade, things were getting off track. I felt like nothing I did was right. I would try to do good work. My teacher would write on my papers: "Needs to concentrate more on answers; Needs to turn in all work; Needs to follow directions."

I really didn't think my teacher liked me. She was very stern, never seemed to smile and was always watching me.

Fourth grade was the year everything fell apart! Before school started my mom took me to see the doctor, like we did every year. The doctor prescribed the same dose as I had taken the year before. He didn't want to raise my dosage unless he really had to.

The first six weeks passed and I didn't do very well, but the doctor said it might be the new school year or getting settled in and used to a new teacher. My mom told the teacher the doctor was considering raising my Ritalin dosage. The teacher said something had to be done because my grades were low. I wasn't always prepared for class, was slow getting my books out, and always needed to go to my locker because I had forgotten something. My doctor did raise my medication to one pill in morning and one pill at lunch. Everyone in the room would say, "Dummy has to go take his pill."

My teacher wanted to make me concentrate better, so one day she put my desk in the far corner, separated from the rest of the class. A few days passed. I still wasn't finishing my work on time, but I was trying to do the work correctly. The teacher didn't care; it wasn't finished. She then put a refrigerator box around my desk so I couldn't see anyone in class. I could hear as other kids in class would make fun of me. It really hurt; I was ashamed of myself and mad at my teacher. I couldn't tell my mom, because I might get in trouble.

I hated school, didn't like my teacher and started not liking myself. Imagine a nine year old going through this day after day. It was hard to face the next day. A week passed, and I poked holes in the cardboard, so I could see who was making fun of me. I started peeping through the holes, making the other kids laugh. The teacher would get so annoyed. So I became the class clown. I was expelled for two days. When my mom found out what was going on, boy, did she get angry.

She was mad that the teacher would do this and mad that the principal allowed it, and no one could see what this was doing to me. Mom called my doctor, explained what was going on, asked him to recommend a specialist. We needed some help! I remember my mom cried over the phone. It scared me. I thought I was really in trouble, but instead, she put me in her lap, kissed my cheek, gave me a hug and said, "You're special to me, and I love you. Together we are going to get through this." It made me feel good because Moms can always fix everything.

This personal story is quite revealing on a number of issues. First, note the depth of the emotional injury that ADHD can inflict on a child, even when the condition is acknowledged and treated. This child was known to have some type of problem as early as the first grade, and both Alan and his mom assumed that with the prescribed medication the problem would be alleviated. Quite often this type of assumption later proves to be incorrect.

Perhaps one of the most telling aspects of work in the ADHD area is the emotional overlay that this disability brings with it. This is recognizable on the part of the children—who feel that they have been cruelly treated—and on the part of parents, who get angry, perhaps justifiably, when they see that the routines of schoolwork constantly injure their children. Indeed, the entire field of ADHD is overburdened to some degree with this emotional intensity. Even though the reasons for such intensity are quite understandable, it often clouds the issue and may not assist in providing services to children who need help.

Alan's embarrassment when taking his medication and when being separated from the other children is also quite telling for both teachers and parents. Whereas some separation to reduce distractions may be appropriate for some children, causing embarrassment is never appropriate. The teacher must always consider how each individual child may respond to particular approaches.

Next, note the constellation of characteristics that this brief remembrance exemplifies. In the early grades, the teacher noted that Alan could not be still. In the elementary years he had problems following directions and concentrating. He demonstrated organizational difficulties (such as with getting his homework done and turned in) and often left material at home. Such behavioral problems could indicate a wide variety of disorders, or these problems could indicate merely that a particular student is not attempting to complete assignments. Still, these problems might be indicative of ADHD. Of course in any event, this constellation of behaviors clearly does not facilitate an effective environment for academic success.

Finally, note that as early as the lower grades, Alan knew he was different and began to not like himself. This is an overwhelming emotional burden for any child to bear. Alan did, however, begin to develop coping strategies. It is not uncommon for students to act as the class clown when academic deficits begin to mount and become embarrassing; apparently this was Alan's strategy. Although this strategy can be very destructive of academic potential over the long run, many students adopt it because it does reduce the embarrassment associated with ADHD during the short term.

Alan's middle school years are even more revealing.

Alan's Middle School Years

Fifth grade came along. It was great! I had the best teacher; she smiled a lot and was flexible yet had a structured day planned. One day I remember she asked me to go to the closet and get the book *Charlotte's Web.* I went to the closet and found the most wonderful book, *King of the Wind.* A story about a horse. I hid the book *Charlotte's Web,* and told the teacher I couldn't find it but that this horse book was there and I really liked horses. All along the teacher knew those books were in that closet. She thought if *King of the Wind* looked that interesting to me, maybe it would be worth doing instead of *Charlotte's Web.* After reading the book, I wrote a report about the story. The teacher was so impressed. She posted the book report in front of the class and made a comment on my report card. I was so proud, proud of myself. I was on track again; life was great. My parents were going to be so proud.

Sixth grade came, and I did fairly well. I had to change classes. It was hard to adjust to better organization skills. I color-coded folders for classes and kept a schedule of where and when classes were.

Seventh grade was a little rocky, but I made it. There were more students. I kind of got lost in the shuffle. By eighth grade it was a struggle every day. More peer pressure to fit in, and I was going through a lot of changes—puberty.

I would find myself daydreaming a lot, wanting to be with my grandfather. In the summer I got to spend a lot of time with him. Grandfather owned his own business, and taught me a lot. Learning was fun that way. It was hands-on learning. Anyway, that year my report card read, "Needs to finish work. Didn't turn in all papers. Needs to show more effort." I dreaded every day. Sometimes I even cried when I was by myself. How could I get these people to understand me? I went into automatic shut-off; everything seemed negative with school.

Once again, the heavy negative emotional aspect of this disorder is apparent. This child has been injured, and he does not enjoy going to school. He may rebel against school quite overtly. More serious defiance and other conduct problems often begin during these years, and schools may respond by placing the child in a class for students with behavioral disorders or emotional problems; suspension and/or expulsion may also result.

Organizational problems become evident in the middle school years, and these problems also tend to affect academic progress negatively. Of course, some teachers seem to understand the various aspects of this condition and assist students to more effectively cope with it, whereas others do not. Recall the example of the teacher who allowed Alan to read what he wanted to and then posted his book report; it was a small action on the part of the teacher, but Alan will remember that success for the rest of his life. Still, even with effective assistance from parents and teachers, students with ADHD will demonstrate some problems, which may become more involved as a student moves into secondary school.

Alan's High School Experiences

High School! What a big step! I was growing up. More things were going to be expected of me. I wanted to fit in and not be a jerk or dork. My parents warned me about wrong crowds and told me high school grades were really important to my future. What pressure! My mom talked to the guidance counselor about my having ADD. The counselor assured her I would do just fine.

I was really nervous the first day, but guess what. All freshmen are. The first six weeks went by. Not all of my teachers had taken the time to read my school records. They didn't realize I had ADD. Boy, did things get out of hand.

Later that year, when mom went in for a conference one of my teachers said, "I would never have guessed Alan was ADD." Mom looked surprised. The teacher said, "He dresses so nice, has a clean hair-cut and shows respect for teachers. He doesn't get into trouble." Mom rolled her eyes but didn't say anything until we got into the car. "Alan, that teacher doesn't understand about ADD. Anyone can get it. It's not a shame to have ADD. At least we know what we are dealing with. Remember, build on your strengths rather than magnify your weaknesses. Ignore that teacher's comment. She needs to be better educated in this field. School isn't just for ABC's anymore!"

I wanted to belong. I acted tough, even started to tell lies. I told stories that made me look big in people's eyes, but everyone knew they were lies. It just made things worse. In high school you are with a lot of people everyday. You meet lots of teachers. Some teachers are there just to earn a paycheck, and there are a few who really care about the students they have. I had such a teacher. She took time for me . . . time to try to understand me better. When I needed someone to stand up for me, this teacher did.

Once, a teacher asked everyone to write a story as if they were in a make-believe world. She asked me about my ideas. I replied, "I deal in the real world." This really puzzled the teacher. I am fifteen now and I have to deal in the real world. Dreaming is nice. Being an ADD student takes all my energy to meet the goals I have set for myself.

Through my years in school so far, I've been through a lot. My mom says I have a good heart; I care about those in need. I am not dumb. You can't always measure smartness by tests. I feel I'm doing better in school. The School Psychologist has become an important tool for me. I can talk to him when I get a teacher who doesn't understand, if I disagree with something or if I'm just having problems. It helps to talk to someone who understands. What I am trying to say is NO MATTER WHAT COMES MY WAY I CAN SURVIVE.

Clearly, the types of problems that Alan experienced during the first eight years of school have not abated, and he is still experiencing difficulties. The problems with organizing work, getting homework done in a timely fashion, and turning it in are debilitating problems for many secondary students with ADHD.

Perhaps more important is the social discomfort that many students with ADHD feel in their peer relationships. Such relationships become progressively more important during the adolescent years, and difficulties that lead to restrictions in social life may seem quite daunting to the adolescent with ADHD. While disturbed peer relationships are not characteristic of every secondary student with ADHD, many of these students demonstrate such problems to some degree (DuPaul & Stoner, 1994).

The resolute affirmation at the end of this story is also characteristic of many students with ADHD. In many ways, these students become very effective at devising survival and coping strategies (we will return to this point in later chapters). This affirmation of a desire to succeed—which is quite common—can also be uplifting. When working with older students with ADHD, one can become impressed with the inner strength and determination that many of these students display. For many of us in the teaching field, finding something to admire about a particular student can be the single factor that makes us take the extra time some students need. We are quite indebted to Alan for sharing both his academic problems and his quiet resolve with us.

Focused on the student, we now begin to ask questions. What is ADHD? What knowledge of etiology, assessment, and interventions do teachers and parents need? How can we, as educators and parents, better facilitate these students' academic and social development? How can we approach the growing body of information available on ADHD, contemplate its meaning, and still remain focused on assisting Alan and other students like him? Answering these questions is our task and challenge.

THE DEFINITION AND REALITY OF ADHD

The Current Definition

Attention-deficit/hyperactive disorder is a set of behavioral symptoms that can be highly disruptive to both the normal home life and the classroom endeavors of a child. These behaviors typically include impulsive participation (which may not be situation appropriate), an inability to attend to task, and overactivity (i.e., making repetitive and inappropriate physical movements). There is considerable debate about specifically what these behaviors are, their causes, and even the utility of the diagnosis based on these behaviors (Maag & Reid, 1994). However, it is clear that many children manifest a similar constellation of inappropriate and maladaptive behaviors, which are presumed to be based on some type of central nervous system abnormality (Maag & Reid, 1994). To be successful, these students require a considerable amount of assistance in both the school and home environments.

The most recent and widely accepted psychiatric definition of ADHD is from the *Diagnostic and Statistical Manual of Mental Disorders* (4th ed.; DSM-IV) (American Psychiatric Association [APA], 1994). The diagnostic criteria for ADHD as published in DSM-IV are presented in Figure 1–1. The definition stipulates several behaviors associated with this disorder, including those mentioned previously—impulsivity, hyperactivity, and inattentiveness—though specific manifestations of these symptomatic behaviors vary widely from child to child.

For a diagnosis to take place based on the indicators mentioned, the child must have demonstrated six or more of the behavioral criteria for either inattention or hyperactivity-impulsivity, and those behaviors must have persisted for at least six months in more than one setting (APA, 1994). Also, some of the symptoms must have been present in the child's life before the age of seven years.

The distinction drawn by some researchers between ADHD and ADD (attention-deficit disorder) is not utilized in this text. We use the omnibus term of *ADHD* to refer to students either with or without hyperactivity, as DSM-IV uses this term and then differentiates between several subtypes of ADHD, as explained later. A more complete description of the subtypes and of the development of this definition is found in Chapter 4.

The ADHD Behavioral Syndrome

As stipulated in the definition, ADHD is a condition characterized by excessive levels of motor activity, impulsivity, and/or inappropriate levels of attention (Barkley, 1990; Maag & Reid, 1994). Most children who have been diagnosed with ADHD demonstrate these three inappropriate behaviors to some degree (APA, 1994), yet some demonstrate only one or

Inattentive Type

- Often fails to give close attention to details or makes careless mistakes in schoolwork or other activities
- Often has difficulty sustaining attention in tasks or play activities
- Often does not seem to listen when spoken to directly
- Often does not follow through on instructions and fails to finish schoolwork, chores, or duties in the workplace (not because of oppositional behavior or failure to understand instructions)
- Often has difficulty organizing tasks and activities
- Often avoids, dislikes, or is reluctant to engage in tasks that require sustained mental effort (such as schoolwork and homework)
- Often loses things necessary for tasks and activities (e.g., toys, school assignments, pencils, books, tools)
- Often is easily distracted by extraneous stimuli
- Often is forgetful in daily activities

Hyperactive-Impulsive Type

Hyperactivity

- Often fidgets with hands or feet or squirms in seat
- Often leaves seat in classroom or in other situations in which remaining seated is expected
- Often runs about or climbs excessively in situations in which such behavior is inappropriate (in adolescents or adults, may be limited to feelings of restlessness)
- Often has difficulty playing or engaging in leisure activities quietly
- Often is "on the go" or often acts as if "driven by a motor"
- Often talks excessively

Impulsivity

- Often blurts out answers before questions have been completed
- Often has difficulty awaiting turn
- Often interrupts or intrudes on others (e.g. "butts into" conversations and games)

FIGURE 1–1

Diagnostic Criteria for ADHD

American Psychiatric Association: *Diagnostic and Statistical Manual of Mental Disorders, Fourth Edition.* Washington, DC, American Psychiatric Association, 1994.

two manifestations of this disorder (Maag & Reid, 1994). For example, hyperactive students may physically move so frequently that they have very little opportunity to learn the material that the teacher is covering, and yet they do not manifest inattention problems when they remain in their seat. Alternatively, students for whom an inability to attend is the primary symptom may be viewed as much better behaved than a hyperactive child (i.e., they don't disrupt others in the class with extraneous movements as often), but at test time they may demonstrate little or no comprehension of the material covered.

Because of these differences in manifestation, DSM-IV identifies several subtypes of ADHD. These include inattentive type, hyperactive-impulsive type, and combined type. Children with merely inattentive behavior problems would be classified as ADHD—inattentive, those with impulsive and hyperactive behaviors would be classified as ADHD—hyperactive-impulsive, and children who demonstrate the entire range of symptomatic behaviors would be identified as ADHD—combined type. The rationale and development of these three subtypes are discussed in more detail in Chapter 4.

Specific behavioral problems that an affected child demonstrates may also change over time, although ADHD tends to be a lifelong disorder. That is, some children may outgrow one or two specific symptoms (e.g., hyperactivity), but other aspects of the disorder tend to continue (e.g., impulse control problems, lack of organizational skills). Moreover, other symptoms (e.g., aggression, disturbed peer relationships, conduct disorders) may develop later. Recall that Alan Brown began to tell lies and became the class clown (i.e., he developed conduct disorders) as a coping strategy during his later school years. In short, the symptoms associated with the disorder may change over time, but that does not mean the disorder has disappeared.

These changing symptoms hold implications for the coping skills of the student with ADHD. A child may develop specific coping skills for one symptom of this disorder during grade three, but by grade seven the disorder may manifest in a different way, which in turn will require different coping skills on the part of the growing child. For Alan, during some years in school things seemed to go well, and during other years things seemed to fall apart. Unfortunately, with the changing manifestation of different symptoms, this up-and-down nature seems to be characteristic for most students with ADHD.

Figure 1–2 identifies several specific manifestations of the general behavior problems associated with ADHD, based on descriptions heard from parents, teachers, and children's peers. To gain a conceptual understanding of ADHD, you may wish to review these examples and compare them with the problems encountered by Alan Brown.

As Described by Teachers

- "I never know what to expect from him!"
- "He doesn't sit still!"
- "She can't seem to concentrate."
- "He doesn't turn his papers in, even when he has them."
- "He can't stay focused on the discussion."
- "She interrupts with irrelevancies in the class."
- "He is like a cyclone; when he comes in, everything is disrupted."
- "Why can't she follow directions like the other children?"
- "Sometimes I wonder how the other students concentrate at all when I am constantly having to call on him to be still."

As Described by Peers and Classmates

- "She's just dumb."
- "He can't even do the work on the board."
- "She's mean. She doesn't understand when she hurts other people's feelings."
- "Why do I have to be a field trip buddy with him?"
- "He never gets his work done."
- "I don't want her on my team."
- "Why does he have to be in our group for the project?"
- "He never tries to get his homework in."
- "Can't we choose someone else?"

As Described by Parents

- "Why can't she get up, get dressed, and get to the breakfast table without a fuss or constant reminding, like my other two kids?"
- "What is it with this kid?"
- "How can he lose one of every pair of shoes we buy?"
- "Whose turn is it to help Jamie get out of bed?"
- "How does all the extra time she requires affect our other kids? Is this fair to them?"
- "I never know with this one. Sometimes it is so draining working with him."

FIGURE 1–2
Common Descriptions of Students with ADHD

Academic Impact of ADHD

Given the behavioral problems that make up the core diagnosis of ADHD, it is not surprising that students with this disorder often demonstrate significant educational problems (Bender & Mathes, 1994). Deficits have been shown in written expression (Resta & Eliot, 1994), listening skills (Forster & Doyle, 1989), impulse control (Korkman & Pesonen, 1994), social functioning (Wheeler & Carlson, 1994), reading (Fergusson & Horwood, 1992; Rowe & Rowe, 1992), and general academic achievement (APA, 1994). These academic deficits will often require significant educational interventions beyond what is required by children without ADHD.

Later chapters in this text recommend a host of educational interventions identified as effective in working with students with ADHD; parents and teachers should become familiar with these options. While no single educational treatment (or medical treatment, for that matter) will alleviate all the problems associated with ADHD, the better prepared that teachers and parents are in using a wide array of effective strategies, the more likely they will be successful in working with ADHD students.

Associated Behavioral Problems

Many children who demonstrate the primary behaviors associated with ADHD also demonstrate other overt behavioral problems. Szatmari, Offord, and Boyle (1989) indicated that as many as 44% of students with ADHD demonstrate some type of related disorder. These related behavioral problems may include conduct disorders, oppositional-defiant behavior, learning disabilities, aggression, and/or other problems (DuPaul & Stoner, 1994; Fletcher, Shaywitz, & Shaywitz, 1994). As one example, Barkley, DuPaul, and McMurray (1990) indicated that 65% of teenagers with ADHD also demonstrate significantly higher rates of oppositional-defiant behavior. Clearly, if behavior problems of this nature are manifested by a student with ADHD, significant problems often result in the school environment. These associated behavioral problems are discussed more fully later in this chapter, and strategies for these behavioral problems are described throughout later chapters.

Prevalence of ADHD

Most researchers estimate that between 3% and 5% of all children demonstrate the characteristics of ADHD to a degree that they could be so diagnosed (Barkley, 1990; APA, 1994; DuPaul & Stoner, 1994). However, estimates on the percentage of children affected with ADHD range from 1% to as high as 23% (Barkley, 1990; Shaywitz & Shaywitz, 1988). Maag and Reid

(1994) indicate that studies depending on parents', teachers', and physicians' estimates yield a lower prevalence percentage than studies done in clinic hospital and/or research settings—usually between 1% and 2%.

Male/Female Ratio

This disorder is much more frequent in males than in females. Almost all reports indicate that many more male children demonstrate ADHD than do female children (APA, 1994; DuPaul & Stoner, 1994). Proportions that range between 3:1 (male:female) and 9:1 are discussed in the literature (APA, 1994; Barkley, 1990).

Typically, the lower ratio is more characteristic of populations that are identified in schools and other community-based placements, whereas the higher ratios are found in studies that used groups of children referred to clinic settings (DuPaul & Stoner, 1994). Consequently, these higher ratios may be somewhat contaminated with other types of behavioral problems (e.g., oppositional-defiant disorders or aggression), since both school and society seem to be somewhat less tolerant of these behaviors. Because males demonstrate these behaviors more frequently, male students may be more likely to be referred to a clinic for treatment, thus resulting in the higher male-to-female ratio (Barkley, 1990; DuPaul & Stoner, 1994).

CONTROVERSIES IN ADHD

As in any new field, perspectives on ADHD vary widely, and certain controversies remain unresolved. Views range from those claiming that ADHD doesn't exist (Goodman & Poillion, 1992; Schwartz, 1995) to those estimating that 23% of all children have the disorder (Shaywitz & Shaywitz, 1988). These issues and the varying perspectives that cloud them must be addressed at the outset.

Subtyping Students with ADHD

Lively discussions are available in the professional literature on issues such as differentiating the subtypes of ADHD and conceptualizing this range of symptoms as multiple disorders (Barkley, 1990, 1995). In other words, some have suggested that ADHD is too broad a category and that placing students with attention problems in the same general group as students with hyperactivity is not consistent with the available data (Barkley, 1995). From the scientific standpoint, numerous studies do seem to indicate that students with attention problems may represent an entirely different group of students from those with impulsive and/or hyperactive types of problems (Barkley, 1990; Maag & Reid, 1994). However, other research has indicated that these problems do in fact co-occur in children more often than not (APA, 1994).

Barkley (1995, 1990) has posited that inattentive disorders and hyperactive-impulsive disorders (subtypes one and two, respectively) are different conditions. As much early research indicates, hyperactivity and impulsivity frequently co-occur in children (Achenbach & Edelbrock, 1983; Milich & Kramer, 1985), whereas inattention problems are somewhat less likely to co-occur with these other primary symptoms. Based on these and similar findings, Barkley (1995) has suggested that inattentive disorders should not be considered part of the same behavioral syndrome as hyperactive and impulsive disorders. If this proposition is supported by additional research, it will have major implications for the field of ADHD, since attention disorders would then be classified as a separate disorder, and new terminology would be required for children manifesting hyperactive-impulsive behaviors.

Moreover, Barkley (1995) suggests that neither hyperactivity nor impulsivity is the primary culprit, even among children who demonstrate these types of problems. Rather, he believes that response inhibition is the primary causal factor that leads to both behavior problems. Barkley (1995) suggests that, since poor impulse control would presumably affect all aspects of a child's behavior, the inhibitory system (based on the central nervous system) may fail to function effectively. The resulting poor impulse control could lead to impulsive answering, for example, as well as hyperactive behaviors. Barkley speculates that poor impulse control may result from some dysfunction of the neurotransmitters in the central nervous system (neurotransmitters are the chemicals upon which brain function is based). If the neurotransmitters do not effectively function to inhibit certain behaviors, then those behaviors would appear to be impulsively demonstrated. Thus, when a child thinks about getting out of his or her seat in the classroom, he or she would do so without concurrently thinking about whether it was an appropriate behavior for that particular time and setting. Consequently, poor impulsive control could lead directly to both impulsive responding and to hyperactivity. Of course, while some evidence supports this poor impulse control theory (Barkley, 1990, 1995), more evidence is needed before this position is widely adopted by the researchers in the field. (Further discussion on the interactions of neurotransmitters is found in Chapter 2.)

Comorbidity with Other Disorders

In addition to the controversies involving the relationship among the primary symptoms of ADHD (impulsivity, inattention, and hyperactivity), there is also considerable controversy concerning related disorders, such as oppositional-defiant disorders, learning disabilities, aggression, and conduct disorders (Cohen, Riccio, & Gonzalez, 1994; DuPaul & Stoner, 1994; Murphy & Hicks-Stewart, 1991). For example, Stanford and Hynd (1994) identified several areas in which the symptoms of students with ADHD—inattentive type and students with learning disabilities were quite similar, but the study also identified several differences between these groups. Fletcher et al. (1994) argued that relationships between attention problems and learning disabilities are so common that researchers should consider the two groups together in their research designs. Clearly, the co-occurrence of ADHD and learning disabilities is an issue that still needs clarification.

Bender and Wall (1994) have suggested that the growth of concern for students with attention-deficit/hyperactive disorders may, in fact, result from changes in the definition of learning disabilities, thus making these two fields intimately related. When the term *learning disability* was first formulated, it was inclusive of children with hyperactivity, impulsiveness, and inattention problems, and those children were served in special education as "children with a learning disability." During the 1960s and early 1970s, children who were impulsive, inattentive, and hyperactive were typically served as "learning disabled" if they were a few years behind their grade placement in academic achievement. However, during the last two decades, the field of special education has restricted the definition of *learning disability* to children who manifest a "significant discrepancy" between intelligence and achievement. This definitional change has taken place at the grassroots level, as state after state adopted this definition, independent of any federal mandate to do so. This resulted in excluding children from special classes unless they met these new criteria. Clearly, some children who were impulsive, inattentive, and/or hyperactive did not meet the new criteria for learning disabilities, and the parents of those children got very angry and subsequently very active in advocacy organizations such as CH.A.D.D. These parents demanded research attention and educational support services for their children.

Given that the new definition of *learning disability* did not fit these children, the application of a label from the American Psychiatric Association seemed to be most expedient (Bender & Wall, 1994). Thus, ADHD and learning disabilities seem to be quite intimately related, and each field will continue to struggle with definitional issues, which may again change this relationship. In another sense, one can only empathize with parents and students who need help when they find the doors to specialized educational assistance closed to them. Provision of some type of specialized educational services for children and youth in need must be the overriding concern.

Other disorders also co-occur with ADHD fairly frequently, and evidence has shown that for many children with ADHD these co-occurring disorders may be quite problematic (DuPaul & Stoner, 1994). Problems with overt aggression, disturbed peer relationships, and/or oppositional disorders are frequently mentioned (Cohen et al., 1994), and these problems can be quite significant in either the home or the school classroom. As parents and practitioners working with children with ADHD, we must realize that students with this disorder will, in many cases, demonstrate other types of behavioral disorders rather than merely impulsivity, hyperactivity, and inattention. Strong oppositional and defiant disorders are not uncommon, and overt aggression is found in most adolescents with ADHD (DuPaul & Stoner, 1994). Figure 1–3 presents some data (admittedly somewhat conflicting) on the probability of co-occurring disorders.

Definitions of all the conditions mentioned in Figure 1–3 may be challenged. For example, definitions of both *learning disabilities* and *conduct disorders* have been modified within recent years, and with the definitions for these conditions still up for debate the relationship between

Learning Disabilities

- Fletcher, Shaywitz, and Shaywitz (1994) indicated that 15% of students diagnosed with ADD were also diagnosed as having learning disabilities.
- Barkley, DuPaul, and McMurray (1990) indicated that 19%–26% of students with ADD could also be classified as having learning disabilities.
- Shaywitz et al. (1988) indicated that 11% of children who met criteria for ADD also met the criteria for having learning disabilities.
- DuPaul and Stoner (1994) stated that students diagnosed as having learning disabilities are seven times as likely to demonstrate ADHD than their counterparts without learning disabilities.

Oppositional-Defiant Disorder/Aggression

- Barkley, DuPaul, and McMurray (1990) demonstrated that 65% of adolescents with ADHD also show indications of oppositional-defiant disorder.
- DuPaul and Stoner (1994) indicated that oppositional-defiant disorder/aggression was the most common disorder co-occurring with ADHD.
- Barkley, DuPaul, and McMurray (1990) demonstrated that 40% of children diagnosed with ADHD demonstrate significant aggression.

FIGURE 1–3
Research Reports of Disorders Co-occurring with ADHD

these conditions and ADHD may yet change. Parents and practitioners should keep abreast of the changing relationships between these varying disabilities and not become wedded exclusively to the labels and terms that happen to be utilized by one professional or another. Rather, when you interact with various professionals, ask them to define the terms they use, and realize that other professionals may express themselves with different terminology.

School Services for Students with ADHD

For a number of years during the mid-1980s, as a result of these definitional issues, students with ADHD were denied specialized services in public schools. Parents and teachers should realize that the American Psychiatric Association (APA) classification system was not intended to serve as a classification system in public school settings. Some researchers have argued that attempts to utilize the term *ADHD* in public schools as a disability category may prove quite problematic (Reid, Maag, & Vasa, 1994). Of course, this had immediate and critical implications for parents of students with ADHD, since the exclusion of students with ADHD from the public school classifications in most states initially resulted in exclusion from the specialized services that some of these students needed.

This issue has been rectified to some degree by a written policy statement by Department of Education officials. In 1991, a memo was written to each state director of special education clarifying the manner in which students with ADHD may receive specialized educational services (Davila, Williams, & MacDonald, 1991). This memo outlined three specific placement options whereby parents of students with ADHD could expect—and indeed demand—specialized educational services for their children.

First, the student with ADHD may expect to receive services from the mainstream or general education teacher in the class. Federal statute (the Rehabilitation Act of 1973, Section 504, sometimes referred to as "the 504 provision" or "the 504 plan" for educational services) stipulates that discrimination against individuals with any form of disability is prohibited and that reasonable accommodations must be made for such individuals. This provision empowered parents to expect a reasonable attempt on the part of the general education teacher to meet the needs of the child within the regular classroom, including provision of necessary "supplementary aids and services" (Davila et al., 1991). It also empowered parents to describe the accommodations that may be needed in the regular education class for their child to succeed and to expect the teacher to meet those needs.

Next, students with ADHD may receive specialized services by virtue of a disability diagnosis if they meet the additional qualifications that states have stipulated for identification as having learning disabilities and/or emotional/behavioral disorders. In other words, if students meet the classification guidelines for either of these disabilities, they could receive specialized education services, by virtue of being identified either as learning disabilities or emotional/behavioral disorders.

Finally, the third option involves the classification of "other health impairment" within the special education legislation. Clearly, because the APA recognizes ADHD as a disorder, affected children and youth who manifest this health impairment may qualify for special education services as "other health impaired."

In addition to this policy statement, the Americans with Disabilities Act (ADA) provides various protections to students with disabilities, including students with ADHD (Aronofsky, 1992). Specifically, both public and private schools must make reasonable modifications in policies, practices, or procedures, including the offer of auxiliary aids and services where such modifications are necessary to meet the needs of the individual, unless those modifications would fundamentally alter school activities (Aronofsky, 1992). Clearly, the net effect of the policy memo and the ADA is to empower parents and students with ADHD to expect reasonable accommodations in the educational environment.

SUMMARY

This chapter has presented basic information currently available on ADHD. While there are many unresolved questions, research has already provided a number of answers to questions posed amid the growing concern for ADHD. Figure 1–4 summarizes the information on ADHD that seems most generally accepted by most researchers in the field.

This chapter has also highlighted several controversies regarding ADHD. Questions on such issues as the appropriate subtypes of this disorder and the relationships between this and other, similar disorders will remain unresolved for the present.

As a parent or practitioner in the field, these issues will probably not affect you a great deal. Rather, your concerns will be much more practical, such as understanding the medical basis for ADHD and the medications used (covered in Chapters 2 and 5, respectively); understanding the assessment practices used with your students and your role in them (Chapter 4); and seeking practical strategies for use at home and in the classroom (Chapters 3, 6, 7, and 8). This text is designed such that chapters can, for the most part, stand alone; parents and teachers may skip around as their needs indicate.

- ADHD is defined by DSM-IV (APA, 1994) as consisting of three subtypes: ADHD—inattentive type, ADHD—hyperactive-impulsive type, and ADHD—combined type.
- Disagreements exist on what percentage of children demonstrate this disorder; the best estimate is that approximately 3%–5% of school-age children have ADHD.
- Males outnumber females with this disorder by at least three to one.
- ADHD frequently overlaps with other disorders, most commonly with oppositional-defiant disorder and aggression but also with learning disabilities and disturbed peer relationships.
- Forty-four percent of persons with ADHD will manifest some other type of disorder.
- ADHD is much more common in relatives of someone with ADHD than in the general population (APA, 1994).
- ADHD may have a very significant negative impact upon the affected child's emotional development. Hating school and having few friends is not uncommon in children with ADHD.
- ADHD often has a significant negative impact upon success both in the home and school environments.

FIGURE 1–4
Fact Sheet on ADHD

REFERENCES

Achenbach, T. M., & Edelbrock, C. S. (1983). *Manual for the child behavior checklist and revised child behavior profile.* Burlington: University of Vermont, Department of Psychiatry.

American Psychiatric Association. (1994). *Diagnostic and statistical manual of mental disorders* (4th ed.). Washington, DC: Author.

Aronofsky, D. (1992). ADD: A brief summary of school district legal obligations and children's educational rights. In M. Fowler (Ed.), *CH.A.D.D. educators' manual: An in-depth look at attention deficit disorders from an educational perspective.* Fairfax, VA: CASET Associates.

Baker, D. B. (1994). Parenting stress and ADHD: A comparison of mothers and fathers. *Journal of Emotional and Behavioral Disorders,* 2(1), 46–50.

Barkley, R. A. (1990). Attention deficit hyperactivity disorder: A handbook for diagnosis and treatment. New York: Guilford Press.

Barkley, R. A. (1995). *A new theory of ADHD.* Paper presented at the first International Conference on Research and Practice in Attention Deficit Disorder, Jerusalem, Israel.

Barkley, R. A., DuPaul, G. J., & McMurray, M. B. (1990). A comprehensive evaluation of attention deficit disorder with and without hyperactivity as defined by research criteria. *Journal of Consulting and Clinical Psychology, 58,* 775–789.

Bender, W. N., & Mathes, M. A. (1994). Teaching students with attention deficit hyperactivity disorder in the inclusive classroom: A hierarchical approach to strategy selection. *Intervention in School and Clinic, 30,* 226–234.

Bender, W. N., & Wall, M. E. (1994). Social-emotional development of students with learning disabilities. *Learning Disabilities Quarterly, 17,* 323–341.

Brown, A. (1994). ADD through the eyes of a child. *Attention!, 1*(3), 32–38.

Cohen, M. J., Riccio, C. A., & Gonzalez, J. J. (1994). Methodological differences in the diagnosis of attention-deficit hyperactivity disorder: Impact on prevalence. *Journal of Emotional and Behavioral Disorders, 2*(1), 31–38.

Davila, R. R., Williams, M. L., & MacDonald, J. T. (1991, September 16). Clarification of policy to address the needs of children with attention deficit disorders within general and/or special education. Unpublished letter to chief state school officers, U.S. Department of Education.

DuPaul, G. J., & Stoner, G. (1994). *ADHD in the schools: Assessment and intervention strategies.* New York: Guilford Press.

Fergusson, D. M., & Horwood, L. J. (1992). Attention deficit and reading achievement. *Journal of Child Psychology and Psychiatry, 33,* 375–385.

Fletcher, J. M, Shaywitz, B. A., & Shaywitz, S. E. (1994). Attention as a process and as a disorder. In G. R. Lyon (Ed.), *Frames of reference for the assessment of learning disabilities: New views on measurement issues.* Baltimore: Paul H. Brooks.

Forster, P., & Doyle, B. A. (1989). Teaching listening skills to students with attention deficit disorders. *Teaching Exceptional Children, 21*(2), 20–23.

Goodman, G., & Poillion, M. J. (1992). ADD: Acronym for any dysfunction or difficulty. *Journal of Special Education, 26,* 37–56.

Korkman, M., & Pesonen, A. E. (1994). A comparison of neuropsychological test profiles of children with attention deficit-hyperactivity disorder and/or learning disorder. *Journal of Learning Disabilities, 27*(6), 383–392.

Maag, J. W., & Reid, R. (1994). Attention-deficit hyperactivity disorder: A functional approach to assessment and treatment. *Behavioral Disorders, 20*(1), 5–23.

Milich, R., & Kramer, J. (1985). Reflections on impulsivity: An empirical investigation of impulsivity as a construct. In K. D. Gadow & I. Bialer (Eds.), *Advances in learning and behavioral disabilities* (Vol. 3). Greenwich, CT: JAI Press.

Murphy, V., & Hicks-Stewart, K. (1991). Learning disabilities and attention deficit-hyperactivity disorder: An interactional perspective. *Journal of Learning Disabilities, 24*(7), 386–388.

Reid, R., Maag, J. W., & Vasa, S. F. (1994). Attention deficit hyperactivity disorder as a disability category: A critique. *Exceptional Children, 60*(3), 198–214.

Resta, S. P., & Eliot, J. (1994). Written expression in boys with attention deficit disorder. *Perceptual and Motor Skills, 79*, 1131–1138.

Rowe, K. J., & Rowe, K. S. (1992). The relationship between inattentiveness in the classroom and reading achievement (Pt. B): An explanatory study. *Journal of the American Academy of Child and Adolescent Psychiatry, 31*, 357–368.

Schwartz, L. (1995). *The myth of attention deficit disorders or potentially gifted.* Paper presented at the first International Conference on Research and Practice in Attention Deficit Disorder, Jerusalem, Israel.

Shaywitz, S. E., & Shaywitz, B. A. (1988). Attention deficit disorder: Current perspectives. In J. G. Kavanagh & T. J. Truss Jr. (Eds.), *Learning disabilities: Proceedings of the national conference* (pp. 369–523). Parkton, MD: New York Press.

Shaywitz, S. E., Escobar, M. D., Shaywitz, B. A., Fletcher, J. M., & Makush, R. (1992). Distribution and temporal stability of dyslexia in an epidemiological sample of 414 children followed longitudinally. *New England Journal of Medicine, 326*, 145–150.

Stanford, L. D., & Hynd, G. W. (1994). Congruence of behavioral symptomatology in children with ADD/H, ADD/WO, and learning disabilities. *Journal of Learning Disabilities, 27*(4), 243–253.

Szatmari, P., Offord, D. R., & Boyle, M. H. (1989). Correlates, associated impairments, and patterns of service utilization of children with attention deficit disorders: Findings from the Ontario child health study. *Journal of Child Psychology and Psychiatry, 30*, 205–217.

Wheeler, J., & Carlson, C. L. (1994). The social functioning of children with ADD with hyperactivity and ADD without hyperactivity: A comparison of their peer relations and social deficits. *Journal of Emotional and Behavioral Disorders, 1*(1), 2–12.

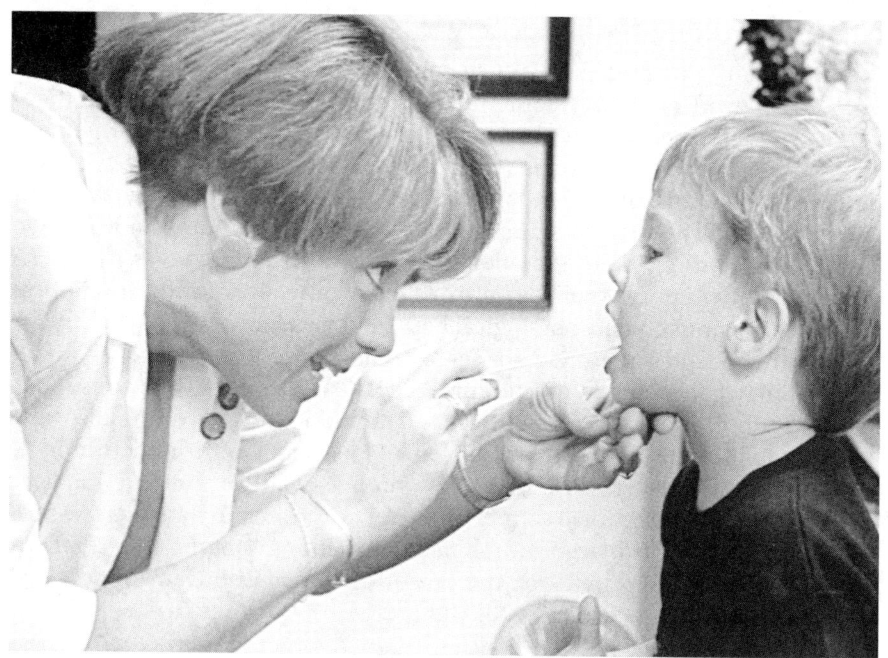

CHAPTER 2

Etiology and Neurobiology of ADHD

Cynthia A. Riccio
University of Alabama

George W. Hynd
University of Georgia
Medical College of Georgia

Morris J. Cohen
Medical College of Georgia
University of Georgia

Since the turn of the century, what is now termed ADHD has been believed to involve some form of brain dysfunction. Various theories have been investigated in an attempt to understand the etiology and nature of this particular brain dysfunction. The past two decades have witnessed an expansion of the research technology available to study ADHD; as a result, significant advances in our understanding have been made with regard to the etiology of this disorder. Changes have also occurred in the conceptualization of ADHD, as well as in the theoretical models regarding the neurobiological basis of this disorder.

In this chapter, we review research studies relating to etiological factors that may contribute to or underlie ADHD. We also review various models and supporting research regarding the neurological basis of the disorder. When feasible, the neurocognitive deficits associated with each model, along with associated research, are presented as well. Further, the implications of these findings for treatment and for future research are discussed. Particular emphasis is placed on the need to examine subtypes of ADHD to decrease the heterogeneity of the larger group of children (and, more recently, adults) diagnosed with ADHD.

ETIOLOGICAL FACTORS

Consistent with the continued conceptualization of ADHD as neurologically based, various theories regarding the etiology of differences in brain function have been postulated (Goodman & Poillion, 1992). However, most of the research findings specific to the etiology of ADHD are correlative and, as a result, cannot definitively indicate a cause–effect relationship. Further, it has become apparent that a number of differing etiologies may lead to ADHD (Barkley, 1990). We present here some of these theories and the current status of research related to them.

Genetic Factors

One of the problems with attributing cause–effect relationships based on association between specific variables is the potential impact of genetic factors underlying ADHD (Barkley, 1990). Evidence for a genetic predisposition has been found in twin studies (Cunningham & Barkley, 1978; Gilger, Pennington, & DeFries, 1992; Goodman & Stevenson, 1989; Heffron, Martin, & Welsh, 1984), as well as in family studies. Based on their findings, Goodman and Stevenson (1989) estimated that the heritability for the traits of hyperactivity is 30–50%, suggesting a significant role for genetic transmission.

Although there has been a number of methodological problems in many of the family studies (see Lahey et al., 1988), it is estimated that 20–32% of parents and siblings of children with ADHD also have the disorder (Biederman et al., 1986; Deutsch et al., 1982; Safer, 1973). More recently, studies have demonstrated that mothers, fathers, and other biological relatives of children with ADHD are significantly more likely to have a history of childhood ADHD (Biederman, Faraone, Keenan, & Tsuang, 1991; Frick, Lahey, Chrits, Loeber, & Green, 1991). Further, findings have demonstrated that family-genetic influences exist that are independent of psychosocial adversity (Biederman et al., 1992) and that the genetic transmission of ADHD is independent of the genetic transmission of learning disabilities (Faraone et al., 1993). Thus, research would suggest that in at least some cases of ADHD, the etiology is genetic/familial in nature.

Nongenetic Factors

Prenatal/Perinatal Factors

Not all cases of ADHD can be traced to a familial predisposition (Sprich-Buckminster, Biederman, Milberger, Faraone, & Lehman, 1993). Researchers have found that many factors during pregnancy and childbirth may result in decreased levels of oxygen to the brain (i.e., anoxia) and, although not resulting in identifiable brain damage per se, these prenatal and perinatal factors are correlated with the occurrence of ADHD (e.g, Barkley, DuPaul, & McMurray, 1990; Nichols & Chen, 1981). In particular, Sprich-Buckminster et al. (1993) found that the association with perinatal complications varied depending on the subgroup. Specifically, the frequency of perinatal complications was greatest for those children with ADHD who had co-occurring disorders and those for whom there was no familial history of ADHD (nonfamilial). In contrast, there were no significant differences in the frequency of perinatal complications between groups of normals, children with ADHD who had no co-occurring disorders, and children with ADHD who had a positive family history. They concluded that perinatal complications may be a factor in the nongenetic etiology of ADHD.

Food Additives/Refined Sugar

In the 1970s, one of the more popular theories about ADHD was that food additives (Feingold, 1975) and/or refined sugar (Smith, 1975) were direct causes of the disorder. Subsequent research, however, has not substantiated either of these hypotheses (see Connors, 1980; Wolraich, Milich, Stumbo, & Schultz, 1985).

Allergies and Atopic Disorders

More recently, researchers have suggested that the relatively high incidence of allergies and atopic disorders (e.g., hay fever, asthma) in children with ADHD implicates a common factor for allergies/atopic disorders and

ADHD (Roth, Beyreiss, Schlenzka, & Beyer, 1991). Allergic reactions have been reported in 20–50% of children with ADHD (e.g., Barkley, 1982; Egger, Carter, Graham, Gumby, & Soothill, 1985); however, most reports have been anecdotal and not substantiated by empirical findings. Further, results of other studies (e.g., Mitchell, Aman, Turbott, & Manku, 1987), do not support an association between ADHD and allergies or atopic sensitivity. More recently—based on parent, teacher, and self-report measures—McGee and colleagues (1993) concluded that there was no association between allergies and atopic disorders and ADHD in children (McGee, Stanton, & Sears, 1993).

Thyroid Disorder

It has been suggested that ADHD is the result of a relatively rare thyroid disorder (Hauser et al., 1993). In their study of 18 families with a history of resistance to thyroid hormone, Hauser and colleagues found that the predominant psychiatric diagnosis was ADHD and that the prevalence of ADHD was significantly higher than in families unaffected by this thyroid disorder. Others, in reviewing this study, have indicated that there is insufficient information to hypothesize a direct causal relationship between ADHD and a thyroid disorder (Alessi, Hottois, & Coates, 1993; Stein & Leventhal, 1993). In a separate study, Elia, Gulotta, Rose, Marin, and Rapoport (1994) investigated the frequency of thyroid disorder in 53 children referred for ADHD and 41 normals. Results of thyroid testing were not suggestive of a causal relationship between ADHD and a thyroid disorder. They concluded that there was no evidence to support measurement of thyroid function in nonfamilial ADHD (Elia et al., 1994).

Psychosocial Factors

Although the impact of psychosocial and environmental factors as a cause of ADHD has been investigated (Block, 1977; Willis & Lovaas, 1977), there is little, if any, evidence that ADHD is the result of social or environmental factors (Barkley, 1990). Differences have been found in the parent–child interactions of children with ADHD (e.g., Barkley, Karlsson, & Pollard, 1985). However, these differences appear to be in response to the difficulty and familial stress resulting from these children's behaviors (e.g., Barkley, Karlsson, Pollard, & Murphy, 1985; Cunningham & Barkley, 1978). Given the familial predisposition toward ADHD evident in genetic studies, it would seem plausible that parent management of these children may in some cases reflect residual effects of ADHD in the parents as well. The inability to attribute the cause of ADHD to psychosocial factors, however, does not lessen the importance of these factors in treatment.

NEUROBIOLOGICAL BASIS OF ADHD

Of the etiological theories discussed, the one for which there is the greatest evidence is that of a genetic predisposition for ADHD that is manifested within the central nervous system. Just as there have been shifts in the conceptualization of ADHD, various etiological theories, and changes in diagnostic nomenclature and criteria (see Chapter 4), research related to the neurobiological basis of ADHD has taken a variety of theoretical approaches (Hynd, Hern, Voeller, & Marshall, 1991). One of the problems facing researchers attempting to localize or identify the neurological basis of ADHD, however, is the inability to map behavioral descriptors onto relevant neurological components. In other words, until very recently this field of study labored under an inability to determine exactly which behaviors could be associated with particular areas within the brain. Further, it has been argued that presumed attentional deficits cannot be linked to specific cognitive operations nor to specific neural systems (Swanson et al., 1991). Although attention is sometimes perceived as a unitary process, several different brain structures and systems are involved in the attention process (Colby, 1991). Problems with localization of attention are complicated by the lack of operationalized criteria for ADHD and the heterogeneity of the clinical group identified as ADHD (Goodyear & Hynd, 1992; Hynd, Semrud-Clikeman, et al., 1991).

ADHD was initially conceptualized as the result of minimal brain damage. In particular, brain damage caused by infection, trauma, or complications during pregnancy or at the time of delivery have been postulated as the chief causes of ADHD (e.g., Cruickshank, Eliason, & Merrifield, 1988). Routine neurological examination of children with ADHD is generally normal, and clinical evaluation with neuroimaging (computerized tomography [CT] and magnetic resonance imaging [MRI]) and electroencephalographic (EEG) studies typically do not reveal specific lesions or abnormalities (Shaywitz, Shaywitz, Byrne, Cohen, & Rothman, 1983; Voeller, 1991). The recent expansion of technology, however, has led to adaptations in traditional imaging and electrophysiological methods. These advances have resulted in evidence of some structural/morphological differences in the brains of children with ADHD as a group (Voeller, 1991). We are witnessing the beginning of an exciting era of study in which specific brain regions and the interaction between them can be more readily understood. These efforts are summarized in Table 2–1.

The variety of attentional mechanisms can be investigated from neuroanatomical, neurochemical, and neurophysiological perspectives. The neuroanatomical approach focuses on the location of brain areas that subserve those systems thought to mediate the regulation of attention and to inhibit motor activity. The neurochemical approach addresses the role of specific neurotransmitters that facilitate communication among the neu-

TABLE 2–1
Studies of Brain Morphology and Function in ADHD

Study	Subjects	Age (years)	Method	Findings
Zambelli, Stamm, Maitinsky, and Loiselle (1977)	9 hyperactive 9 control	X = 14.04 X = 14.07	EP	Results suggested impairment both on evoked potential and behavioral measures of selective attention in the hyperactive group.
Lou, Henriksen, and Bruhn (1984)	11 ADD/H* 9 control 2 dysphasic	6–15 7–15	rCBF	Decreased blood flow (hypoperfusion) noted in all ADD subjects in the frontal lobes; 7 of 11 also demonstrated hypoperfusion in the area of the caudate.
Lou, Henriksen, Bruhn, Borner, and Nielsen (1989)	19 ADHD 9 control	6–15 7–15	rCBF	Subjects with ADHD demonstrated hypoperfusion (decreased blood flow) in the striatal regions as compared with controls; differences decreased with medication (methylphenidate).
Hynd, Semrud-Clikeman, Lorys, Novey, and Eliopulos (1990)	10 dyslexic 10 ADD/H 10 normal	X = 9.9 X = 10.0 X = 11.8	MRI	ADHD group and dyslexic group demonstrated reversed asymmetry of frontal lobes (left greater than right); ADD/H subjects had normal posterior asymmetry (left greater than right).
Zametkin et al. (1990)	25 hyperactive 10 normal	Adults Adults	PET	Differences were found on both global and regional measures of glucose (sugar) metabolism, with reduced metabolism in the hyperactive group; greatest differences found to be in the frontal area.

Study	Subjects	Age (years)	Method	Findings
Hynd, Hern, Voeller, and Marshall (1991)	7 ADHD 10 control	X = 9.08 X = 11.79	MRI	ADHD children had smaller corpus callosum, particularly in the region of the most anterior portion (genu), most posterior portion (splenium), and the area anterior to splenium.
Hynd et al. (1993)	11 ADHD 11 control	X = 11.03 X = 11.08	MRI	Of the ADHD children, 63.6% had reversed asymmetry of the caudate due to a significantly smaller left caudate as compared with controls; this finding was most notable in males.
Zametkin et al. (1993)	10 ADHD 10 normal	X = 14.5 X = 14.3	PET	Using an auditory attention task, ADHD subjects were not significantly different on global measures but demonstrated reduced glucose (sugar) metabolism in 6 of 60 regions; symptom severity was found to be correlated with reduced metabolism in the left frontal (anterior) lobe.

*Some of the ADD subjects were also dysphasic.

Notes: ADHD = attention-deficit/hyperactive disorder based on DSM-III-R(evised); ADD/H = attention-deficit disorder with hyperactivity based on DSM-III; EP = evoked potentials; rCBF = regional cerebral blood flow; MRI = magnetic resonance imaging; PET = positron emission tomography.

ronal circuits implicated in this disorder. The neurophysiological perspective attempts to explain the dynamic interaction between the neurochemical and anatomical components that together form the functional system on which the attentional process is based. Each of these areas of study has witnessed advances in recent years, and we are now beginning to develop a much more accurate portrait of brain functioning.

Neuroanatomical Basis

Typically, hypotheses relating to neuroanatomical differences emphasize the involvement of cortical structures (e.g., frontal lobes) and/or subcortical structures (e.g., brain stem reticular activating system, thalamus, hypothalamus, and basal ganglia). These are identified in Figure 2–1.

Frontal Lobe Involvement

The frontal lobes (i.e., the cortical structures at the front, or anterior, of the brain) are believed to be involved in functions of motor planning, problem solving, organizing, and executive functioning (Kolb & Whishaw, 1990). Parallels have been drawn between the behavioral symptomatology associated with known damage to the frontal lobes and symptoms of ADHD, suggesting that the most anterior portion of the frontal lobes (i.e., the prefrontal region) is involved in ADHD (Chelune, Ferguson, Koon, & Dickey, 1986; Gualtieri & Hicks, 1985; Hynd, Semrud-Clikeman, Lorys, Novey, & Eliopulos, 1990; Mattes, 1980; Voeller & Heilman, 1988). One possible explanation for the involvement of the prefrontal region is that of a delay in the development of the sheaths that cover the nerve fibers (i.e., myelination); this would affect nerve transmission in the prefrontal area (Mattes, 1980).

Support for frontal lobe involvement as a possible causal factor in ADHD comes from positron emission tomographic (PET) scan studies. These studies indicate reduced whole brain glucose or sugar utilization, particularly in the right frontal area and specifically in the area of the orbit of the eyes (i.e., the posterior-medial orbital areas; Zametkin et al., 1990). Because sugar utilization is associated with cognitive activity in that brain region, this may indicate a potential cause for ADHD; other research seems to support this lack of activity in the prefrontal region. Results of single-positron-emission-computed tomography indicate that 65% of the subjects with ADHD demonstrated prefrontal deactivation in response to an intellectual task, as compared with 5% of the patient controls (Amen, Paldi, & Thisted, 1993). On comparisons of regional cerebral blood flow in children with ADHD and control children, the children with ADHD showed decreased metabolic activity in the frontal lobes and basal ganglia (the basal ganglia is involved in regulation of movement and is connected to the frontal lobes;

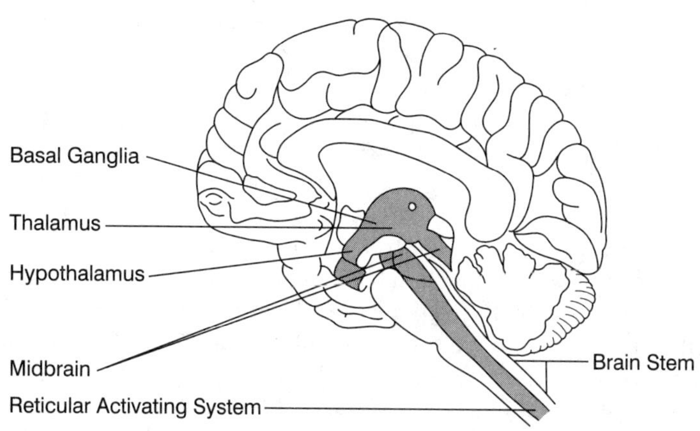

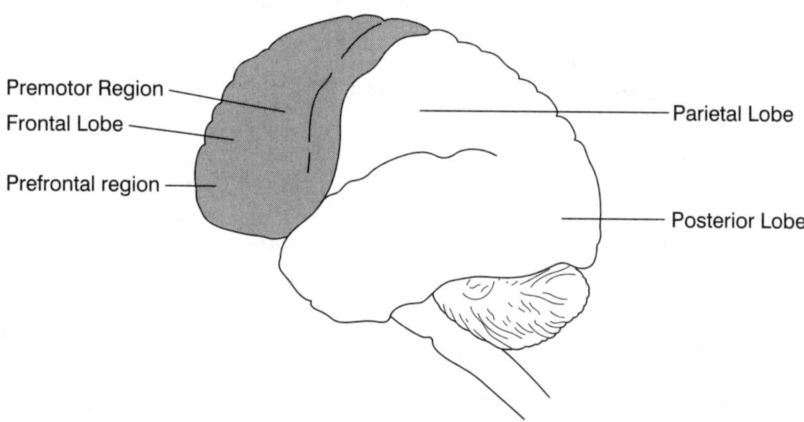

FIGURE 2–1
Neuroanatomical Structures

see Figure 2-1), with increased metabolic activity in the primary sensory and sensorimotor regions (Lou, Henriksen, & Bruhn, 1984; Lou, Henriksen, Bruhn, Borner, & Nielsen, 1989). Quantitative analysis of electroencephalographs (EEGs) in boys with ADHD revealed increased slow wave activity predominantly in the frontal regions and decreased activity of the wave form associated with intense mental activity (i.e., beta waves) in the temporal regions, compared with normal controls matched for age and sex (Mann, Lubar, Zimmerman, Miller, & Muenchen, 1992).

Hynd et al. (1990) used MRI to examine the relative size of various portions of the brain (specifically, the asymmetry of the frontal lobes) in children with ADHD, in children with reading problems, and in normal controls. Findings revealed decreased right frontal width measurements in children with ADHD relative to normals.

This body of evidence, including findings from various other studies, indicates decreased cortical arousal and/or structural differences in the brains of children with ADHD in those anterior areas of the brain. This is particularly relevant, as these are the same areas of the brain most frequently associated with behavioral control and attention.

Results of neuropsychological studies of frontal lobe functioning in ADHD children are equivocal, and Welsh and Pennington (1988) caution against the interpretation of developmental alterations in prefrontal function as evidence of ADHD. Specifically, not all studies focusing on the neurocognitive functioning of children with ADHD have demonstrated significant frontal dysfunction (Loge, Staton, & Beatty, 1990). Further, it has been argued that the neurological basis of ADHD appears to be related to more-widespread brain dysfunction (Benson, 1991). Thus, while the frontal/prefrontal area has been implicated using neuroimaging techniques, this finding has not been consistently supported by neuropsychological studies (e.g., Loge et al., 1990). Further, the frontal lobes are not the only regions of the brain where differences in morphology have been identified.

The Caudate

The caudate is one portion of the group of structures referred to collectively as the basal ganglia (see Figure 2-1). Numerous fibers connect the caudate to the frontal lobes. The fibers form the caudate-frontal axis, a system in the brain known to be important in motor regulation and behavioral inhibition. The resemblance of ADHD to the spectrum of behaviors associated with dysfunction in the caudate-frontal axis suggests possible involvement of the caudate in ADHD (Pontius, 1973; Zambelli, Stamm, Maitinsky, & Loiselle, 1977). Evidence to support possible dysfunction of the caudate includes cerebral blood flow studies with findings of decreased metabolism in the caudate, particularly the right caudate (Loun et al., 1989).

Consistent with this notion, neuroimaging studies using MRI have revealed differences in the size of the right caudate, relative to the left, in children with ADHD when compared with normal controls (Hynd et al., 1993). Specifically, as with the frontal lobes, the normal asymmetry of the caudate (i.e., the right side being greater than the left) appears to be absent in children with ADHD, compared with nondisabled children.

Corpus Callosum

Another structure implicated in ADHD is the corpus callosum (see Figure 2-1). The corpus callosum is made up of 200 million to 800 million nerve fibers and serves to connect the right and left hemispheres of the brain (Kolb & Whishaw, 1990). In particular, the interhemispheric fibers in these regions interconnect the two hemispheres of the brain, including the left and right frontal, occipital, parietal, and posterior temporal regions (Hynd, Semrud-Clikeman, et al., 1991). Analysis of data from MRI scans of children with ADHD has also identified differences in the size of the corpus callosum. Specifically, it has been found that children with ADHD have a smaller corpus callosum in the anterior region (genu), the posterior region (splenium), and the area just anterior to the splenium (Hynd, Semrud-Clikeman, et al., 1991). While these differences are subtle, they may ultimately affect the cooperative as well as individual functioning of the hemispheres.

Right Hemisphere Differences

At the same time as some researchers have implicated specific neuroanatomical structures in the etiology of ADHD, historically there has been a tendency to implicate those same structures specific to the right hemisphere. It has been argued that the right hemisphere is specialized for attentional processes in adults (Vallar & Perani, 1986) and for the control of various aspects of motor response (Heilman, Voeller, & Nadeau, 1991). For example, adult patients with right central-posterior lesions have shown less arousal when compared with patients with left hemisphere lesions (Heilman, Schwartz, & Watson, 1978). Further, it has been found that there is a higher incidence of attentional deficits, problems with vigilance, distractibility, and difficulty performing intentional motor activities in children and adults with documented right hemisphere lesions (Heilman et al., 1991; Heilman & Van Den Abell, 1980).

Research conducted on the neurobehavioral characteristics of children with evidence of right hemisphere dysfunction provides some additional support for involvement of the right hemisphere in ADHD (Heilman et al., 1991; Voeller & Heilman, 1988). In examining the behavioral, neurological, and neuropsychological characteristics of children with evidence of right hemisphere dysfunction, Voeller (1986) found that 93% of the children met criteria for ADHD. Results of a prospective study comparing children with right hemisphere dysfunction with children with left hemisphere dysfunction revealed group differences on measures of impulsivity, with the right hemisphere dysfunction group evidencing significantly more impulsivity, in the form of errors of commission on a computerized continuous performance task (Branch, Cohen, & Hynd, in press). However, results indicated that there were no significant group differences on rating scales sensitive to ADHD (Branch et al., in press). Further, results of a study comparing children with attention deficit disorder (ADD) with hyperactivity, children with ADD without hyperactivity, and children with learning disabilities on various neuropsychological measures of right and left hemisphere functioning indicated that ADHD is not simply attributable to right hemisphere dysfunction but may involve a number of different brain systems, possibly implicating different functional systems in those children with or without the hyperactivity component (Matazow & Hynd, 1992b).

Anterior-Posterior Hypothesis

The anterior-posterior hypothesis refers to the hypothesis that children with ADHD who do not demonstrate hyperactivity and impulsivity have evidence of more brain structure involvement in the posterior regions (i.e., the parietal lobes) of the brain, whereas children with ADHD who do manifest hyperactivity seem to have more involvement in the anterior regions (i.e., the frontal lobes) of the brain. Thus, this hypothesis refers to evidence implicating structures in the anterior portion of the brain as contrasted with structures located in the posterior of the brain as one causal factor for the behavioral differences between students with ADHD who demonstrate hyperactivity compared with those who do not.

While this hypothesis has received some support, it is still somewhat controversial. Specifically, several investigators have documented the relationship between the hyperactivity/impulsivity aspects of ADHD and anterior functioning based on neurocognitive tasks (Chelune et al., 1986; Luria, 1980). Others have explored the relationship between the attentional aspects of ADHD and right hemisphere posterior functioning (Ogden, 1985; Schaughency & Hynd, 1989). Based on the results of these investigations, it has been posited that anterior-posterior dysfunctions may well result in differential behavioral effects (Schaughency & Hynd, 1989). Those differential behaviors—resulting in subgroups with differing symptom predominance—would in part explain the inconsistent findings of research studies that used more heterogenous groups of children with ADHD.

The relationship between neuroanatomical/behavioral subtypes has not, however, been borne out by a neuropsychological study of subgroups as previously defined (Matazow & Hynd, 1992a). Research specific to group comparisons based on the more recent subtypes identified in the *Diagnostic and Statistical Manual of Mental Disorders* (4th ed.; DSM-IV) (American Psychiatric Association [APA], 1994) may yield further information regarding the validity of the anterior-posterior hypothesis.

Neurochemical Basis

Various chemicals, referred to as neurotransmitters, are involved in the transmission of information from one neuron to another throughout the brain and the central nervous system (Kolb & Whishaw, 1990). It has generally been accepted that several of these chemicals, the catecholamines (i.e.

dopamine, norepinephrine), are implicated in ADHD and appear to affect a wide variety of behaviors, including attention, inhibition and response of the motor system, and motivation (Clark, Geffen, & Geffen, 1987a, 1987b). The focus on the neurochemistry of ADHD, and specifically this neurotransmitter system, has been reviewed in detail by Zametkin and Rapoport (1987).

Related to the focus on neurotransmitters, it was postulated that an imbalance in the formation of dopamine or norepinephrine resulted in the decreased stimulation of certain portions of the brain stem—specifically, the locus coeruleus, within the brain stem reticular activating system (see Figure 2-1) (Mefford & Potter, 1989). It has also been argued that frontal lobe dysfunction may be due to impairment of the dopamine system, specifically in the midregions of the brain (Heilman et al., 1991). Some support for these conceptualizations is provided from the efficacy of treatment with clonidine (Hunt, Minderra, & Cohen, 1985), as well as with psychostimulants (e.g., Ritalin) in some children with ADHD (Pelham et al., 1990), since these medicines are known to affect those areas of the brain.

Further, it has been suggested that attentional control involves two separate neural systems. The first of these is believed to be an activation system centered in the left hemisphere that specializes in analytic and sequential cognitive operations (such as motor responses) and is modulated by dopaminergic transmitters. The second is postulated to be an arousal system that is centered in the right hemisphere; is responsible for holistic, parallel, and novel cognitive functions (such as perceptual orienting responses); and is modulated by norepinephrinergic neurotransmitters (Tucker, 1986; Tucker & Williamson, 1984).

In a restatement of this causal theory concerning dopaminergic explanations of arousal, Levy (1991) suggested that the underlying dysfunction is a disorder of dopaminergic circuits between the prefrontal and striatal centers (basal ganglia). The impact of such a disorder would include disorders of planning and automatic instinctual motor programming, which are often found to be characteristics of students with ADHD. In conjunction with the dopaminergic models, it has been suggested that the frontal lobe is the locus of the attentional system whereas the parietal lobe is involved in covert shifting of visual attention and that both work together to regulate attentional processes as a complex functional system (Posner, Inhoff, & Fredrich, 1987).

Neurophysiological Basis

While evidence has supported the role of both neurochemical and neuroanatomical differences in children with ADHD, neither theory has been found to fully account for the myriad behaviors associated with this syndrome (Voeller, 1991). Most recently, a more complex model has been proposed to explain the multifaceted, heterogeneous population identified as having ADHD. This model proposes that we have certain ascending/arousal and descending/inhibitory pathways, which are defined as connections between the frontal lobes, the basal ganglia, and the thalamus. These pathways for attention arousal (i.e., the ascending pathway) and behavior inhibition (i.e., the descending pathway) are presumed to constitute a functional system that involves activation and inhibition of other regions of the brain at the cortical and subcortical levels. The complex interaction of ascending and descending pathways, and various dysfunctions along these pathways, could account for the wide variety of behavioral problems associated with ADHD.

The ascending pathway is the pathway by which neurotransmitters reach various cortical structures, thus maintaining adequate levels of arousal (e.g., attention). When this functional system is disrupted along the ascending/arousal pathway, this component is no longer able to maintain an adequate level of arousal to the specifically targeted brain regions at the level of the cortex (e.g., the frontal lobes).

Conversely, the descending pathways are the pathways by which neurotransmitters leave various cortical structures, thus balancing arousal with appropriate inhibitory behavior. When the functional system is disrupted along the descending/inhibitory loop, an adequate level of inhibition (e.g., selective attention) cannot be maintained (Eichler & Antelman, 1979; Magoun, 1952; Moruzzi & Magoun, 1949). Thus, it is hypothesized that interference at any level of this loop may lead to a cluster of clinically similar signs, with diversity depending on the level(s) affected. This complex interaction of ascending and descending pathways, and various dysfunctions along these pathways, could account for the wide variety of behavioral problems associated with ADHD.

Involvement of the subcortical limbic system along with the frontal lobe might result in behavior disorders that occur comorbidly with ADHD. This model, therefore, provides an explanation for arousal (Watson, Valenstein, & Heilman, 1981) and accounts for the variability of behaviors and characteristics attributed to children with ADHD.

Certain research studies, when taken together, support this "functional system" model. Specifically, it has been found that parietal, frontal, and limbic pathways terminate in the caudate (Goldman & Nauta, 1977; Selemon & Goldman-Rakic, 1990), with a similarly organized system between the somatosensory and premotor cortices to another component of the basal ganglia, the putamen (Alexander, DeLong, & Strick, 1986). Thus, the basal ganglia has emerged as a "hub" of influence over the thalamus and motor structures because of the number of crossing pathways that lead to and from the cortex (Selemon & Goldman-Rakic, 1990).

This model neither contradicts nor conflicts with neurochemical and neuroanatomical findings reviewed previously. Since the pathways and structures that constitute the functional system are intricately involved in the regulation of neurochemical levels, neurochemical differences are an integrated part of the model. Neuroanatomical differences are also incorporated in that the structures identified as demonstrating subtle differences in brain morphology in children with ADHD are also part of the system in question. Thus, Voeller (1991) has suggested that this model currently provides the best explanation of the various clusters of behavior associated with ADHD. However, while this theory has appeal for understanding the diverse characteristics associated with ADHD, it lacks empirical support.

COMORBIDITY AND SUBTYPES: UNRESOLVED QUESTIONS

It is unlikely that the questions regarding the etiology and neurological basis of ADHD will be answered unless a set of reliable, research-based criteria can be established and consistently employed in the diagnosis of the disorder (Cohen, Riccio, & Gonzalez, 1994; Goodyear & Hynd, 1992; Riccio, Gonzalez, & Hynd, in press). In the absence of clear neurological evidence, diagnosis will continue to be made based on behavioral observations. It is important, however, to establish operationally defined behavioral criteria so that appropriate differential diagnoses of ADHD, learning disability, and conduct disorder can be made and an appropriate intervention program be designed (Cohen et al., 1994).

The research relative to subtypes of ADHD (inattentive type, hyperactive-impulsive type, and combined type) indicates that a perspective on the diagnosis of ADHD as unidimensional is questionable (Goodyear & Hynd, 1992). It may be more appropriate to view ADHD as a cluster of different behavioral deficits (attention, hyperactivity, and impulsivity), each with a specific neural substrate of varying severity and variable etiology, occurring in variable constellations and sharing a common response to psychostimulants (Voeller, 1991). This type of multidimensional diagnosis may also be beneficial in addressing issues of comorbidity of ADHD with learning disabilities and other behavior disorders.

SUMMARY

Since the turn of the century, ADHD has been presumed to have an underlying neurological basis. Extensive research has provided empirical and theoretical support for the conceptualization of ADHD as a neurological disorder. There is now strong evidence for a genetic/familial transmission of ADHD, and, in these cases, it is presumed that the underlying cause is neurological in nature. Additional research, however, is needed to identify the impact of various nongenetic factors on the predisposition of ADHD such that preventive steps as well as appropriate early intervention can occur. Research is also needed with regard to the impact of psychosocial and other factors, such as the co-occurrence, or comorbidity, between ADHD and other disorders on the presentation of ADHD in the face of predisposition for the disorder. Further, research specific to any differences in etiology between subtypes of ADHD is needed. This is particularly important in planning an adequate, individualized, and multifaceted intervention program.

Current research provides evidence of morphological differences in the ADHD population based on electrophysiological measures, regional cerebral blood flow, PET studies, and MRI tests. As yet, however, limited progress has been made in characterizing definitive neurological mechanisms that account for the primary manifestations and associated characteristics of ADHD. There is evidence implicating the frontal lobes, basal ganglia, and brain stem as well as one of the major neurotransmitter systems in ADHD. Also, some evidence points specifically to the right hemisphere as being selectively more involved in some children with ADHD. Research findings to date have not supported any of these possible explanations unequivocally or when considered individually.

Of late, attention has been focused on the role of a "functional system" comprising cortical and subcortical structures and the pathways that interconnect them as a possible model for the neurological basis of ADHD. This functional system model effectively incorporates the research relating to both neurochemical models and neuroanatomical models. It has been suggested that viewing ADHD as the result of a deviation in this functional system provides an explanation for the high level of heterogeneity associated with ADHD. Additional research, with more stringent methodological considerations specific to this model as well as other models, is clearly needed to address the question of the neurological basis of ADHD.

REFERENCES

Alessi, N., Hottois, M. D., & Coates, J. K. (1993). The gene for ADHD? Not yet. *Journal of the American Academy of Child and Adolescent Psychiatry, 32,* 1073–1074.

Alexander, G. E., DeLong, M. R., & Strick, P. L. (1986). Parallel organization of functionally segregated circuits linking basal ganglia and cortex. *Annual Review of Neuroscience, 9,* 357–381.

Amen, D. G., Paldi, J. H., & Thisted, R. A. (1993). Brain SPECT imaging. *Journal of the American Academy of Child and Adolescent Psychiatry, 32,* 1080–1081.

American Psychiatric Association. (1994). *Diagnostic and statistical manual of mental disorders* (4th ed.). Washington, DC: Author.

Barkley, R. A. (1982). Specific guidelines for defining hyperactivity in children (Attention Deficit Disorder with Hyperactivity). In B. Lahey & A. Kazdin (Eds.), *Advances in clinical child psychology* (Vol. 5, pp. 137–180). New York: Plenum Press.

Barkley, R. A. (1990). *Attention deficit hyperactivity disorder: A handbook for diagnosis and treatment.* New York: Guilford Press.

Barkley, R. A., DuPaul, G. J., & McMurray, M. B. (1990). A comprehensive evaluation of Attention Deficit Disorder with and without Hyperactivity. *Journal of Consulting and Clinical Psychology, 58,* 775–789.

Barkley, R. A., Karlsson, J., & Pollard, S. (1985). Effects of age on the mother–child interactions of hyperactive children. *Journal of Abnormal Child Psychology, 13,* 631–638.

Barkley, R. A., Karlsson, J., Pollard, S., & Murphy, J. (1985). Developmental changes in the mother–child interactions of hyperactive boys: Effects of two doses of Ritalin. *Journal of Child Psychology and Psychiatry, 26,* 705–715.

Benson, D. F. (1991). The role of frontal dysfunction in attention deficit hyperactivity disorder. *Journal of Child Neurology, 6* S, S9–S12.

Biederman, J., Faraone, S. V., Keenan, K., Benjamin, J., Krifcher, B., Moore, C., Sprich-Buckminster, S., Ugaglia, K., Jellinek, M. S., Steingard, R., Spencer, T., Norman, D., Kolodny, R., Kraus, I., Perrin, J., Keller, M. B., & Tsuang, M. T. (1992). Further evidence for family-genetic risk factors in attention deficit hyperactivity disorder. *Archives of General Psychiatry, 49,* 728–738.

Biederman, J., Faraone, S. V., Keenan, K., & Tsuang, M. T. (1991). Evidence of familial association between attention deficit disorder and major affective disorders. *Archives of General Psychiatry, 48,* 633–642.

Biederman, J., Munir, K., Knee, D., Habelow, W., Armentano, M., Autor, S., Hoge, S. K., & Waternaux, C. (1986). A family study of patients with attention deficit disorder and normal controls. *Journal of Psychiatric Research, 20,* 263–274.

Block, G. H. (1977). Hyperactivity: A cultural perspective. *Journal of Learning Disabilities, 110,* 236–240.

Branch, W. B., Cohen, M. J., & Hynd, G. W. (in press). Academic achievement and attention deficit/hyperactivity in children with left or right hemisphere dysfunction. *Journal of Learning Disabilities.*

Chelune, G. J., Ferguson, W., Koon, R., & Dickey, T. O. (1986). Frontal lobe disinhibition in attention deficit disorder. *Child Psychiatry and Human Development, 16,* 221–234.

Clark, C. R., Geffen, G. M., & Geffen, L. B. (1987a). Catecholamines and attention: 1. Animal and clinical studies. *Neuroscience and Biobehavioral Research, 11,* 341–352.

Clark, C. R., Geffen, G. M., & Geffen, L. B. (1987b). Catecholamines and attention: 2. Pharmacological studies in normal humans. *Neuroscience and Biobehavioral Research, 11,* 353–364.

Cohen, M. J., Riccio, C. A., & Gonzalez, J. J. (1994). Methodological differences in the diagnosis of attention deficit hyperactivity disorder: Impact on prevalence. *Journal of Emotional and Behavioral Disorders, 2,* 31–38.

Colby, C. L. (1991). The neuroanatomy and neurophysiology of attention. *Journal of Child Neurology, 6* S, S88–S116.

Connors, C. K. (1980). *Food additives and hyperactive children.* New York: Plenum Press.

Cruickshank, B. M., Eliason, M., & Merrifield, B. (1988). Long-term sequelae of cold water near-drowning. *Journal of Pediatric Psychology, 13,* 379–388.

Cunningham, C. E., & Barkley, R. A. (1978). The effects of methylphenidate on the mother–child interactions of hyperactive twin boys. *Developmental Medicine and Child Neurology, 20,* 634–642.

Deutsch, C. K., Swanson, J. M., Bruell, J. H., Cantwell, D. P., Weinberg, F., & Baren, M. (1982). Over-representation of adoptees in children with attention deficit disorder. *Behavioral Genetics, 12,* 231–238.

Egger, J., Carter, C. M., Graham, T. J., Gumley, D., & Soothill, J. S. (1985). Controlled trial of oligoantigenic treatment in hyperkinetic syndrome. *Lancet, 14,* 540–545.

Eichler, A. J., & Antelman, S. M. (1979). Sensitization to amphetamine and stress may involve nucleus accumbens and medial frontal cortex. *Brain Research, 176,* 412–416.

Elia, J., Gulotta, C., Rose, S. R., Marin, G., & Rapoport, J. L. (1994). Thyroid function and attention-deficit hyperactivity disorder. *Journal of the American Academy of Child and Adolescent Psychiatry, 33,* 169–172.

Faraone, S. V., Biederman, J., Lehman, B. K., Keenan, K., Norman, D., Seidman, L. J., Kolodny, R., Kraus, I., Perrin, J., & Chen, W. J. (1993). Evidence of the independent familial transmission of attention deficit hyperactivity disorder and learning disabilities: Results from a family genetic study. *American Journal of Psychiatry, 150,* 891–895.

Feingold, B. (1975). *Why your child is hyperactive.* New York: Random House.

Frick, P. J., Lahey, B. B., Chrits, M. A. G., Loeber, R., & Green, S. (1991). History of childhood behavior problems in biological relatives of boys with attention-deficit hyperactivity disorder and conduct disorder. *Journal of Clinical Child Psychology, 20,* 445–451.

Gilger, J. W., Pennington, B. F., & DeFries, J. C. (1992). A twin study of the etiology of comorbidity: Attention-deficit hyperactivity disorder and dyslexia. *Journal of the American Academy of Child and Adolescent Psychiatry, 31,* 343–348.

Goldman, P. S., & Nauta, W. J. H. (1977). An intricately patterned prefronto-caudate projection in the rhesus monkey. *Journal of Comparative Neurology, 171,* 369–386.

Goodman, G., & Poillion, M. J. (1992). ADD: Acronym for any dysfunction or difficulty. *Journal of Special Education, 26,* 37–56.

Goodman, R., & Stevenson, J. (1989). A twin study of hyperactivity. 2: The aetiological role of genes, family relationships, and perinatal adversity. *Journal of Child Psychology and Psychiatry, 30,* 691–709.

Goodyear, P., & Hynd, G. W. (1992). Attention-deficit disorder with (ADD/H) hyperactivity and without (ADD/WO) hyperactivity: Behavioral and neuro-psychological differentiation. *Journal of Clinical Child Psychology, 21,* 273–305.

Gualtieri, C. T., & Hicks, R. E. (1985). Neuropharmacology of methylphenidate and a neural substrate for childhood hyper-activity. *Psychiatric Clinics of North America, 8,* 875–892.

Hauser, P., Zametkin, A. J., Martinez, P., Vitiello, B., Matochik, J. A., Mixson, A. J., & Weintraub, B. D. (1993). Attention deficit-hyperactivity disorder in people with generalized resistance to thyroid hormone. *New England Journal of Medicine, 328*(14), 997–1001.

Heffron, W. A., Martin, C. A., & Welsh, R. J. (1984). Attention deficit disorder in three pairs of monozygotic twins: A case report. *Journal of the American Academy of Child and Adolescent Psychiatry, 23,* 299–301.

Heilman, K. M., Schwartz, H. D., & Watson, R. T. (1978). Hypoarousal in patients with the neglect syndrome and emotional indifference. *Neurology, 28,* 229–232.

Heilman, K. M., & Van Den Abell, T. (1980). Right hemisphere dominance for attention: The mechanism underlying hemispheric asymmetries of inattention (neglect). *Neurology, 30,* 327–330.

Heilman, K. M., Voeller, K. K. S., & Nadeau, S. E. (1991). A possible pathophysiological substrate of attention deficit hyperactivity disorder. *Journal of Child Neurology, 6* S, S76–S81.

Hunt, R. D., Minderra, R., & Cohen, D. J. (1985). Clonidine benefits children with attention deficit and hyperactivity. *Journal of the American Academy of Child and Adolescent Psychiatry, 24,* 617–629.

Hynd, G. W., Hern, K. L., Novey, E. S., Eliopolus, D., Marshall, R., Gonzalez, J. J., & Voeller, K. K. (1993). Attention-deficit hyperactivity disorder (ADHD) and asymmetry of the caudate nucleus. *Journal of Child Neurology, 8,* 339–347.

Hynd, G. W., Hern, K. L., Voeller, K. K., & Marshall, R. M. (1991). Neurobiological basis of attention-deficit hyperactivity disorder (ADHD). *School Psychology Review, 20,* 174–186.

Hynd, G. W., Semrud-Clikeman, M., Lorys, A. R., Novey, E. S., & Eliopulos, D. (1990). Brain morphology in developmental dyslexia and attention deficit disorder/hyperactivity. *Archives of Neurology, 47,* 916–919.

Hynd, G. W., Semrud-Clikeman, M., Lorys, A. R., Novey, E. S., Eliopulos, D., & Lyytinen, H. (1991). Corpus callosum morphology in attention-deficit hyperactivity disorder: Morphometric analysis of MRI. *Journal of Learning Disabilities, 24,* 141–155.

Kolb, B., & Whishaw, I. Q. (1990) *Fundamentals of human neuropsychology* (3rd ed.). New York: W. H. Freeman and Co.

Lahey, B. B., Piacentini, J. C., McBurnett, K., Stone, P., Hartdagen, S., & Hynd, G. (1988). Psychopathology in the parents of children with conduct disorder and hyperactivity. *Journal of the American Academy of Child and Adolescent Psychiatry, 27,* 163–170.

Levy, F. (1991). The dopamine theory of attention deficit hyperactivity disorder (ADHD). *Australian and New Zealand Journal of Psychiatry, 25,* 277–283.

Loge, D. V., Staton, R. D., & Beatty, W. W. (1990). Performance of children with ADHD on tests sensitive to frontal lobe dysfunction. *Journal of the American Academy of Child and Adolescent Psychiatry, 29,* 540–545.

Lou, H. C., Henriksen, L., & Bruhn, P. (1984). Focal cerebral hypoperfusion in children with dysphasia and/or attention deficit disorder. *Archives of Neurology, 41,* 825–829.

Lou, H. C., Henriksen, L., Bruhn, P., Borner, H., & Nielsen, J. B. (1989). Striatal dysfunction in attention deficit and hyperkinetic disorder. *Archives of Neurology, 46,* 48–52.

Luria, A. (1980). *Higher cortical functions in man.* New York: Basic Books.

Magoun, H. W. (1952). An ascending reticular activating system in the brain stem. *Archives of Neurology and Psychiatry, 67,* 145–154.

Mann, C. A., Lubar, J. F., Zimmerman, A. W., Miller, C. A., & Muenchen, R. A. (1992). Quantitative analysis of EEG in boys with attention-deficit hyperactivity disorder: Controlled study with clinical implications. *Pediatric Neurology, 8,* 30–36.

Matazow, G. S., & Hynd, G. W. (1992a, February). *Analysis of the anterior-posterior gradient hypothesis as applied to attention deficit disorder children.* Paper presented at the 20th convention of the International Neuropsychological Society, San Diego, CA.

Matazow, G. S., & Hynd, G. W. (1992b, February). *Right hemisphere deficit syndrome: Similarities with subtypes of children with attention deficit disorder (ADD).* Paper presented at the 20th convention of the International Neuropsychological Society, San Diego, CA.

Mattes, J. A. (1980). The role of frontal lobe dysfunction in childhood hyperkinesis. *Comprehensive Psychiatry, 21,* 358–369.

McGee, R., Stanton, W. R., & Sears, M. R. (1993). Allergic disorders and attention deficit disorder in children. *Journal of Abnormal Child Psychology, 21,* 79–88.

Mefford, I. N., & Potter, W. Z. (1989). A neuroanatomical and biochemical basis for attention deficit disorder with hyperactivity in children: A defect in tonic adrenaline mediated inhibition of locus coeruleus stimulation. *Medical Hypotheses, 29,* 33–42.

Mitchell, E. A., Aman, M. G., Turbott, S. H., & Manku, M. (1987). Clinical characteristics and serum essential fatty acid levels in hyperactive children. *Clinical Pediatrics, 26,* 406–411.

Moruzzi, G., & Magoun, H. W. (1949). Brain stem reticular formation and activation of the EEG. *Electroencephalography and Clinical Neuropsychology, 1,* 455–473.

Nichols, P. L., & Chen, T. C. (1981). *Minimal brain dysfunction: A prospective study.* Hillsdale, NJ: Erlbaum.

Ogden, J. A. (1985). Anterior-posterior interhemispheric differences in the loci of lesions producing visual hemineglect. *Brain and Cognition, 4,* 59–75.

Pelham, W. E., Greenslade, K. E., Vodde-Hamilton, M., Murphy, D. A., Greenstein, J. J., Gnagy, E. M., Guthrie, K. J., Hoover, M. D., & Dahl, R. E. (1990). Relative efficacy of long acting stimulants on children with attention deficit-hyperactivity disorder: A comparison of standard methylphenidate, sustained release methylphenidate, sustained release dextroamphetamine, and pemoline. *Pediatrics, 86,* 226–237.

Pontius, A. A. (1973). Dysfunction patterns analogous to frontal lobe system and caudate nucleus syndromes in some groups of minimal brain dysfunction. *Journal of American Medical Women's Association, 28,* 285–292.

Posner, M. I., Inhoff, A. W., & Fredrich, F. S. (1987). Isolating attentional systems: A cognitive-anatomical analysis. *Psychobiology, 15,* 107–121.

Riccio, C. A., Gonzalez, J. J., & Hynd, G. W. (in press). Attention-deficit hyperactivity disorder (ADHD) and learning disabilities. *Learning Disabilities Quarterly.*

Roth, N., Beyreiss, J., Schlenzka, K., & Beyer, H. (1991). Coincidence of attention deficit disorder and atopic disorders in children: Empirical findings and hypothetical background. *Journal of Abnormal Child Psychology, 19*(1), 1–13.

Safer, D. J. (1973). A familial factor in minimal brain dysfunction. *Behavioral Genetics, 3,* 175–186.

Schaughency, E. A., & Hynd, G. W. (1989). Attentional control systems and the Attention Deficit Disorders. *Learning and Individual Differences, 14,* 423–449.

Selemon, L. D., & Goldman-Rakic, P. S. (1990). Topographic intermingling of striatonigral and striatopallidal neurons in the rhesus monkey. *Journal of Comparative Neurology, 297,* 359–376.

Shaywitz, B. A., & Shaywitz, S. E. (1991). Comorbidity: A critical issue in attention deficit disorder. *Journal of Child Neurology, 6* S, S13–S20.

Shaywitz, B. A., Shaywitz, S. E., Byrne, T., Cohen, D. J., & Rothman, S. (1983). Attention deficit disorder: Quantitative analysis of CT. *Neurology, 33,* 1500–1503.

Smith, L. (1975). *Your child's behavior chemistry.* New York: Random House.

Sprich-Buckminster, S., Biederman, J., Milberger, S., Faraone, S. V., & Lehman, B. K. (1993). Are perinatal complications relevant to the manifestation of ADD? Issues of comorbidity and familiality. *Journal of the American Academy of Child and Adolescent Psychiatry, 32,* 1032–1037.

Stein, M. A., & Leventhal, B. L., (1993). "Attention deficit-hyperactivity disorder in people with generalized resistance to thyroid hormone": Comment. *New England Journal of Medicine, 329*(13), 966.

Swanson, J. M., Posner, M., Potkin, S., Bonforte, S., Youpa, D., Fiore, C., Cantwell, D., & Crinella, F. (1991). Activating tasks for the study of visual-spatial attention in ADHD children: A cognitive anatomic approach. *Journal of Child Neurology, 6* S, S119–S127.

Tucker, D. M. (1986). Hemisphere specialization: A mechanism for unifying anterior and posterior brain regions. In D. Ottoson (Ed.), *Duality and unity of the brain: Unified functioning and specialization of the hemispheres.* New York: Plenum Press.

Tucker, D. M., & Williamson, P. A. (1984). Asymmetric neural control systems in human self-regulation. *Psychological Review, 91,* 185–215.

Vallar, G., & Perani, D. (1986). The anatomy of unilateral neglect after right-hemisphere stroke lesions: A clinical CT-scan correlation study in man. *Neuropsychologia, 24,* 609–622.

Voeller, K. K. S. (1986). Right-hemisphere deficit syndrome in children. *American Journal of Psychiatry, 143,* 1004–1009.

Voeller, K. K. S. (1991). Toward a neurobiologic nosology of attention deficit hyperactivity disorder. *Journal of Clinical Neurology, 6* S, S2–S8.

Voeller, K. K. S., & Heilman, K. M. (1988, September). Motor impersistence in children with attention deficit hyperactivity disorder: Evidence for right hemisphere dysfunction. Paper presented at the 17th annual meeting of the Child Neurology Society, Halifax, Nova Scotia.

Watson, R. T., Valenstein, E., Heilman, K. M. (1981). Thalamic neglect, possible role of the medial thalamus and nucleus reticularis in behavior. *Archives of Neurology, 38,* 501–506.

Welsh, M. C., & Pennington, B. F. (1988). Assessing frontal lobe functioning in children: Views from developmental psychology. *Developmental Neuropsychology, 4,* 199–230.

Willis, T. J., & Lovaas, I. (1977). A behavioral approach to treating hyperactive children: The parent's role. In J. B. Millichap (Ed.), *Learning disabilities and related disorders* (pp. 119–140). Chicago: Year Book Medical.

Wolraich, M., Milich, R., Stumbo, P., & Schultz, F. (1985). The effects of sucrose ingestion on the behavior of hyperactive boys. *Pediatrics, 106,* 675–682.

Zambelli, A. J., Stamm, J. S., Maitinsky, S., & Loiselle, D. L. (1977). Auditory evoked potentials and selective attention in formerly hyperactive adolescent boys. *American Journal of Psychiatry, 134,* 742–747.

Zametkin, A. J., Liebenauer, L. L., Fitzgerald, G. A., King, A. C., Minkunas, D. V., Herscovitch, P., Yamada, E. M., & Cohen, R. M. (1993). Brain metabolism in teenagers with attention-deficit hyperactivity disorder. *Archives of General Psychiatry, 50,* 333–340.

Zametkin, A. J., & Rapoport, J. L. (1987). Neurobiology of attention deficit disorder with hyperactivity: Where have we come in 50 years? *American Academy of Child and Adolescent Psychiatry, 26,* 676–686.

Zametkin, A. J., Nordahl, T., Gross, M., King, A. C., Semple, W. E., Rumsey, J., Hamberger, S., & Cohen, R. M. (1990). Cerebral glucose metabolism in adults with hyperactivity of childhood onset. *New England Journal of Medicine, 323,* 1361–1366.

CHAPTER 3

Family Interactions and Social Development

Dr. Diane Knight
University of Georgia

The families of children with ADHD experience unique challenges that often are not present in the homes of children without the disorder. While parents will assume the primary role in the development of the child, other family members, such as siblings and grandparents, are actively involved. Also, the extra demands placed on the parents' time and energy will affect the extended family unit.

Children with ADHD often pose a complicated puzzle to their parents. Their inattentiveness, hyperactivity, and impulsivity tend to create a constant state of disruption in the home. If additional children are present, the parents are frequently confused by the behavior of the child with ADHD and his or her inability to conform to the family's daily routine, particularly when the siblings are able to do so (Goldstein & Goldstein, 1986).

Parents frequently report that the child with ADHD appears to want to comply with their requests but seems unable to do so. As a point of further frustration, these children are also capable of appearing caring and considerate at other times. They are often described by parents as "having good days and bad days, good hours and bad hours, even good minutes and bad minutes" (Accarado, 1991–1992, p. 18). Parents have a difficult time understanding why children with ADHD are able to display exemplary behavior in one instance but are unable to repeat their performance a short time later.

The vignette in this chapter describes the behavior of Tim, a child with ADHD. Tim's behavioral problems are typical of those that parents of children with ADHD must face on a daily basis.

Tim's Story

At four years of age, Tim has been an extremely difficult and frustrating child for his parents. As an infant, Tim was often irritable, overactive, and moody. He had trouble fitting in with routines, and his irritable, high-pitched crying resulted in his parents frequently curtailing their family outings.

At four years of age, he is still extremely overactive and temperamental. He rarely sits still and provides his parents with very little pleasure. He acts impulsively and appears to engage in a very high degree of risk-taking behavior. This has resulted in numerous bumps, bruises, and half a dozen trips to the hospital emergency room. With his siblings and peers, Tim is extremely aggressive, and his parents have been asked to remove him from two preschool settings. He continues to frustrate easily and [has] tantrums on a daily basis.

Tim's parents are at their wits' end. They are angry, frustrated, and unhappy. Despite all of his difficulties, Tim, too, is well aware of his parents' unhappiness (Goldstein & Goldstein, 1986, p. 1).

This chapter examines the dynamics of the family relationship when a child with ADHD is present in the home. It discusses issues such as adjustment to the presence of a child with ADHD, codependency, family stress, management of home behavior, behavioral interventions and strategies, as well as family training programs. Unique aspects of the child's social development are also discussed for parental consideration.

FAMILY INTERACTIONS

Stages of Grief

Parents of children with ADHD must adjust to the presence of a child with special needs in their home. It is not uncommon for these parents to experience feelings of sadness, isolation, denial, and depression. In fact, these same feelings are faced by the families of children with significant physical and/or mental disabilities, although usually at earlier stages in the child's development. ADHD typically manifests itself in the child's preschool or primary-grade years, whereas more noticeable disabilities, such as sensory deficits, motor problems, and mental impairments, are noted shortly after birth.

Research has found that, despite the child's age at onset of difficulty, parents progress through a series of identifiable stages, which allow them to adjust to the sense of loss and new limitations placed on their lives. Initially, these stages were identified in parents experiencing a sense of loss because of their children's terminal illness (Kübler-Ross, 1969); later research included parents of children with severe medical problems (Klauss & Kennel, 1981) and of those with attention-deficit disorder (Whitman & Smith, 1991). The stages are universal, and progressing through them is considered a normal reaction toward acceptance of the child's problem and planning for his or her future. The grieving process cannot be accelerated, and individuals must work through each phase as new challenges arise; the sequence of stages may also vary from person to person and challenge to challenge (Silver, 1992).

The following stages should be considered by parents of children with ADHD as expected and normal (Lerner, Lowenthal, & Lerner, 1995):

1. *Denial.* This stage is accompanied by varying degrees of shock and disbelief that a problem exists and that one's child is not as perfect as expected. Often, the refusal to admit that a problem exists is evident, and the need to withdraw from reality occurs (Falik, 1995).
2. *Anger.* This stage may manifest as self-pity and resentment toward others. Parents may feel guilty and may examine

their lives for indications of why the child has problems. Guilt may be internalized or displaced onto each other as causes are desperately sought. Professional confirmation of the existence of the problem, as well as its prognosis, may be sought from doctors, therapists, teachers, and ministers (Falik, 1995). Parents may turn from one resource to another in a desperate search for a cure or treatment.

3. *Bargaining.* This stage involves the parent attempting to rationalize the child's problems and deal with them in more abstract, detached terms. The child's actual impairment, such as ADHD, may be used to excuse the child's behavior; "quick cures," such as medication, may be tried instead of dealing with the actual behavioral issues of concern. Parents may try to make a pact with themselves, sometimes through religion, believing that if they change their actions and thoughts or commit their time and energy to socially acceptable causes (such as working with groups/individuals with disabilities) their child will be all right.
4. *Depression.* This stage involves sadness and discouragement. Despair at not locating a source to blame for the child's problems is realized. Physical illness may be exhibited, due to increased stress and anxiety. Temporary relief through alcohol and/or drugs may be pursued. Prolonged helplessness may require professional counseling. Both children and adults may be greatly affected during this stage, as a sense of isolation creeps into daily routines and employment situations. The need to control the child's environment begins to develop and accelerates rapidly.
5. *Acceptance.* This stage marks the parents' coming to terms with the child's disability. They reconcile themselves to the fact that the child possesses unique qualities and needs that may require medical intervention through medication and/or psychological intervention through counseling. Increased demands on energy, time, and finances will be required from the family unit. Participation in support groups and the child's education may be pursued, as plans are made to assist the child in recognizing his or her full potential.

Codependency

Parents of a child with ADHD often overlook their own well-being and enter into a codependent relationship with the child (Gehret, 1993). This type of relationship may be characterized by the parents' catering to the demands of the child while often neglecting each other, other children, or members of the extended family. The family environment may change from one of spontaneity and freedom to one of anxiety and control. Parents may become dependent on the disability, as well as on the child, for making life decisions.

The child's needs for consistent structure, mental and physical stimulation, direct instruction, assistance with task completion, and guidance in social situations pose a challenge for the parents. As this child grows older, demands for extra attention often interrupt a myriad of established daily routines—such as conversations, household chores, family outings, and recreational activities. These demands for attention and time may even affect the parents' employment (e.g., when they are called away from work to deal with problems at school or when they arrive at work already emotionally exhausted from the challenges of getting the child ready for school).

For these reasons, a concerted effort must be made to maintain the family as a total unit and prevent codependent behaviors from developing. Such behavior is evident when "an individual's life has become unmanageable, because he lives in a committed relationship with emotionally or mentally disturbed people, such as those who have disabilities, chronic illness, or behavior problems . . . codependent people let another's behavior affect them so much that they become obsessed with that effort to control" (Gehret, 1993, p. 2).

To bring a degree of normalcy into the family environment, parents will often increase family stress and anxiety by attempting to control every aspect of the life of the child with ADHD. Parents, while believing they are operating with the best of intentions, are actually preventing the child from learning to solve problems, show initiative and creativity in meeting challenges, and assume responsibility for successes and failures. They may establish a codependent relationship, which will only grow stronger over time and extend into adulthood if the child is not taught to assume mature behavior.

As is often exhibited by parents of children with mental and/or physical disabilities, parents of children with ADHD often subconsciously show special attention to them, which may be perceived as favoritism by the siblings involved. The ADHD topic may dominate family conversation, as well as become the topic of discussion with relatives and friends. The child with ADHD is often viewed as having a "higher status" than either siblings or the spouse in the family unit. Personal and financial sacrifices by both parents may be made, resulting in burdens for the entire family. Mothers often choose to become the child's primary advocate, rather than share this role with their spouse, and that choice can create marital discord (Falik, 1995). When both parents assume an equal role, the experience of having a child with ADHD is perceived as positive rather than as a family burden (Stickney, 1994).

As a result of the inappropriate behavior associated with ADHD, the child may be isolated by his or her siblings. An inability to follow rules may cause embarrassment when around nonfamily members. Demands for extra parental attention may create jealousy and frustration, which leads to further alienation. Parental attempts to forcibly include the child in the hobbies and pursuits of siblings may be resented. Siblings may also view the child with ADHD as a "scapegoat" and cause parental blame for misbehavior to be improperly placed upon him or her (Goldstein & Goldstein, 1986). Parents must take extra care to not automatically discipline children with ADHD for misbehavior because of their past negative behaviors. Each circumstance of inappropriate behavior must be viewed through unbiased eyes. These potential sibling conflicts can lead to strengthening parental codependency.

The codependent relationship between the parents and the child with ADHD may be exacerbated by the child's perceived lack of respect for them. Since parents are investing a great deal of time and effort in meeting the demands of the child with ADHD, a degree of resentment may develop. Parents often grow to want the child to need them and to love them for their "special" efforts. In contrast, however, many children respond with continued boredom, diminished self-esteem, and lack of initiative, because all challenges have been removed in the name of parenting and protection (Falik, 1995; Gehret, 1993). A sense of "learned helplessness" may develop in which the child believes he or she is not responsible for his or her own behavior; the child becomes passive and dependent in assuming responsibility for his or her own actions.

In summary, the codependent relationship that develops in families with ADHD individuals can be quite destructive. The relationship is interactive in the sense that, as parents "protect" the child with ADHD more, the family becomes more codependent upon the presence of the disability, and the child becomes increasingly less capable of dealing with the realities of the environment. This in turn leads many parents to provide more "protection," resulting in a self-perpetuating cycle that embroils the family even more in codependency.

Family Stress

Aside from the overt codependency described above, numerous other stress factors affect families. Three common behavior problems creating family stress stem directly from the tendencies toward impulsivity, hyperactivity, and inattention demonstrated by the child with ADHD. Impulsive behavior—the habit of acting without considering the consequences of one's actions—may cause the inability to follow rules and learn from experiences. Impulsive individuals seek immediate reward. Despite having been disciplined several times for the same inappropriate behavior and understanding the family's preestablished rules, a child with ADHD may act impulsively on a whim (Stickney, 1994).

Another key problem is inattention—difficulty with critical listening, causing the child to miss out on such things as parental directions and instructions. While the child may appear to be attending, he or she is not practicing "selective listening." Thoughts are wandering, and the child doesn't internalize what is expected of him or her; therefore, the child doesn't comply with family requests in a timely manner (Goldstein & Goldstein, 1986).

A third problem causing stress for family members has its roots in the child's hyperactivity—a constant state of overarousal and excessive motor activity. Others are often annoyed by the ADHD child's aggressive acting-out behaviors, and negative feedback may result. This becomes cyclical in nature and may lead to the child's belief that he or she cannot meet others' expectations and is always wrong (Falik, 1995).

When the child's behavior pattern reaches the point of creating physical and mental exhaustion in the parents, obsession with ADHD on the part of the parents may result. Parents become unable to think about or participate in anything not related to the child's needs. A decrease in healthy physical and mental stimulation may lead to anxiety, stress, and physical illness. Minor situations may appear as crises and be treated as such, since reacting to crises feels familiar and expected. The ability to view events along a continuum of importance may be lost, because of the parents' pattern of past negative experiences with the child with ADHD.

An additional source of family stress derives from the home–school relationship. While the teachers and school administrators feel they are merely expressing "concern" for the child, communication between the school and home is often viewed as negative by the parents (Falik, 1995; Chesapeake Institute, 1994). Mothers, in particular, may internalize blame for their children's behavior and become resentful toward what they view as a constant barrage of communication that appears to be labeling their child with ADHD. A combination of school disciplinary actions and management of home behaviors may lead to parents' avoiding consistent contact and collaboration with school personnel. A common reaction is to move the child from school to school, often several times during a single semester or year. The hope that a "new start" awaits them at the next school inspires continued moves, and each move only compounds the stress.

Research on Family Stress

The effects of parental stress on the family of a child with ADHD are well documented in the professional literature. Research has noted that ADHD may occur over several generations, and it is not uncommon for parents to exhibit it to some degree. ADHD may also be a precursor to some forms of psychiatric illness in adulthood (Lerner et al., 1995; Schaughency, Vannatta, & Mauro, 1993).

Cantwell's study (1972) of parents of 100 boys between the ages of five and nine years (50 diagnosed with hyperactivity and 50 without) documented these problems. A high rate of alcoholism and sociopathy in the fathers and hysteria in the mothers was found. In addition, 10% of the parents with children labeled "hyperactive" had been considered hyperactive when they were children.

Morrison's examination (1980) of the parents of 231 children yielded similar findings. Both boys and girls between the ages of 11 and 13 were included in the research, although 80% of the subjects were male. Of the participants, 140 had been diagnosed with hyperactivity and 91 with other psychiatric illnesses such as affective disorder, schizophrenia, and personality disorder. A high prevalence of antisocial personality and hysteria was, again, noted in the parents. However, a less significant degree of alcoholism was exhibited. Approximately 11% of the children with hyperactivity had an alcoholic parent.

Parental stress in handling the day-to-day behavior of the child with ADHD has been documented as taking a violent turn in the form of child physical abuse. Heffron, Martin, Welsh, Perry, and Moore (1987) reviewed the medical records of 115 children ranging in age between 2 and 17 years. Of those children, 75 were said to have ADHD and 40 were said to be hyperactive only; 90% of the children in the former group were boys, while 80% in the latter group were boys. Data analysis revealed that the subjects with ADHD were somewhat more likely to encounter physical abuse than those with hyperactivity alone and six to seven times more likely to experience physical abuse than children of the same age in the general population. The authors speculate that the presence of hyperactivity may be the key, contributing to or resulting from physical abuse.

The effects of stress on family functioning has been the topic of several research studies involving parental interviews and the completion of questionnaires. One such study was conducted by Mash and Johnston (1983b) and consisted of 91 families (40 with children exhibiting ADHD and 51 without). Results determined that the mothers of the children with ADHD behavior demonstrated significantly more parenting stress than did the mothers of the children without ADHD. Parenting stress was associated with feelings of social isolation, self-blame, and depression and with the child displaying a high degree of bother and distractibility.

Further writings have compared the parental stress perceived by mothers and fathers when ADHD is present. Baker's examination (1994) of 20 couples, each parenting a son with ADHD behavior, found little difference between maternal and paternal parenting stress, but fathers reported feeling significantly less attached to the child. The data indicated a significant difference based on the length of marriage and socioeconomic status. Higher socioeconomic status and fewer years married tended to contribute more to parenting stress than did parental gender.

Similar questions were explored by Cunningham, Benness, and Siegel (1988) when they queried 52 two-parent families (26 with an ADHD child and 26 without). These researchers examined the degree of parental stress present in the family unit. The average age of the children was 10 years, and 90% were male. Parents of children with ADHD reported fewer extended-family contacts, and mothers find such contacts less helpful than extended family contacts in families where ADHD was not present. Mothers of these children reflected higher depression scores than did fathers or the mothers of children without ADHD. Marital disturbances were higher in the families of children with ADHD, as was alcohol consumption, especially by the fathers.

Parental stress and sibling interactions were the topics of concern in a study by Mash and Johnston (1983a), in which they conducted parental interviews and child observations. Twenty-three boys with hyperactivity and 23 boys without such were each paired with one sibling, male or female, and observed in play situations. Children with hyperactivity tended to show higher levels of conflict with their siblings than did those without hyperactivity. The mothers of these siblings perceived themselves as having higher levels of stress and lower levels of self-esteem in regard to parenting skills and the parenting role.

When the impact of parental stress is viewed in terms of the family unit, parents of children with ADHD must take care to not let it get the best of them. While some stress is expected in normal daily interactions, it can be kept at a minimum. This will benefit both adults and children (the immediate family as well as the extended family unit). Parents of children with ADHD may find the following guidelines beneficial in establishing mental well-being and in reducing stress.

Express Your Feelings. Learn to express grief and anger by discussing attitudes and concerns. Keeping negative emotions confined inside prevents one from dealing with relationships, positive emotions, and crises in a realistic, timely manner. Reaching out to the spouse and scheduling regular family conferences to discuss problems are means of effectively making both adults and children feel they are valuable, worthwhile members of the family unit. Joining a support group, reading literature on ADHD, and talking to a counselor or minister allows one to gain additional knowledge on the subject, while interacting with others sharing common experiences and concerns (Gehret, 1993).

Parents must remember that their needs and desires and those of their other children are just as important as those of the child with ADHD. They must learn to let go of guilt when they are forced to discipline that child or deny his or her wishes. Sometimes a few sessions with an effective counselor can assist parents in doing this.

Allocate Time Wisely. Parents must plan quality time for themselves that does not involve the child with ADHD. Just as a person's job should not occupy 24 hours of each day, parenting a child with ADHD should not either. Engaging in hobbies, participating in volunteer activities, and exploring hidden talents, such as in art, music, and sports, should be pursued (Gehret, 1993). The marital relationship must be strengthened and not allowed to deteriorate because of neglect and too much concern being placed on the misbehavior of the child with ADHD.

Siblings should be allowed to pursue their own talents and interests. Enroll the child with ADHD in worthwhile pursuits that will allow development of a sense of self-worth, creativity, and responsibility. Participation in community organizations (such as the Boy Scouts and Girl Scouts), on neighborhood athletic teams, in church-sponsored activities, and in summer camp will provide structured, learning experiences while allowing for "breathing" time away from the familiarity of the family. New friendships can be forged with children of approximately the same age, ability, and interests.

Acquire "Surrogate" Parent(s). Arranging for another adult to serve as a mentor to the child with ADHD is a valuable method of encouraging the development of new relationships and teaching respect for authority. The parents will also be provided with the opportunity to pursue their own desires or take a more active role in parenting other children. This is especially important if the child is an only child, if the presence of an extended family is limited, and if the child is being reared in a one-parent family.

The selection of a male role model for boys identified with ADHD is particularly needed when the boys are being reared by their mothers in a single-parent family. Since these boys are usually being taught in school by females, the existence of an adult male mentor is lacking and needed. Indeed, research has shown that the only group of children who survive divorce with no measurable negative emotional consequences are males who are placed in either joint custody or paternal-custody homes; this suggests that the absence of a same-sex role model in the postdivorce home, rather than divorce itself, may be destructive of children's emotional well-being (see Warshak, 1992, chap. 7). At any rate, male children with ADHD need a same-sex role model mentor, and a healthy relationship with such a person can positively affect the child's behavior.

This surrogate parent should be introduced into the child's life slowly, so that a sense of mutual trust and respect can evolve. A child is quick to sense deception, as well as feel insecure. Therefore, active participation in selecting a mentor is beneficial. Likewise, the chosen surrogate should be cautioned regarding the child's likes and dislikes and other unique needs. Clearly, the surrogate parent may not react in the same way as the biological parent and may recognize worthy attributes in the child not commonly seen by the parent.

Conserve Your Energies. Make time for regular exercise. When the body is operating at peak performance, the mind is better able to deal with the stressful demands of daily life, and the family unit benefits. Participation in outdoor and group activities is recommended for the parent who spends most of the time at home, while the person who works outside the home may find that the quiet of an indoor individual activity relieves stress.

Since the parents of children with ADHD gradually become accustomed to more and more demands on their energies, they often don't realize the degree to which they have overextended themselves. Over time, their needs for self-control and control of their environment often place them in the role of "superparent," and they may find it difficult to delegate tasks or say no to requests from others. Emotional burnout can result from too many volunteer efforts. Parents must learn to wisely choose activities in which to participate.

Promote Individuality. Parents of children with ADHD must come to realize that they are not their children—that is, that their children have their own identities. Parents should attempt to differentiate their successes and failures from those of their child and allow the child to acquire his or her own attitudes, beliefs, and sense of self (Gehret, 1993).

The child must be guided toward developing an independent identity, making appropriate choices, solving problems, setting goals, and weighing the consequences of his or her actions. The parent cannot go through life doing this for the child with ADHD. Rather, the parent must encourage independence early in the child's development and allow it to expand as the child matures into adolescence and adulthood.

HOME BEHAVIOR MANAGEMENT

Children with ADHD often earn negative attention from parents and siblings without making a concentrated effort to do so. Because of stress, anxiety, and the need to establish environmental control, parents often provide negative direction that does not let the child clearly know what is expected. Instead, positive direction, which eliminates negative feedback, must be given. Figure 3–1 discusses the foundations for promoting positive interaction, which Goldstein and Goldstein (1986) believe are essential when managing the behavior of the child with ADHD at home.

Parent Training Programs

Because of negative feedback received from the school and individuals outside the immediate family, most parents of children with ADHD eagerly seek professional advice from physicians and therapists and incorporate recommended treatment into their daily routines. Although this may involve giving the child medication, such treatment often does not benefit families directly—the effects of medication generally wear off just as parents and children are getting back together after school (Anastopoulos, 1993, p. 9). Instead, parents come to realize that training is warranted to modify and/or refine parenting skills, which will increase the amount and quality of positive interaction between them and their ADHD child.

Parents must strive to develop a "prosthetic" home environment, which will assist the child in developing compensatory skills for coping with misbehavior. The goal of parent training is to restructure the types of

- *Be Positive*. Draw attention to misbehavior by telling the child what is expected in regard to appropriate behavior, rather than pointing out mistakes and faults. Place emphasis on what is to be done, as opposed to what is to be stopped. For instance, when a child throws a temper tantrum because a friend has taken his toy, teach the child to share instead of verbally scolding or allowing the tantrum to continue. The parent must learn to separate the child's behavior, which is negative, from the child as a person.
- *Match Punishment with Misbehavior.* Punish the child only for factors within his or her control and ability level. If daydreaming while completing homework is a significant area of concern, make sure that lack of motivation, rather than lack of knowledge to perform the expected task, is the cause of the unwanted behavior.
- *End Interactions Successfully.* Since many children with ADHD experience repeated failure, it is important that they be afforded the opportunity to correct their inappropriate behavior, succeed, and receive praise. If the child is supposed to be sent to the bedroom as discipline for failure to complete assigned chores in a timely manner, he or she should also be allowed to complete the chores and be praised for doing so.

FIGURE 3–1
Positive Interaction Guidelines

demands that parents make on their children with ADHD—to be less taxing of behavioral problems while restructuring the environment and to be more conducive toward stimulating motivation, compliance, task completion, and rule-governed behavior.

Several parent training programs have been developed by leading professionals in the field. Common elements of these programs include detailed assessments of parenting skills and children's problem behaviors; treatment extending over several sessions, which teaches parents to attend to a child's compliant/noncompliant behavior and provides consistent, positive feedback; reinforcement approaches, which emphasize the rewarding of positive behaviors through token, point, or social reinforcement; and punishment procedures, which enforce the use of "timeout," either through isolation of the child in the same area as the parent or through removal to a more distant location. Three of the most popular programs are presented next.

The Barkley Parent Training Program

The Barkley program is based on the following three major goals: to improve parenting skills for dealing with childhood misbehavior, particularly noncompliance; to increase parental knowledge of causes of childhood misbehavior; and to develop the child's compliance to parental rules and commands (Barkley, 1990). Parent training consists of 6 to 12 sessions that may be conducted either in an individual family format or in a multifamily format. Sessions have been found to be most effective when both parents are active participants and the children with ADHD are between 2 and 11 years of age. The program is behavioral in nature and designed to modify parenting skills through the implementation of a 10-step procedure. Parents are assigned activities and procedures to complete at home, which are then demonstrated and discussed in clinic sessions. These steps are briefly described here (Barkley, 1990; Anastopoulos, DuPaul, & Barkley, 1991):

1. *Program orientation and review of ADHD.* A detailed discussion of ADHD is presented—history, primary symptoms, assessment, prevalence rates, child and family characteristics, causes, and treatment approaches.
2. *Understanding parent–child relations and principles of behavior management.* The dynamics of parent–child interactions, as well as the family unit relationship, are examined. The principles of behavioral management (analyzing what caused the misbehavior to occur and what the results were) are introduced. Parents inventory their own family stressors and identify behavioral problems to be addressed.

3. *Enhancing parental attending skills.* The concept of "special time," during which the parents spend quality time with the child while remaining nondirective and noncorrective, is discussed. Parents are taught to observe and describe playtime activities in positive terms while ignoring inappropriate behavior. The appropriate use of praise to reinforce positive behavior is demonstrated.
4. *Paying positive attention to appropriate independent play and compliance; giving commands more effectively.* The manner in which parents make requests and give commands is considered. Parents are taught to modify their verbal and nonverbal communication to increase child compliance to tasks. A "shaping" procedure to encourage children to play independently is presented, and parents are encouraged to begin providing periodic positive attention during this time and to then gradually decrease the amount of such and increase the duration of independent play.
5. *Establishing a home token system.* Parents receive instruction in increasing desired behavioral outcomes through the implementation of a "home token system," which emphasizes the use of rewards. This method is designed to strengthen the parents' ability to positively attend to their child and recognizes only good behavior. It is described in detail later in this chapter.
6. *Using response costs and timeout from reinforcement.* The use of penalties for misbehavior (response costs) is introduced into the home token system previously initiated. The deduction of tokens for inappropriate behavior and the actual physical removal of the child to an isolated area of the room for a predetermined period of time is emphasized. Both techniques are presented in detail later in this chapter.
7. *Extending timeout for other misbehaviors.* Parental efforts at integrating a home token system, response costs, and timeout are refined. Problems are analyzed, and the use of these techniques for other types of rule violations and/or noncompliance are suggested.
8. *Managing the child's behavior in public places.* Generalizing the previously learned home management skills to outside settings (e.g., churches, restaurants, movie theaters, grocery stores) is encouraged. Parents are also taught how to avoid potential difficult situations with the child by reviewing preestablished rules prior to leaving the home, agreeing

upon an incentive for compliance, and establishing a disciplinary response for noncompliance.

9. *Handling future behavior problems.* All techniques presented in the training program and progress made by the child are reviewed. Potential behavioral problems and means of dealing with each are considered.
10. *Having a booster session.* This usually occurs approximately one month after Step 9 is completed. Further review and refinement of parenting skills and the home management plan are conducted. An explanation of the child's progress is made. Future sessions may be scheduled, if needed.

The Patterson Parent Training Program

The Patterson program has as its main goal the reduction of coercive interactions between parents and children. Misbehaviors, such as inattention, impulsivity, hyperactivity, and aggression, respond best to this program. Children under the age of 12 are especially good candidates for intervention, and family treatments during six to eight sessions are recommended. Home activities are also an integral part of this training. The program consists of the following three phases (Newby, Fischer, & Roman, 1991; Patterson, Cobb, & Ray, 1972):

1. *Phase One.* The concepts of compliant behavior (the child doing what is requested without engaging in undesirable behaviors) and noncompliant behavior (any response that does not fulfill the command) are discussed. The importance of positive parental feedback that is both immediate and consistent is reinforced. Parents begin monitoring and recording their child's compliance and noncompliance and targeting specific problem behaviors.
2. *Phase Two.* The "positive point program" is implemented, which requires parents to identify one or two chores for their child to complete daily, as well as rewards that can correspondingly be earned. Parents are taught to break complex, multistep behavior into smaller, manageable tasks that the child can perform and the parent can observe. Points are earned for task completion and later traded for rewards. Parents are also encouraged to issue requests more effectively through utilization of eye contact and clear statements.
3. *Phase Three.* The effective implementation of timeout is introduced, which requires the parent to physically remove

the child to another room for a predetermined amount of time. Certain concerns (such as the child's safety and negative reactions) and the implementation of this procedure are discussed. Techniques for extending timeout to outside the home are then considered. Participation in "booster sessions" is afforded to ensure maintenance of the program and continued behavioral change.

Forehand and McMahon's Parent Training Program

Forehand and McMahon's program fosters the main goals of improving children's compliance with family rules and making family interaction more pleasurable. At least one parent of children ranging in age from three to eight years participates in 10 or more training sessions. Direct training of the parent(s) and child using instruction, role playing, and coaching is provided in actual interaction sessions in both clinic and home. The program employs these two phases (Forehand & McMahon, 1981; Newby et al., 1991):

1. *Phase One.* Parents are taught to attend to their child's behaviors, administer social reinforcement immediately after positive ones, and ignore negative behaviors. Parents are encouraged to maintain records of their efforts to increase desired behaviors.
2. *Phase Two.* The administering of specific, direct, positive commands and the application of consequences for compliance/noncompliance are presented to parents. Effective timeout procedures are discussed; these involve ignoring the child or physically removing the child to another area of the room for a predetermined period of time.

Making Parent Training Work

Several suggestions may be offered to increase the efficacy of parent training. For parent training programs to be effective, parents must be open to suggestions regarding their parenting styles. It is all too easy for them to feel that their ability to parent is being questioned and their self-esteem as adults, as well as parents, is being threatened. Parents must realize that their parenting styles, not their role as parents, are being examined. Parents must be willing to examine the various interactions occurring within their family unit (spouse/spouse, parent/child, sibling/child, grandparent/child) and share these with a professional whose expertise lies in behavioral and family therapy. This person will offer a new perspective on existing family dynamics in the role of mediator and can identify existing strengths and weaknesses not realized by parents because of their day-to-day family involvement. This detachment from the actual family unit will also allow a recommendation regarding the best approach for improving the behavior of the child with ADHD within existing family parameters. Figure 3–2 introduces three basic guidelines that therapists consider before initiating a parent training program. Parents should be aware of these so that they can better understand the role of the professional as mediator.

OTHER HOME BEHAVIOR MANAGEMENT TECHNIQUES

Parent training programs appeal to parents of children with ADHD because parents "often have the greatest investment in bringing about positive behavior change in their child, as well as the best opportunity to alter the child's environment to bring about this change" (Newby et al., 1991, p. 252). The approaches fostered in these programs can be used for an array of problematic behaviors in a variety of situations on a daily basis. The underlying bases of these approaches have their roots in behavioral and cognitive psychology, both of which view the child as an active participant in acquiring new behavioral skills. However, parents do not necessarily have to participate in specific parent training to utilize these techniques. In fact, many

- Establish that the child's ADHD behavior is preventing positive parent–child interactions and daily routines. Clarify that difficulties arise from the existence of the ADHD, not from other physical, sensory, and/or psychological impairments, such as severe language delay, deafness, and depression.
- Realize that parents present ADHD-related clinical concerns, such as stress, low self-esteem, and marital discord. Parent training programs are often warranted even when parents feel they are "in control" of the situation, as they may not be cognizant of the family stress that surrounds them. More time-efficient and energy-efficient methods of dealing with the child's misbehavior must be taught.
- Encourage parents to set realistic expectations regarding the outcome of their training. They may feel that once the training sessions end, the child will be "cured" and there will no longer be a need to employ specialized skills. They must understand that these new effective skills are supplanting formerly utilized, less effective ones and will need to be continued in a consistent, cohesive fashion.

FIGURE 3–2
Foundations of Parent Training

of the same techniques used in public school classrooms (described elsewhere in this text) may also be used at home. Several techniques representative of these approaches are described next.

Behavioral Contracts

The technique of using behavioral contracts is representative of the behavioral approach and emphasizes positive reinforcement. It requires that the parent develop a written contract with the child, which specifies what target behavior will be changed and the reward that will be earned. After discussing behaviors of concern with the child with ADHD, a target behavior (task) should be decided upon and properly defined so that it is understood by all. It is particularly important that the child be an active participant in this process; if the procedure is to be implemented in a time-efficient manner and the results are to be long term, the child should agree upon the need for change. The conditions under which the behavior will be performed are then identified, followed by the reward, which will be earned when the behavior has been changed/completed.

Figure 3–3 is a behavioral contract between a father and his nine-year-old daughter (Bender, 1992). This contract was developed for a parent whose child experienced difficulty remaining at her desk during a daily 60-minute time period set aside for completing homework. It was designed for a period of four months, to correspond with the fall semester of the school year. The child agreed with her parent that lack of attention to her homework was causing her to lose valuable points at school. Of particular concern was the reading assignment in her social studies workbook. Two points were normally awarded daily, for a cumulative weekly total of 10 points, which were then applied to the weekly social studies test grade. Both the father and daughter felt that the ability to complete the reading assignment was not the issue; instead, the issue was lack of attention to task. As the contract shows, the child decided that she wanted to work toward the goal of getting to stay up 30 minutes later on Friday nights than she was normally allowed to do and that obtaining a total of 8 of the 10 extra points for completion of her social studies workbook pages was a reasonable goal toward which to strive. The father agreed to check his daughter's homework daily, and a kitchen timer was used so that both could monitor the 60-minute time period in question.

The Token Economy

The token economy is another behavioral technique in which positive reinforcement is applied, creating reward options for appropriate behavior.

This is a contract between Emily and her father. The contract starts on 9/11/95 and ends on 1/19/96. We will renegotiate it on 10/30/95.

During homework, we agree to increase the specific behavior of completing social studies workbook assignments. This will be measured by points applied to weekly test grade. The contract will continue, until the behavior is increased to 80% completion.

When the appropriate level of behavior is reached, Emily will stay up 30 minutes later on Friday nights. The parent will help by monitoring daily homework.

Parent's Signature: Daniel Hunter

Child's Signature: Emily Hunter

Date: 9/11/95

FIGURE 3–3
Behavioral Contract

Tokens are awarded to the child over a period of time; the tokens can then be exchanged for a specific child-selected reward at a later date. As with the behavioral contract, both parent and child should mutually agree upon the target behavior as well as the type of tokens to be awarded and the reward to be earned. This technique involves plotting the progress of the child on a chart that is easily constructed by the parent. The chart of behavioral performance across different days serves as an aid to both the parent and the child. The tokens may be poker chips, marbles, play money (coins or bills), slips of paper with "I OWE YOU" printed on them, index cards designed to look like credit cards, colored paper clips, or anything else that is easily and inexpensively obtained.

Figure 3–4 shows the charting of a seven-year-old son's behavior by his mother over a four-week period. A token economy was implemented to improve the child's ability to independently dress and groom himself for school each morning within a 30-minute time period so that he could be at his bus stop on time. Both parent and child felt too much time was being spent in this routine, causing the child to sometimes miss breakfast. The four specific tasks to be completed were washing his face, brushing his teeth, combing his hair, and dressing himself with clothes selected by him and laid out the night before. It was decided that the mother would award the son a marble for each of the four tasks completed daily without her reminding him. These marbles were then placed in a special "bank." When 20 marbles were earned, he could then trade them in for baseball cards to add to his collection.

The baseline phase (represented by the letter "A" on the chart) is a time period in which the four target behaviors were measured without any intervention. That took up the first five days. This time period reflected 8 tasks completed out of a possible 20 (i.e., 4 specific tasks per day), with an average of 2 performed each day.

During the intervention phase (days 6–10, indicated as "B" on chart), the child was reinforced with one marble for each daily task completed. A kitchen timer was used for time management. If his mother had to remind him to perform one of the four tasks, the child was not awarded a marble for it. During these five days, the son earned 14 marbles out of a possible 20, which indicated that he showed improvement in his morning dressing habits.

On days 11–13, a second baseline phase was initiated (indicated as "AA" on chart). A second baseline is typically used to establish that the improved behavior is really the result of the token economy. As the chart indicates, the child reverted back to previously exhibited behavior, completing a total of nine tasks independently without reminding from his mother. Since the intervention was determined to be effective, it was reinstated (indicated as "BB" on chart). This second intervention phase occurred over days 14–20 with positive results. An analysis of the chart for this phase showed an average of three tasks independently completed each day, for a total of 22 tokens awarded. Thus, for this parent, a measurable improvement was seen in the child's preparation behaviors as a result of this simple token economy reward system.

Response Cost Strategies

Another behavioral technique may be used to decrease inappropriate behavior. It is similar to the token economy method in that a chart is used to note inappropriate behavior. However, rather than using tokens and rewards, each time a misbehavior is observed, something that the child enjoys is taken away in an effort to decrease the misbehaviors.

To implement a response cost approach, the parent and child should first agree upon a target behavior and the need to reduce or eliminate it. Then, over a certain period of time, each time the misbehavior occurs the child is penalized through limiting of participation in a favored activity.

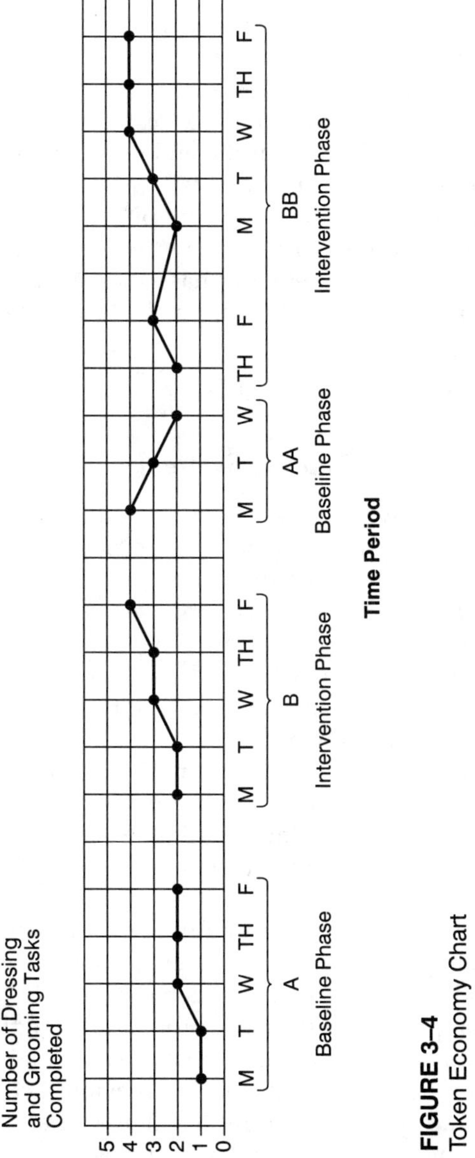

FIGURE 3–4
Token Economy Chart

Figure 3–5 depicts the recording of a six-year-old girl's behavioral change over a 14-day period. Both the child and her mother had decided that the girl's inability to participate in the family's 45-minute dinner session without getting out of her chair or playing with her food was an area in need of change. Punishment involved a reduction in the amount of time the child could play outside in the afternoons. Normally, 30 minutes were allotted for playtime when the child returned from school. The mother kept a pad of paper numbered 1–30 by her dinner plate. Each time the daughter was observed getting out of her chair and/or playing with her food, the highest number on the pad was crossed off, indicating a reduction in the number of minutes the child could have to play outside the next afternoon. If all 30 numbers were crossed off at the end of the dinner session, no time was permitted for playing outside the next day.

Data were collected during a baseline phase of seven days, in which time the daughter was observed to display the inappropriate behaviors an average of 20 times. The intervention phase showed a significant decrease in this behavior, to an average of 10 times daily during the 45-minute family dinner session.

Timeout Strategies

Timeout strategies involve the removal of something that the child enjoys and may involve moving the child to a specific location where enjoyment is less likely (e.g., a room in which there is no television, a room where the child is told to sit quietly). Such strategies are very effective when the potential of an "audience" for the child's misbehavior exists. Although several types of timeout procedures may be used, four are easily incorporated into the daily routine by parents. These are presented in Figure 3–6.

When implementing timeout procedures, the same type of charting system utilized for the token economy method is initiated. A mutually agreed upon target behavior should be selected and baseline data gathered. Once this is accomplished, an intervention phase employing timeout is implemented. If necessary, second baseline and intervention phases can be incorporated.

Children who display severe aggressive behaviors (e.g., temper tantrums, physical aggression toward others/pets, destruction of property, swearing) respond especially well to this technique. To be most effective, timeout must be applied consistently for the entire length of the predetermined time. It should be structured in such a manner as to make the child want to return as quickly as possible to the previous activity. Children are often already well acquainted with this technique because this is a popular form of behavioral management in today's schools.

Self-Monitoring Strategies

Self-monitoring strategies involve the child more directly in learning how to pay attention to particular tasks. Emphasis is placed on developing responsibility for one's own behavior. Initially, external cues are employed to

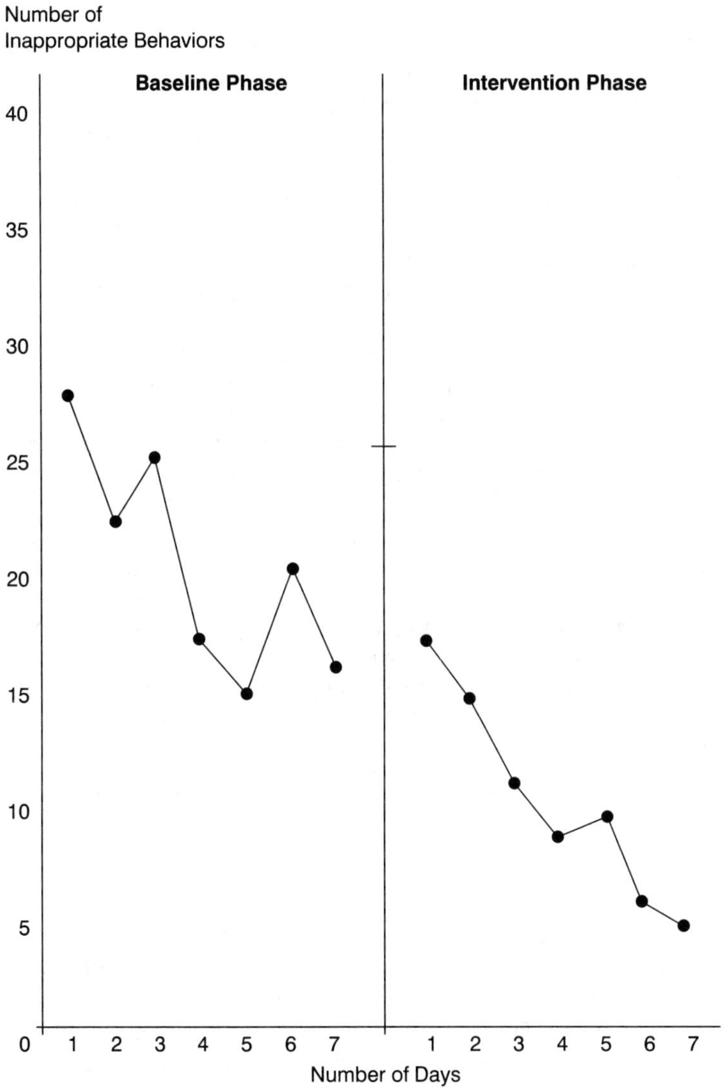

FIGURE 3–5
Response Cost Chart

remind the child to monitor his or her behavior. As appropriate behavior increases, external cues are removed and internal cues (e.g., giving oneself directions for appropriate behavior) replace them. Self-monitoring should be implemented when a child possesses understanding of the task and can independently perform it but has difficulty maintaining attention long enough to do so. It is a particularly effective approach with older children who need to develop self-regulatory behaviors.

- *Activity Timeout*—A favored activity or item is removed from the child when he or she begins exhibiting inappropriate behavior. The removal should be for a predetermined period of time. The toy or item may then be returned to the child if appropriate behavior is resumed.
- *Contingent Observation*—The child is physically removed from participation in a group (family) activity. This removal should be for a predetermined period of time, during which the child is allowed to observe the family's activity but not actively participate in it. After the removal period is over, the child may then be allowed to rejoin the group on a participatory basis.
- *Exclusion Timeout*—The child is physically removed to a different area of the same room, such as to a corner, for a predetermined period of time. A partition may be used to create a sense of isolation. This area should not be near a window, door, or heavy traffic area. All possible distractions (toys, pets, radio, television) should be excluded from this area. Parental monitoring should be as unobtrusive as possible.
- *Seclusion Timeout*—The child is physically removed from the immediate environment to a separate area, such as a bathroom, for a predetermined period of time. This area should be safe and free of distractions but allow for easy parental monitoring that is unobserved by the child. As some children are fearful of small, dark places, the seclusion area should be carefully chosen. If the child is prone to self-injury, all possible items, which could be utilized for this purpose, should be removed or secured.

FIGURE 3–6
Possible Timeout Procedures

After the targeted behavior has been selected by both parent and child, a means of monitoring it must be determined. One simple method of initiating this technique is to prepare a cassette tape with a bell tone or a verbal command, which the child will hear at varying intervals (these can range from 30 seconds to one minute in length) and should last the entire length of the task. As the sound is heard, the child asks the question, "Was I paying attention?" The child then records his or her behavior on a chart or registers it internally and returns promptly to task.

Figure 3–7 is a self-monitoring chart, which can be used to record behavior. It was designed for a 12-year-old boy who experienced difficulty maintaining attention long enough to complete his daily 60-minute saxophone practice session. His father had frequently observed that the boy would periodically stop playing the instrument to watch television, listen to his stereo, or play games at his computer. The son would have to be reminded several times to return to task.

Task/Behavior: Saxophone Practice Date: 12/2/95

WAS I PAYING ATTENTION?

	Yes	No		Yes	No
1.		✓	21.		
2.		✓	22.		
3.		✓	23.		
4.	✓		24.		
5.		✓	25.		
6.	✓		26.		
7.	✓		27.		
8.	✓		28.		
9.		✓	29.		
10.		✓	30.		
11.	✓		31.		
12.		✓	32.		
13.	✓		33.		
14.	✓		34.		
15.	✓		35.		
16.	✓		36.		
17.		✓	37.		
18.	✓		38.		
19.	✓		39.		
20.	✓		40.		

FIGURE 3–7
Self-Monitoring Chart

The father gathered baseline data to determine the period of time on-task and off-task. During a five-day period, the child was on-task only approximately 45% of the expected time. The father then prepared a cassette tape with the verbal command "saxophone" recorded at varying intervals and instructed his son as to how the procedure would work. Appropriate on-task behavior was defined, and examples of off-task behavior were given. Modeling of such behaviors might also be included, depending upon the age and/or mental abilities of the child. The son was required to monitor his behavior, using the auditory command, for a one-week period. A decision was mutually reached that after this time the boy was capable of periodically recording his behavior without external reinforcement. Self-praise was then substituted for the actual paper-and-pencil recording.

Summary of Home Management Techniques

Home management techniques provide parents with flexible methods for curtailing inappropriate behavior and replacing it with behavior deemed appropriate. Each method is easily incorporated into the daily routine and readily implemented by both parent and child. Specific behaviors that parents often need assistance enforcing include adhering to home schedules, following family rules, understanding parental instructions, and completing daily homework. Figure 3–8 provides suggestions for modifying behavior, which may prove beneficial to parents in these areas.

Research Support for Home Behavioral Management

Favorable reviews have been reported concerning the implementation of parent training programs and home management techniques. In general, parent-targeted intervention has been shown to have greater impact on parent behavior than on child behavior. An investigation by Horn, Ialongo, Popovich, and Peradotto (1987) reflected significantly improved home behaviors when parent training or child self-control instruction, or a combination of the two treatments, was utilized.

Pisterman et al. (1989) examined 46 families with children exhibiting ADHD behavior between the ages of three and six. A parent training program was conducted for 12 weeks and consisted of 10 parent group sessions and 2 individual in-clinic sessions with the parent and child. Instruction was offered regarding providing differential attention for appropriate behavior, issuing appropriate commands, and implementing timeout for noncompliance. Results of both posttesting and follow-up assessment during free play, compliance tasks, and parent-supervised activities revealed positive effects concerning the decrease of noncompliant behavior in the child and the development of more effective parental management skills (e.g., use of appropriate commands; consistent, structured, positive reinforcement; less directiveness). Evidence of generalization to nontargeted child behavior was not noted, suggesting that parents had difficulty applying newly learned skills to other areas of behavioral concern.

Family-based behavioral training programs involving preschool-age children have also been a source of interest for Erhardt and Baker (1990).

Two mothers and their five-year-old sons diagnosed with ADHD behavior participated in 10 weekly individual and group training sessions designed to teach observation techniques, identification of strengths and behavioral problems, application of behavioral management techniques, and methods of coping with daily behaviorally related stress. Improvement occurred in the mothers' knowledge of behavior modification principles/techniques, their confidence regarding behavioral home management, and child/parent interaction. Although long-term significant decreases in noncompliant behavior were not exhibited, other targeted behaviors, such as tantrums and pervasive rocking movements, registered a decline in frequency.

Similar findings supporting the effectiveness of parent training programs have been documented when adolescents were included. Sixty-one teenagers ages 12 to 18 years and their mothers participated in training sessions conducted by Barkley, Guevremont, Anastopoulos, and Fletcher (1992). The sessions were developed to assess the effectiveness of three different therapy approaches. Eight to 10 weekly sessions provided instruction in behavior management training, problem solving and communication training, and structured family therapy. Both the mothers and the adolescents attended the second and third types of training sessions; however, only the mothers attended the first type. The issues addressed depended on the program's focus, such as behavioral reinforcement systems, communication during family conflicts, and family dynamics. Both posttesting and follow-up examinations indicated significant reductions in negative communication, number of conflicts, severity of anger during conflicts, internalizing (e.g., anxiety, depression, withdrawal) and externalizing (e.g., aggression, delinquency) symptoms, and maternal depression, as well as improved school adjustment.

The effectiveness of parent training programs emphasizing either the behavioral or the communication approach was studied by Dubey, O'Leary, and Kaufman (1983). Parents of 37 children between the ages of 6 and 10 (32 males, 5 females) who had been identified as possessing ADHD behavior were randomly assigned to one of the two approaches and attended nine weekly training workshops. General skills of child management and their relationship to learning principles, rather than solutions to specific behavior problems, were explored. Posttesting and follow-up monitoring indicated that both treatment methods led to significant reductions in parental reports of hyperactivity, severity of problem behaviors, and frequency of occurrences. Parents exposed to the behavioral approach reported more improvement than those exposed to the communication training; they also noted greater applicability to the home setting.

Research regarding behavioral management with children experiencing ADHD behavior has generally yielded positive results. Studies have attempted to increase on-task behavior, task completion, compliance, impulse control, and social skills while decreasing aggression, off-

Schedules

- Set specified time periods for waking, chores, playtime, meals, bedtime, etc., and consistently enforce them.
- Allow the child to participate in schedule planning, so that a sense of "ownership" and control in the daily routine will be felt.
- Provide choices within established schedule from time to time, so that the child will develop initiative and self-control.
- Explain changes in daily routine ahead of time, and make sure the child understands that they are temporary and necessary.

Rules

- As a family unit, develop a behavioral management plan for the home, which specifies what is considered acceptable, as well as unacceptable, behavior.
- Write rules down and post them in a prominent place for frequent review. Consequences for breaking rules, as well as rewards for appropriate behavior, should also be addressed.
- Firmness and consistency must be followed. Previously agreed upon punishment and rewards should be administered as promptly as possible.
- Respond to misbehavior in a quiet, slow voice. Do not become visibly irritated, or the effect of the punishment will be compromised.
- Face the child when talking to him or her. Facial expressions will help the child learn to use and understand proper body language.
- Avoid being trapped into arguments. No one wins, and emotions are wasted in nonproductive verbal banter.

Instructions

- Provide simple, clear, concrete directions, and physically demonstrate them when needed.
- Ask the child to orally repeat directions in his or her own words to check for understanding.

FIGURE 3–8
Home Interventions

task behavior, hyperactivity, and disruptive behavior (Fiore, Becker, & Nero, 1993).

Other avenues of research have examined the long-term results of parent training programs comparing behavioral and cognitive approaches, as well as their interaction with psychostimulant medication. Specifically, programs with behavioral bases have proven superior to those with a cognitive focus; however, medication, either alone or in combination with

- Give directions, which involve only one or two steps at first; these can be expanded upon later if the child proves they can be handled.
- For more difficult tasks, perform a "task analysis," which breaks multistep, complicated procedures into single steps that can be performed separately.
- With small chores, use a timer to instill a sense of passing time.

Homework

- Provide a quiet, designated "corner," which the child can call his or her own and associate with school.
- Limit environmental stimulation, so that the opportunity for distraction will be minimal—proper lighting, comfortable furniture, no windows, toys stored, no background noise, etc.
- Allow for breaks in studying for snacks and such, but monitor that they are not too frequent nor unnecessary.
- Frequently check on child's progress. Assist with assignment when needed, but be careful to not assume the primary role in its completion. Use a charting system to plot progress and a timer to teach time management and self-monitoring.
- Maintain close contact with child's teacher, and establish a system for being informed of upcoming due dates of tests and long-term projects. Write these on a calendar and display in ready view for frequent reference.
- Have child keep assignment notebook with homework and needed supplies listed. Arrange for teacher to check at end of school day, before child leaves for home.
- Provide space at home to display child's work and creative efforts. This will foster a sense of pride and build self-esteem.

behavior therapy or cognitive training, has been shown to be more effective than either approach alone (Gomez & Cole, 1991). Certain data suggest that cognitive training can reduce one feature of ADHD—impulsivity (Kendall, 1993). Horn (1991) also found that parent training was not superior to medication alone but that, with a combination of medication and behavioral treatments, less medication was needed to achieve positive behavioral changes.

Through participation in training sessions, parents become active members of a team of concerned individuals (health care professionals, therapists, teachers) seeking to positively shape the behavior of the child displaying ADHD behavior. Many of the systematic parent training programs and behavioral management techniques were initially developed to alleviate aggressive, acting-out behaviors. However, over time they have been shown to be just as effective with noncompliance, impulsivity, hyperactivity, and inattention (Barkley, Fischer, Edelbrock, & Smallish, 1990). Figure 3–9 lists social behaviors common to children with ADHD that may interfere with their ability to experience positive relationships with parents, siblings, peers, and teachers (Guevremont, 1992). Parent training programs and behavioral management techniques emphasizing behavioral and/or cognitive approaches can be effective tools in equipping parents with the necessary knowledge and skills to assist children in overcoming these inappropriate behaviors.

Whether actively engaged in parent training programs, implementing behavioral management techniques at home, or participating in support groups, families of children displaying ADHD behavior often need to locate additional information to assist them in refining their parenting skills (Lerner et al., 1995). Figure 3–10 lists resources that parents may find helpful in achieving this goal.

High-Rate, Intrusive Behaviors

- Excessive talking
- Disruptive behavior
- Domination of activities
- Noisy interactions
- Obnoxious behavior
- Monopolization of discussions

Deficient Communication Skills

- Limited turn-taking in conversations
- Less responsive to others' initiations
- Tendency to ignore peers' questions
- Problems shifting roles between giving and receiving information
- Inappropriate and/or disagreeable verbal exchanges
- Difficulty remaining on-task or on same topic
- Poor eye contact and motor regulation

Biased or Deficient Social Cognitive Skills

- Limited self-awareness
- Less knowledgeable about appropriate behavior
- Deficient in social problem-solving
- Overattribution of hostility to actions of others toward them
- Inattentiveness to important social cues

Poor Emotional Regulation

- Aggressive behavior
- Temper outbursts
- Excitability
- Overreactions to minor events
- Poor at transitioning from one activity to another

FIGURE 3–9
Inappropriate Social Behaviors

ADD: Stepping Out of the Dark

- A.D.D. Video
  P.O. Box 622
  New Palz, NY 12561

  An award-winning video for parents, educators, and health professionals. This documentary features perspectives from families, a doctor, adults with ADD, and an educator. $32.95.

Why Won't My Child Pay Attention?

- Neurology, Learning and Behavior Center
  230 South 500 East, Suite 100
  Salt Lake City, UT 84102

- ADD Warehouse
  300 N.W. 70th Ave., Ste. 102
  Plantation, FL 33317

  Features Sam Goldstein, a leading researcher on ADHD, and presents information on ADD for parents. 76 minutes. $30.00.

A.D.D. from A to Z: A Comprehensive Guide to Attention Deficit Disorders.

A curriculum package consisting of four videotapes and curriculum materials intended for professional staff development and parent information. $195.00.

Sopris West
1140 Boston Ave.
Longmont, CO 80501

Home Token Economy

ADD Warehouse
300 N.W. 70th Ave., Ste. 102
Plantation, FL 33317

By Jack Alvord. This book describes a home token ecomony. Uses a token system for rewards and lost rewards. Designed for parents to use in the home. $11.00.

Listen, Look, and Think: A Self-Regulation Program for Children.

ADD Warehouse
300 N.W. 70th Ave., Ste. 102
Plantation, FL 33317

By Harvey Parker. This book presents a program that will help children learn to pay attention in school and when doing homework. $20.00.

FIGURE 3–10
Resources for Parents with Children with ADHD

REFERENCES

Accarado, P. (1991–1992, December/January). My child has an attention deficit disorder. Now what? *PTA Today, 17*(3), 17–19.

Anastopoulos, A. (1993, February). Parent training: It's not just for kids anymore. *The ADHD Report, 1*(1), 8–9.

Anastopoulos, A., DuPaul, G., & Barkley, R. (1991). Stimulant medication and parent training therapies for attention deficit-hyperactivity disorder. *Journal of Learning Disabilities, 24*(4), 210–218.

Baker, D. (1994). Parenting stress and ADHD: A comparison of mothers and fathers. *Journal of Emotional and Behavioral Disorders, 2*(1), 46–50.

Barkley, R. (1990). *Attention-deficit hyperactivity disorder: A handbook for diagnosis and treatment.* New York: Guilford Press.

Barkley, R., Fischer, M., Edelbrock, G., & Smallish, L. (1990). The adolescent outcome of hyperactive children diagnosed by research criteria: An 8-year prospective follow-up study. *Journal of the American Academy of Child and Adolescent Psychiatry, 29*(4), 546–557.

Barkley, R., Guevremont, D., Anastopoulos, A., & Fletcher, K. (1992). A comparison of three family therapy programs for treating family conflicts in adolescents with attention-deficit hyperactivity disorder. *Journal of Consulting and Clinical Psychology, 60*(3), 450–462.

Bender, W. (1992). *Learning disabilities: Characteristics, identification, and teaching strategies.* Boston: Allyn & Bacon.

Cantwell, D. (1972). Psychiatric illness in the families of hyperactive children. *Archives of General Psychiatry, 27*, 414–417.

Chesapeake Institute. (1994). *Attention deficit disorder: What parents should know.* Author (ERIC Document Reproduction Service No. ED 370 337).

Cunningham, C., Benness, B., & Siegel, L. (1988). Family functioning, time allocation, and parental depression in the families of normal and ADHD children. *Journal of Clinical Child Psychology, 17*(2), 169–177.

Dubey, D., O'Leary, S., & Kaufman, K. (1983). Training parents of hyperactive children in child management: A comparative outcome study. *Journal of Abnormal Child Psychology, 11*(2), 229–246.

Erhardt, D., & Baker, B. (1990). The effects of behavioral parent training on families with young hyperactive children. *Journal of Behavioral Therapy and Experimental Psychiatry, 21*(2), 121–132.

Falik, L. (1995). Family patterns of reaction to a child with a learning disability: A mediational perspective. *Journal of Learning Disabilities, 28*(6), 335–341.

Fiore, T., Becker, E., & Nero, R. (1993). Educational interventions for students with ADD. *Exceptional Children, 60*(2), 163–173.

Forehand, R. L., & McMahon, R. J. (1981). Helping the noncompliant child: A clinician's guide to parent training. New York: Guilford Press.

Gehret, J. (1993). *Before the well runs dry: Taking care of yourself as the parent of an LD/ADD child.* Paper presented at the annual Learning Disabilities of America International Conference, San Francisco, CA (ERIC Document Reproduction Service No. ED 361 986).

Goldstein, S., & Goldstein, M. (1986). *A parent's guide: Attention deficit disorders in children.* Salt Lake City: Neurology, Learning, and Behavior Center.

Gomez, K., & Cole, C. (1991). Attention deficit hyperactivity disorder: A review of treatment alternatives. *Elementary School Guidance and Counseling, 26*(2), 106–114.

Guevremont, D. (1992, Fall/Winter). The parents' role in helping the ADHD child with peer relationships. *CHADDER, 6*(2), 17–18.

Heffron, W., Martin, C., Welsh, R., Perry, P., & Moore, C. (1987). Hyperactivity and child abuse. *Canadian Journal of Psychiatry, 32*(5), 384–386.

Horn, W. (1991). Additive effects of psychostimulants, parent training, and self-control therapy with ADHD children. *Journal of the American Academy of Child and Adolescent Psychiatry, 30,* 233–240.

Horn, W., Ialongo, N., Popovich, S., & Peradotto, D. (1987). Behavioral parent training and cognitive-behavioral self-control therapy with ADD-H children: Comparative and combined effects. *Journal of Clinical Child Psychology, 16,* 57–68.

Kendall, P. (1993). Cognitive-behavioral therapies with youth: Guiding theory, current status, and emerging developments. *Journal of Consulting and Clinical Psychology, 61*(2), 235–247.

Klauss, M., & Kennel, J. (1981). *Parent-infant bonding.* St. Louis: C. V. Mosby.

Kübler-Ross, E. (69). *On death and dying.* New York: Macmillan.

Lerner, J., Lowenthal, B., & Lerner, S. (1995). *Attention deficit disorders: Assessment and teaching.* Pacific Grove, CA: Brooks/Cole Publishing.

Mash, E., & Johnston, C. (1983a). Parental perceptions of child behavior problems, parenting self-esteem, and mothers' reported stress in younger and older hyperactive and normal children. *Journal of Consulting and Clinical Psychology, 51,* 86–99.

Mash, E., & Johnston, C. (1983b). Sibling interactions of hyperactive and normal children and their relationship to reports of maternal stress and self-esteem. *Journal of Clinical Child Psychology, 12*(1), 91–99.

Morrison, J. (1980). Adult psychiatric disorders in parents of hyperactive children. *American Journal of Psychiatry, 137*(7), 825–827.

Newby, R., Fischer, M., & Roman, M. (1991). Parent training for families of children with ADHD. *School Psychology Review, 20*(2), 252–265.

Patterson, G. R., Cobb, J. A., and Ray, R. S. (1972). A social engineering technology for restraining aggressive boys. In H. Adams & L. Unike (Eds.), *GA symposium in experimental clinical psychology.* Vol. 2 (pp. 139–210). Oxford: Permagon Press.

Pisterman, S., McGrath, P., Firestone, P., Goodman, J., Webster, I., & Mallory, R. (1989). Outcome of parent-mediated treatment of preschoolers with attention deficit disorder with hyperactivity. *Journal of Consulting and Clinical Psychology, 57*(5), 628–635.

Schaughency, E., Vannatta, K., & Mauro, J. (1993). Parent training. In J. L. Matson (Ed.), *Handbook of hyperactivity in children* (pp. 256–281). Boston: Allyn & Bacon.

Silver, L. (1992). *The misunderstood child: A guide for parents of children with learning disabilities.* Blue Ridge Summit, PA: Tab Books.

Stickney, J. (1994, October). *Attention deficit hyperactivity disorder (ADHD): Perceptions of parents, siblings, and children with ADHD.* Poster session presented at CH.A.D.D. Sixth Annual Conference, New York, NY.

Warshak, R. (1992). *The custody revolution: The father factor and the motherhood mystique.* New York: Poseidon Press.

Whitman, B., & Smith, C. (1991). Living with a hyperactive child: Principles of families, family therapy, and behavior management. In P. Accardo, T. Blondis, & B. Whitman (Eds.), *Attentional deficit disorder and hyperactivity in children* (pp. 176–221). New York: Marcel Dekker.

CHAPTER 4

Assessment and Diagnosis of ADHD

Kerry A. Schwanz

Randy W. Kamphaus
University of Georgia

In this chapter we provide a practical guide for teachers who deal with children having attention-deficit/hyperactivity disorder (ADHD) in their classrooms and who may have only limited experience in the assessment and diagnosis of ADHD. Information is given on teacher rating scales, methods for conducting direct observations of behavior, and collaboration with other professionals in the assessment and diagnosis of ADHD. We discuss teacher rating scales that involve a broad spectrum of children's emotional and behavioral functioning, as well as scales that focus exclusively on the core problems of children with ADHD. In addition, real-world cases and sample assessments are presented to better illustrate some of the practical uses of the instruments and methods discussed here.

DIAGNOSTIC ISSUES

Although the syndrome of childhood hyperactivity and its primary behavioral manifestations have long been recognized, the diagnostic features have undergone numerous reconceptualizations, redefinitions, and changes in nomenclature. In the past, children with hyperactive symptoms were identified as having "minimal brain dysfunction," which was thought to be due to central nervous system damage (Barkley, 1990). However, early studies failed to indicate consistent neurological dysfunction in hyperactive children. With the publication of the *Diagnostic and Statistical Manual of Mental Disorders* (2nd ed., DSM-II), the name was changed to "hyperactive child syndrome" or "hyperkinetic reaction of childhood," reflecting a time when the primary feature of the disorder was considered excess motor hyperactivity (American Psychiatric Association [APA], 1968). For a discussion of the changes in the diagnostic criteria of ADHD in DSM-III, DSM-III-R, and DSM-IV, see Figure 4–1.

Although the specific diagnostic definition of ADHD has changed over the years, there is a general consensus that the primary essential features of the disorder are developmentally inappropriate degrees of inattention, impulsivity, and motor hyperactivity. Problems of inattention include problems with alertness, arousal, selectivity, sustained attention, and distractibility, among others (Hale & Lewis, 1979, cited in Barkley, 1990). Typically, children with problems of impulsivity are noted to respond quickly to situations without waiting for directions to be completed or without adequately appreciating the results of their actions. Careless errors are often the result. They also tend to fail to consider potentially negative, destructive, and even dangerous consequences that may be associated with certain behaviors or situa-

Portions of this chapter have been adapted from R. W. Kamphaus and P. J. Frick, *Clinical Assessment of Children's Personality and Behavior* (Needham Heights, MA: Allyn & Bacon, in press).

tions (i.e., they may engage in frequent, unnecessary risk taking) (Barkley, 1990). Hyperactivity is characterized by excessive or developmentally inappropriate levels of motor and/or vocal activity (Barkley, 1990).

Another characteristic of these primary symptoms that is important to consider in the diagnosis, assessment, and treatment of children with ADHD is that they all have a high degree of situational variability. In other words, certain situations are typically more problematic than others for children with ADHD (Frick & Lahey, 1991). For example, attention deficits are often most apparent in situations requiring sustained attention to unstimulating or repetitive tasks (Milich, Loney, & Landau, 1982, cited in Frick & Lahey, 1991). Such classroom behaviors as using math formulas, spelling words, and memorizing history facts may be particularly trying. Also, a child may appear overactive, fidgety, or restless in situations with a high degree of structure but less so in situations where fewer demands are placed on the child (Porrino, Rapoport, & Behar, 1983, cited in Frick & Lahey, 1991).

Some children with ADHD demonstrate problem behaviors in only a few situations, whereas others do so in most situations. These children have been referred to as "situationally" and "pervasively" hyperactive, respectively (Schachar, Rutter, & Smith, 1981). Research suggests that the situational and pervasive distinction may be important in identifying valid subtypes of children with ADHD. For example, several studies have demonstrated that pervasively hyperactive children have a poorer prognosis, more cognitive deficits, and more neurodevelopmental problems than do situationally hyperactive children.

COMORBIDITIES

Children with ADHD are at risk for several co-occurring problems in other areas; this is referred to as comorbidity of disorders. Problems that occur with ADHD have important clinical implications because they often cause more disruptions for the child than do the primary symptoms of ADHD (Kamphaus & Frick, in press). Thus, these secondary factors often become a major focus of intervention efforts (Abikoff & Klein, 1992).

Comorbidity among disruptive disorders is extremely common. For example, 60%–75% of children referred to clinics with ADHD show significant levels of conduct problems and/or aggression (Hinshaw, 1987). Also, according to Barkley (1990), the co-occurrence of oppositional-defiant disorder and conduct disorder among children with ADHD occurs in approximately 20% of clinic cases. Unfortunately, children displaying the combination of hyperactivity/inattention and conduct problems/aggression tend to have the worst features of both domains, particularly regarding observed behavior, peer status, and outcomes (Hinshaw, 1987).

With the publication of the *Diagnostic and Statistical Manual of Mental Disorders*, third edition (DSM-III; American Psychiatric Association [APA], 1980), the first detailed definition of what is now referred to as ADHD was provided. The manual renamed the disorder attention-deficit disorder (ADD) and specified three main branches of defining symptoms: inattentiveness, impulsivity, and overactivity or motor restlessness (Henker & Whalen, 1989). Although this threefold classification system had an impact on research and practice, it was short-lived and replaced by the definition provided in the revised classification (DSM-III-R). The term for the disorder under the DSM-III-R definition was attention-deficit/hyperactivity disorder, which marked a return to a single, undifferentiated list of symptoms (Henker & Whalen, 1989). Under this unidimensional definition, a child was considered to manifest ADHD if he or she exhibited 8 or more of 14 symptoms that reflected difficulties in attention, impulsivity, and motor hyperactivity and if the onset of symptoms was prior to age 7 (Frick & Lahey, 1991). The definition of ADHD under DSM-III-R implies that there is a single unitary dimension of maladaptive behavior that encompasses attention difficulties, impulsivity, and motor hyperactivity. The DSM-III definition, on the other hand, was based on the idea that difficulties in inattention could exist independent of impulsivity and motor hyperactivity. A body of evidence (namely, factor analytic studies of teacher rating scales) contradicted the unidimensional conceptualization of ADHD. Specifically, these studies have demonstrated that items describing attention deficits and items describing motor hyperactivity loaded on separate factors (Carlson & Lahey, 1983; Lahey, Stempniak, Robinson, & Tyroler, 1978; Neeper, Lahey, & Frick, 1990; Quay, 1986; cited in Frick & Lahey, 1991). In addition, Frick and

Figure 4–1
Attention-Deficit/Hyperactivity Disorder as Defined in DSM-III, DSM-III-R, and DSM-IV

Children with ADHD are quite frequently rejected by their peers; those with comorbid ADHD and aggressive features are almost universally rejected by agemates (Milich & Landau, 1989, cited in Hinshaw, 1992). Given the strong predictive power of peer rejection in childhood for a host of problems later in life (Parker & Asher, 1987, cited in Hinshaw, 1992), it is not surprising that children with ADHD often show low self-esteem that persists throughout childhood and into adolescence (Weiss, Hechtman, & Perlman, 1978). Academic underachievement and learning disabilities also tend to co-occur with ADHD. It is estimated that 30% of children with ADHD show such learning problems (Frick et al., 1991). It is important for clinicians, parents, and educators to be aware that such additional problems can exist along with ADHD so that interventions can be designed to help the child in all problem areas.

Lahey (1991) reviewed research studies that demonstrated that significant differences exist between children diagnosed with attention-deficit disorder with hyperactivity (ADD/H) and those with attention-deficit disorder without hyperactivity (ADD/WO) under DSM-III. For example, children with ADD/H tended to exhibit more conduct problems and more impulsivity and to be rejected more often than children with ADD/WO. However, children with ADD/WO tended to be more sluggish and drowsy, to be more anxious and shy, and to be more likely to show an optimal response to low doses of stimulant medication than children with ADD/H.

In DSM-IV, the most recent revision of DSM, the new definition of ADHD seems to better reflect past research findings that suggest that there is more than just a single core feature of the disorder and that the subtypes of ADHD needed to be redefined. For starters, there are two symptom lists in DSM-IV that closely correspond to two core features of attention-deficit/hyperactivity disorder, which are inattention-disorganization (e.g., difficulty sustaining attention, easily distracted) and impulsivity-hyperactivity (e.g., difficulty awaiting turn, difficulty sitting). DSM-IV also acknowledges the existence of subtypes based largely on the presence of hyperactivity. The *ADHD—inattentive type* identifies children with problems of inattention-disorganization but who do not exhibit problems of impulsivity and overactivity, the *ADHD—hyperactive-impulsive type* and *ADHD—combined type* diagnose children with significant problems of impulsivity-hyperactivity, either in combination with or independent from problems of inattention and disorganization.

ETIOLOGIES AND ASSESSMENT

There are several theories about the possible causes of ADHD, including both environmental etiologies and genetic causes. During the 1960s and 1970s, brain damage was proposed as a major cause of ADHD symptoms. However, fewer than 5% of children with ADHD have neurological problems that are consistent with this theory (Goldstein & Goldstein, 1990). Others theorize that possible neurotransmitter imbalances are the cause of ADHD because of responses of children with the disorder to various drug therapies. However, there is little direct evidence available to confirm this theory, and many studies have shown conflicting results (Mash & Barkley, 1989). According to Barkley (1990), there is little if any evidence to support the notion that ADHD can arise purely out of social or environmental factors, such as poverty, family problems, diet, and poor parental management of children. It appears that most investigators of the possible etiologies of ADHD endorse a biological predisposition to the disorder, much like mental retardation, in which a number of neurological etiologies (e.g., pregnancy and birth complications, acquired brain damage, toxins, infections, and heredity) can give rise to the disorder through some problem in a final common pathway in the nervous system (Barkley, 1990). This issue is discussed more fully in Chapter 2; in the context of in-school assessment, we need only point out that the search for etiology has not affected school assessment practices for ADHD in any major way.

ASSESSMENT ISSUES

Typically employed in the assessment of ADHD is a multimethod assessment battery, including parent and teacher interviews, behavior rating scales, direct observations, and clinic-based testing (Barkley, 1988a, cited in DuPaul, 1991). Multiple assessment methods are used to determine the presence and severity of ADHD symptoms across settings, tasks, and caretakers, as well as to rule out other conditions that could account for the child's attention problems (DuPaul, Anastopoulos, Shelton, Guevremont, & Metevia, 1992).

Standardized, clinic-based measures of sustained attention and impulse control have been widely used in the evaluation of ADHD. One of the most popular clinic-based measures of sustained attention and vigilance is the Continuous Performance Test (CPT; DuPaul et al., 1992). Many different CPT versions are available, but most require the child to observe the rapid presentation of letters or numbers on a screen and to make a response such as pressing a button when a certain pair of stimuli appears in succession (Conners, 1985). Three scores are usually derived: the total number of correct responses, the number of target stimuli missed (omission errors), and the number of nontarget stimuli to which the child responded (commission errors). The number of correct responses and the number of omission errors are considered to be measures of sustained attention, whereas the commission error score is considered to assess both vigilance and impulse control (Sostek, Buchsbaum, & Rapoport, 1980, cited in DuPaul et al., 1992). As a group, children with ADHD demonstrate higher frequencies of omission and commission errors relative to normal controls (DuPaul et al., 1992). Also, significant correlations between CPT scores and teacher ratings of inattention, impulsivity, and hyperactivity have been found (DuPaul et al., 1992).

Despite the utility of CPT measures, some investigators have questioned the ecological validity of these evaluation techniques (DuPaul et al., 1992). In addition, few studies have been done to determine whether these techniques, when used as part of a multimodal assessment paradigm, provide diagnostic data that are consistent with other components of the evaluation (e.g., parent interview responses, teacher ratings).

INTERVENTION ISSUES

Some of the intervention strategies that have the greatest research support in the treatment of ADHD are behavior modification procedures and prescription psychostimulant medications (e.g., Ritalin). A number of issues must be taken into consideration during the process of choosing appropriate recommendations for a child with ADHD.

Initially, the severity of the child's ADHD should be determined (e.g., borderline, mild, moderate, severe) based on the number of symptoms the child exhibits. The greater the severity of ADHD symptoms, the more likely a referral to a physician for a medication assessment will be necessary (DuPaul, 1992). Then, a behaviorally based intervention treatment is usually used, employing reinforcement techniques designed to increase task-related attention and completion of assigned work (DuPaul, 1992). A third factor to consider is the possible comorbid existence of a learning problem or conduct disorder. For example, a child with ADHD who also exhibits severe aggressive behavior may benefit from a referral to a community-based professional such as a psychologist for intervention rather than presenting a danger to himself or herself or others in a classroom situation.

Another important factor to consider in designing the treatment plan is a child's response to previous interventions. For example, if a behavioral program has been implemented in the classroom and yet the child continues to demonstrate a high frequency of ADHD-related behaviors, other treatment modalities (e.g., prescription medication) may be recommended. A final factor to consider is the availability of treatment resources in the child's community. For example, some children will be referred to a community-based professional such as a clinical psychologist; for others, home-based interventions will be designed by a school psychologist.

ADHD is an incurable problem for 3%–5% of school-age children and can have long-term implications and effects on the child throughout his or her lifetime. Therefore, information must continue to be generated to keep clinicians, educational personnel, and parents better informed about the diagnostic, assessment, and treatment issues related to the disorder.

DIAGNOSTIC/ASSESSMENT METHODS

Various assessment methods are necessary for the evaluation of ADHD. The typical assessment battery for a child suspected of having ADHD would include developmental history, child interview, classroom observation, parent and teacher interviews and rating scales, and intelligence and achievement assessment. The size of the assessment battery virtually assures the need for multidisciplinary assessment.

A detailed developmental history is required to properly establish age of onset prior to seven years of age. Historical information is of central importance when a child older than seven is being considered for evaluation (see DSM-IV criteria in Chapter 1). History taking can also reveal other types of problems that may account for the child's behavior.

Parent and teacher ratings of the core symptoms of inattention, hyperactivity, and impulsivity are necessary to document the symptoms' severity and to assess for the existence of problems in at least two settings (e.g., home and school; see DSM-IV criteria). Structured and unstructured interviews with teachers and parents, as well as classroom observations, also assist in the documentation of significant problems in two settings.

Another reason to assess on multiple dimensions is to rule out comorbid problems, such as aggression and conduct disorders. The use of rating scales that assess ADHD symptoms exclusively may result in some problems remaining untreated. Aggression, for example, may be prominent in a child with ADHD, and yet this problem may not respond to Ritalin therapy. If aggressive behavior remains unchecked, this could result in poorer outcomes for the child than in difficulties that may be attributed to the core symptoms of ADHD. Furthermore, multiple aspects of cognitive function must be evaluated to rule out learning disabilities.

Teacher Rating Scales

As mentioned earlier, we focus here on teacher rating scales that assess either a broad spectrum of children's emotional and behavioral functioning or those focusing exclusively on the core problems of children with ADHD. Teacher rating scales that assess multiple dimensions of behavior are preferred for two reasons. First, research on children's emotional and behavioral problems consistently shows that children with school adjustment problems typically have problems in multiple domains. Second, domain-specific rating scales (i.e., those that assess ADHD symptoms only) often do not add much to the assessment of the core symptoms of ADHD beyond that provided within the global rating scales. Some of the more popular broad-based teacher rating scales are briefly described next. For a comparison of these rating scales, see Figure 4–2.

Behavior Assessment System for Children—Teacher Rating Scales (BASC—TRS)

The Behavior Assessment System for Children—Teacher Rating Scales (BASC—TRS) was presented by Reynolds and Kamphaus (1992b). There are

Scale	Authors	Publisher	Content Items	Ages
BASC—TRS	Reynolds & Kamphaus (1992)	American Guidance Service	Externalizing, internalizing, learning, attention, and adaptive, (109–148 items)	4–18
CBCL—TRF	Achenbach (1991)	Author, University of Vermont	Internalizing, externalizing, social, and attention (113 items)	5–18
CBRSC	Neeper, Lahey, & Frick (1990)	Psychological Corporation	Attention, anxiety, learning, cognitive, conduct, and social (70 items)	6–14
CTRS-39 and CTRS-28	Conners (1989)	Multi-Health Systems, Inc.	CTRS-39: Attention, Hyperactivity, conduct, and anxiety; CTRS-28: conduct, hyperactivity, and attention	CTRS-39: 4–12; CTRS-28: 3–17
DBRS—SF	Naglieri, LeBuffe, & Pfeiffer (1993)	Psychological Corporation	Interpersonal problems, inappropriate behaviors/feelings, depression, and physical symptoms/fears (40 items)	5–18
ADDES	McCarney (1989)	Hawthorne Educational Services	Inattention, impulsivity, and hyperactivity (60 items)	5–18

FIGURE 4–2

Overview of Broad-Based Teacher Rating Scales

Note: BASC—TRS = Behavior Assessment System for Children—Teacher Rating Scales; CBCL—TRF = Child Behavior Checklist—Teacher's Report Form; CBRSC = Comprehensive Behavior Rating Scale for Children; CTRS = Conners Teacher Rating Scales; DBRS—SF = Devereux Behavior Rating Scale—School Form; ADDES = Attention Deficit Disorders Evaluation Scale—School Version.

three forms of the BASC-TRS: one for preschool children (ages 4–5), one for elementary-grade children (ages 6–11), and one for adolescents (ages 12–18). Each form contains behavioral descriptors that are rated by the teacher on a four-point scale of frequency, ranging from "Never" to "Almost always." The scales for elementary-grade children are listed here.

Hyperactivity	Learning problems
Aggression	Atypicality
Conduct problems	Withdrawn
Anxiety	Adaptability
Depression	Social skills
Somatization	Leadership
Attention problems	Study skills

According to Kamphaus and Frick (in press), the BASC-TRS is a psychometrically sophisticated rating scale for teachers that is attractive for clinical use for several reasons. It is part of a multimethod, multi-informant system that allows it to fit into a more comprehensive clinical evaluation. The item content covers the major domains of classroom behavioral and emotional functioning, similar to many other teacher rating scales, but it also has some fairly unique content features. Specifically, the BASC-TRS covers several aspects of adaptive behavior (adaptability, leadership, social skills, and study skills), it includes separate anxiety and depression scales, and it has separate hyperactivity and attention scales. The BASC-TRS is also unique in having a preschool version for children ages 4–5, an age group often not included in the development of other teacher rating scales. The BASC-TRS has a large nationwide normative sample on which several norm-referenced scores are based.

Child Behavior Checklist—Teacher's Report Form (CBCL—TRF)

Achenbach (1991) has proposed the Child Behavior Checklist—Teacher's Report Form (CBCL—TRF), which is designed for children between the ages of 5 and 18. The major feature of this scale consists of 113 items describing problem behaviors and emotions that the teacher rates on a three-point scale as being "Not true," "Somewhat true or sometimes true," or "Very true or often true" of the child. The scale allows for calculation of a total problem score, which is an overall score reflecting a child's classroom adjustment, and two broad band scores consisting of internalizing and externalizing behaviors. The CBCL—TRF is part of a system that allows better cross-informant integration of information. The scales included on the CBCL—TRF for children of ages 6–11 are listed next.

Withdrawn	Thought problems
Somatic complaints	Attention problems
Anxious/depressed	Delinquent behavior
Social problems	Aggressive behavior

The CBCL—TRF has been shown to be valuable for identifying children in need of services. Its results correlate with observations of children's behavior in the classroom and with diagnoses offered by clinicians (Kamphaus & Frick, in press).

Comprehensive Behavior Rating Scale for Children (CBRSC)

The Comprehensive Behavior Rating Scale for Children (CBRSC) is a 70-item teacher rating scale designed to assess the classroom functioning of children ages 6 to 14 (Neeper, Lahey, & Frick, 1990). Teachers rate 70 behaviors on a five-point scale based on whether the child exhibits the behavior as ranging from "Not at all" (1) to "Very much" (5). The CBRSC scales are as follows:

Reading problems	Daydreaming
Cognitive deficits	Oppositional-conduct disorders
Sluggish tempo	Anxiety
Inattention-disorganization	Social competence
Motor hyperactivity	

The CBRSC results closely approximate DSM-III and DSM-III-R definitions of emotional and behavioral problems. Several scales have been found to be associated with DSM definitions of attention-deficit disorders (Kamphaus & Frick, in press). The inattention-disorganization scale was positively correlated with teacher ratings of DSM-III symptoms of inattention (.79) and impulsivity (.72), and the motor hyperactivity scale was significantly correlated with DSM-III symptoms of overactivity (.79). Three CBRSC scales differentiated children with DSM-III attention-deficit disorder with hyperactivity from children with attention-deficit disorder without hyperactivity. Children without hyperactivity scored lower on the motor hyperactivity scale and higher on the sluggish tempo and daydreaming scales than children with hyperactivity in this study (Kamphaus & Frick, in press). These findings make the CBRSC a viable measure for the classroom assessment of ADHD.

Conners Teacher Rating Scales (CTRS)

Conners (1989) has presented two teacher rating scales. The Conners Teacher Rating Scales-39 (CTRS-39) has 39 items describing behaviors that are scored on a four-point frequency scale, ranging from "Not at all" (0) to "Very much" (3). The CTRS-39 has been normed for use with children between the ages of 4 and 12. The CTRS-28 is a 28-item version of the CTRS-39 that includes three scales and is for use with children of ages 3–17. For both versions of the CTRS there is a 10-item hyperactivity index, composed of the "ten items most sensitive to drug effects" (Conners, 1989, p. 2) in the treatment of childhood hyperactivity. The scales of the CTRS-39 and CTRS-28 are as listed:

CTRS-39
Hyperactivity
Conduct problems
Emotional-overindulgent
Anxious-passive
Asocial
Daydream-attention problems
Hyperactivity index

CTRS-28
Conduct problems
Hyperactivity
Inattentive/passive
Hyperactivity index

The often-cited definitive finding across the various forms of the CTRS is the sensitivity of the hyperactivity index to treatment effects in samples of children with attention-deficit disorders, especially in studies on the effects of Ritalin on classroom behavior (see Conners, 1989; Piacentini, 1993). However, the CTRS has some noteworthy psychometric weaknesses. Most important, the normative base is of questionable value because it was normed only on Canadian children.

Devereux Behavior Rating Scale—School Form (DBRS—SF)

The Devereux Behavior Rating Scale—School Form (DBRS—SF) contains two 40-item forms, one for children of ages 5–12 and one for adolescents of ages 13–18 (Naglieri, LeBuffe, & Pfeiffer, 1994). The behaviors are rated on a five-point frequency scale ranging from "Never" to "Very frequently" based on their occurrence during the four weeks prior to the rating being taken. The scales of the DBRS-SF are listed here:

Classroom disturbance
Impatience
Disrespect-defiance
External blame
Achievement anxiety
External reliance
Comprehension
Inattentive/withdrawn
Irrelevant/responsiveness
Creative/initiative
Need closeness to teachers

The validity information provided for the DBRS-SF demonstrates the ability of the scales to differentiate children receiving special education services or psychiatric services from normal control children in six samples. No research is available to date, however, to demonstrate the ability of the DBRS—SF to differentiate ADHD symptoms from symptoms of other clinical disorders.

Attention Deficit Disorders Evaluation Scale—School Version (ADDES)

The Attention Deficit Disorders Evaluation Scale (ADDES) is a 60-item rating scale with three subscales designed to assess the three primary dimensions of attention-deficit disorder: inattention (27 items), impulsivity (18 items), and hyperactivity (15 items) (McCarney, 1989). The ADDES provides a comprehensive list of items related to these three dimensions, with proven reliability and a nationwide normative base. However, there is limited information on the validity of the ADDES scales, making the types of interpretations that can be made from the scores unclear (Kamphaus & Frick, in press). The scale is designed for children of ages 5–18.

USING TEACHER RATINGS

Educators currently have a substantial number of teacher rating scales from which to choose. However, the instruments vary considerably in content and validity for various purposes. The ADDES and CTRS scales focus on the assessment of ADHD problems, whereas the CBCL—TRF and BASC-TRS are broad-based measures that may be more useful for ruling out other difficulties. The CBRSC is intermediate in terms of domains assessed.

As mentioned previously, teacher rating scales represent only a small portion of the interdisciplinary information that needs to be collected to make a diagnosis. Such rating scales, however, contribute valuable information to the assessment of ADHD and may be useful for a variety of purposes. For example, they may be useful for screening purposes. A teacher who suspects that a child has serious behavior problems may complete a teacher rating to decide whether further referral or intervention is necessary. A T-score of 65 or greater on inattention, attention problems, hyperactivity, or overactivity should trigger further assessment to rule out ADHD. Moreover, a score at this level should cue the child's teachers that this child may be suffering from problems that require more intensive and perhaps creative intervention. The child's teachers may then begin to implement strategies that they have found useful for children with ADHD, or they may seek behavioral consultation from a colleague.

Teacher ratings may also be helpful for targeting behavioral interventions. Teachers may list the individual problems that have been acknowledged and rank them by their frequency. Such a list will help teachers focus intervention first on the most problematic behavior across classrooms. Analogously, infrequently noted adaptive behaviors may be targeted for instruction.

Finally, teacher ratings provide a valuable tool for intervention evaluation. Such ratings may be used to more objectively evaluate the effects of pharmacological and behavioral interventions. These evaluation results are also potentially useful for demonstrating intervention effects to parents and others in conferences and team meetings.

DIRECT OBSERVATIONS

In addition to rating scales, direct observations of a child's or adolescent's overt behavior is yet another useful tool for teachers/practitioners in the assessment of ADHD. Direct observations are popular for the assessment of youth primarily for two reasons (Kamphaus & Frick, in press). First, observations of overt behavior are viewed as not being filtered through a parent's, teacher's, or child's own perceptions. Thus, these direct observations may eliminate some of the informant's potential biases that may otherwise make the interpretation process more complex. Second, direct observations of overt behavior allow for the assessment of environmental factors associated with a child's behavior. For example, a direct observation is more likely to reveal environmental factors that may exacerbate a child's attention problem (e.g., the noise level of a classroom, a seat placement in the back of the classroom). Thus, direct observations are more likely to help a teacher/practitioner detect environmental factors that seem to be associated with or that elicit certain behaviors. These two benefits of direct observations make them an integral part of any behavior assessment and particularly useful for the development of a written Individualized Education Plan (IEP) or intervention for a child diagnosed with ADHD.

In the next section we will describe a popular standardized observation system, the Behavior Assessment System for Children—Student Observation Scale (BASC—SOS; Reynolds & Kamphaus, 1992a). We will discuss how such a direct observation technique is used by teachers/practitioners in a classroom setting.

Behavior Assessment System for Children—Student Observation System (BASC—SOS)

The BASC—SOS is a short (15-minute), easy-to-use observational system designed for use in a classroom setting. It defines 65 specific target behaviors that are grouped into 13 categories—4 categories of positive/adaptive behaviors and 9 categories of problem behaviors. The BASC—SOS is designed so that the observer uses a time-sampling approach in recording data. There is a 15-minute observational period, which is divided into 30-second intervals. At the end of each 30-second interval, the child's behavior is observed for 3 seconds. A checklist allows the observer to mark each category of behavior that occurred during the 3-second interval. At the end of the observation period, the observer is asked to provide narrative information on the interactions between the child and teacher. Classroom observations for a child with ADHD are presented in the following vignette.

Classroom Observations for a Case of ADHD

Martin was observed from 8:15 to 9:00 in Mrs. Kerry's first-grade class. At the beginning of the observation, some children were settling in at their desks and some were returning from a book fair. Mrs. Kerry introduced a writing activity, and then the children worked on their writing independently. Some children shared their stories, and then they all had snacks. When the observer left, the children were coloring in their workbooks.

From 8:20 to 8:35, time sampling under the BASC Student Observation System was used to observe Martin; with BASC—SOS, the child's behavior is observed for 3 seconds every 30 seconds for 15 minutes. Consequently, there are 30 observation points. This period covered the time from the children settling in to the time they were working independently at their desks on the writing activity. During this time, Mrs. Kerry moved around the room, sat in a rocking chair a few feet away from Martin, and sat at her desk, which is approximately 15 feet away from Martin.

Martin was responding to the teacher (e.g., attending, raising hand, responding, standing at the teacher's desk) during 15 of the observations. He was moving inappropriately (e.g., fidgeting in chair, playing with hands, dancing) during 8 of the observations. During 4 of the time samplings he was making inappropriate vocalizations (e.g., calling out, making noises). Twice he was interacting with a peer through talking. Once he was inattentive and staring into space. He was once observed in a transition movement as the class shifted from opening singing activities to writing instruction. Thus, during a little more than half the time samplings, Martin was acting appropriately. For the entire 45-minute observation, he acted most appropriately during Mrs. Kerry's introduction of the writing activity. Much of the time sampling took place during that time. Consequently, his behavior during the time samplings was more appropriate than it was during the remainder of the observation.

The contributions of Allison Morgan to this observation are gratefully acknowledged.

Numerous behavior patterns were observed during the 45-minute observation. As noted in the time sampling, Martin made many inappropriate movements, which were typically ignored by the teacher. For example, he frequently fidgeted in his chair and "popped" out of the seat. During the singing of "It's a Grand Old Flag," he danced by his desk while everyone else was singing. He also frequently went up to the teacher when it did not appear necessary, perhaps to get attention. For example, when Mrs. Kerry commented that not everyone was back from the book fair, Martin ran up to her and offered to go get them. While Mrs. Kerry was talking about an assignment, Martin ran up to the board, picked an eraser off the floor, erased a mark on the board, put the eraser on the chalk ledge, and returned to his seat. Later, when Mrs. Kerry had already explained the assignment, Martin went up twice to her desk with a question. Mrs. Kerry commented that it had already been explained, but she helped him anyway. Another example of inappropriate movement took place while Mrs. Kerry was rocking in her chair during snack time. Martin stood in front of her and mimicked the rhythm of the rocking chair with his body. Later, when Mrs. Kerry began instruction and the other students were seated and paying attention, Martin went to his backpack to get something. As he was standing at his backpack compartment, he turned his head around, stuck out his tongue, and then made an additional rude gesture shaking his body. He then laughed. The gesture may have been directed at the observer or at other students.

Martin also made frequent inappropriate vocalizations (e.g., grunting noises), which were typically ignored. In addition, he frequently blurted out comments, many of them inappropriate. For example, when Mrs. Kerry was having children read their letter to Mother Nature, Martin at first had his hand raised and called out, "I want to read mine," although the only thing he had written on his paper was the starter sentence Mrs. Kerry had provided all students on the board. When he wasn't called on, Martin blurted out "I'll write to Mother Nature that I hate her." Then after scribbling something on his paper, he announced to the students at his table, "I wrote I hate her." While Mrs. Kerry was talking during writing instruction, Martin twice called out, "Can we color?" During a transition period, Martin talked and sang to himself.

Martin displayed some appropriate and some inappropriate social behaviors. At snack time, he asked a girl if she wanted to trade snacks. The girl said no. Martin went around and swung his snack in the faces and around the heads of the other girls at the table in an attempt to get them to trade. The girls ignored his behavior.

Martin displayed a mixture of inattentive/attentive and nonproductive/productive behaviors. As noted previously, he appeared to be paying attention when Mrs. Kerry was explaining the writing exercise. He also sometimes held his hand up to be called on, although he sometimes blurted out while his hand was raised. During the writing exercise, however, he did not accomplish as much as his other classmates. At one point he erased everything he had done, and, as noted, he went up to the teacher's desk twice to ask questions and receive attention. He also looked around the room at some points during the letter writing period and meddled in the work of others. Consequently, as noted previously, his only addition to the sentence provided by Mrs. Kerry was about hating Mother Nature. At times during the observation, he appeared to have missed some of the teacher's comments and directives. For example, Mrs. Kerry told the children they would return to the letter later in the day and to put it away. When Martin was again reminded to put it away, he complained that he had not finished.

The overall impression was that Martin was displaying disruptive behaviors, although his teacher typically ignored them so that they did not become an issue. He was very active and frequently made noises and blurted out inappropriate comments. Often his behavior was silly and perhaps attention seeking. Although he did not appear to be actively rejected by his peers, they did not appear to initiate interactions with him. Martin displayed some task-appropriate behaviors, such as sometimes listening to the teacher, raising his hand, and attempting to write the letter, but he did not accomplish much during seatwork.

INTERVENTION ISSUES

The importance of using behavior rating scales to assist in planning interventions cannot be overemphasized. Some additional practices are suggested next.

Prioritize Among a Group of Possible Target Behaviors

Often the assessment process reveals a variety of related, and sometimes rather unrelated, behaviors in need of change through intervention. For example, results obtained through parent interviews, observations of a child, and individually administered test results may produce a long list of possible behaviors to change (e.g., decreasing aggressive behavior, improving attention span). When more than one possible target behavior exists, the question becomes: Which behavior should be changed first? Particularly important for a child with ADHD in a classroom is the question of how disruptive or bothersome a particular behavior is. However, since rating scales do not always assess the bothersomeness of a child's behavior, another method needs to be developed to prioritize a group of behaviors on the basis of disruptiveness.

Teachers may use curriculum-based measurement methods to monitor students. Thus, behavior rating scale follow-up techniques may be helpful for prioritizing among target behaviors for intervention. One such method could involve the teacher using a likert scale to rate the degree of disruptiveness of a child's behaviors. For example, on a scale from 1 to 5 a particular behavior could be rated as not at all disruptive (1), a bit disruptive (2), disruptive (3), highly disruptive (4), or extremely disruptive (5). This format would not only allow teachers to identify a significant amount of behaviors with the rating scale but would also allow for a sampling of some of the most disruptive behaviors for the purpose of intervention.

For example, if a teacher rated a child's behavior of interrupting others as extremely disruptive (5) and of daydreaming as not at all disruptive (1), the teacher may choose to first provide intervention techniques to try to reduce the child's interruptions since this particular behavior seems to be the most disruptive.

Formulate Operational Definitions of the Target Behavior for Intervention

An operational definition defines a behavior in terms of the operations that it has on the environment. It also answers the question: What is the behavior and what functions does it have in the environment? For example, you may define certain behaviors as follows:

> Being on-task: Billy works on his assignments 100% of the time.
>
> Being aggressive: Sarah hits, bites, pushes, jabs other children.
>
> Interrupting others: Candace makes verbalizations or gestures while others are talking.

Note the Frequency of the Target Behavior

Frequency information is important to successfully monitor progress of the intervention. Examples include the following:

> Study skills—amount of time spent on task
>
> Homework completion—how frequently homework is done or how frequently it is incomplete
>
> Interruption of others—how often? how many times a day (week, etc.)?

A sample assessment of ADHD is presented in Figure 4–3. Note in particular the utility of behavior rating scales and the complementary nature of the other assessment methods. A graph depicting momentary time sampling results from behavior observations of a child with ADHD both on and off Ritalin therapy is presented in Figure 4–4.

CONCLUDING REMARKS

The epidemiology of ADHD and the frequency of this referral problem beckon all teachers to become steeped in issues of assessment and intervention. This chapter has provided necessary background regarding the syndrome, advice regarding the use of teacher rating scales, and a strategy for intervention planning.

It is advisable for teachers to share the burden of ADHD diagnosis and intervention. While we now know considerably more about ADHD than a decade ago, there are still more questions than answers. For this reason, ADHD should be evaluated and treated by teachers in a multidisciplinary context so that the efforts of many can be marshaled to solve classroom problems. When faced with issues regarding ADHD, teachers should seek the guidance of valued team members to maximally enhance the development of each child.

Name: Austin
Chronological Age: 10 years, seven months
Grade: Fourth

Assessment Procedures

Differential ability scale
Kaufman Test of Educational Achievement
Child interview
Structured Interview for the Diagnostic Assessment of Children (SIDAC)
Behavior assessment scale for children
- Self-report
- Structured developmental history
- Parent rating scale
- Teacher rating scale

Achenbach teacher rating scale
Achenbach parent rating scale
Teacher interview
Classroom observation

Referral Information

Austin Mason was referred by his mother to determine the cause of his increasing behavior problems at school in the past few months. She is also interested in knowing more about why he is poorly motivated. Austin makes "B" and "C" grades in class and does not complete homework assignments, despite his being in the gifted program. At school he misbehaves and shows disrespect toward adults. In the past couple of months disciplinary action was taken in the form of two days of in-house suspension and one day of at-home suspension. Other behaviors of concern were temper flare-ups when corrected and an uncooperative attitude.

Mrs. Mason first became concerned about Austin when he had behavior problems in the first grade, although she states those problems were not as serious as they are now. At that time the teachers reported uncooperativeness, inattention, and resistance to authority. These problems required Mrs. Mason to visit the principal several times, and she thought perhaps the problem was a personality conflict with teachers.

Second grade was better in that Austin was more cooperative. Mrs. Mason states that the teacher was clear, firmer with boundaries, and more in control of the classroom.

Background Information

Austin's mother's pregnancy and labor were of normal length. Birth was by cesarean section. Developmental milestones were within normal limits. During Austin's first four years he was prone to temper tantrums. Austin's early medical history is unremarkable. There were ordinary childhood diseases and illnesses such as measles, chicken pox, and ear infections.

FIGURE 4–3
Sample Psychological Assessment

Vision and hearing screenings were done at school within the past year. Austin is nearsighted and has been prescribed glasses but has lost them in recent weeks. However, he did wear them most of the time when he had them because he cannot see well at a distance.

Behavioral Observations

During the assessment session, Austin repeatedly declined to cooperate and complained about being there. Finally, the examiner "cut a deal," exchanging a promise of cooperation for an opportunity to play with Play-doh. During administration of the tests, effort and cooperation were sufficiently variable to question the validity of the results.

Austin is an appealing-looking, somewhat overweight boy who uses language well. Motor coordination appeared normal, though Austin used an awkward pencil grip. Attention and task completion were good when Austin elected to cooperate. The intellectual and academic assessment was likely affected by Austin's poor cooperation.

Assessment Results and Interpretation

Intellectual

On the differential ability scales, Austin obtained a "general cognitive ability" score within the average range. Verbal skills were well above average. Nonverbal abilities, reflecting the matrices, sequential and quantitative reasoning subtests were average. Spatial abilities scores were significantly below average. However, this was the first instrument used with Austin and was likely affected by his considerable opposition.

Achievement

The Kaufman Test of Educational Achievement yielded a wide range of scores, from well below to well above average. A wide discrepancy is seen between math applications and math computations. A gap is also seen between reading decoding and reading comprehension. While there may be some variability in Austin's competency in academic skills, it is impossible to evaluate this on the basis of these results because of his variable effort and cooperation.

Behavioral/Personality

The Behavior Assessment System for Children—Parent Rating Scales (BASC—PRS) were completed by Mrs. Mason. Her responses were at a clinically significant level in the areas of hyperactivity, aggression, conduct problems, and attention. On the Achenbach parent rating scale, which assesses social competence and behavior problems, Mrs. Mason's responses yielded an overall score within the clinically significant range. Areas of concern were somatic complaints, social problems, and aggressive behavior.

Austin's classroom teacher completed the Behavior Assessment System for Children—Teacher Rating Scales (BASC—TRS) and the Achenbach teacher rating scale. The results were clinically significant in regards to delinquent and aggressive behavior, with the latter being the predominant area of concern. Some difficulty was seen in the area of attention.

The Structured Interview for the Diagnostic Assessment of Children (SIDAC) was also administered to Mrs. Mason. Mrs. Mason gave a strong endorsement to the presence of symptoms related to attention-deficit/hyperactivity disorder. She acknowledged Austin frequently getting into trouble at school and home but did not endorse symptoms associated with a diagnosis of conduct disorder.

Child Interview

Austin was interviewed according to a structured format about his views on a variety of subjects, including self-image, moods, friends, school, and family. He showed interest and emotional involvement in responding to the questions during this interview. His affect was appropriate, showing a range of emotion from pleasure to sadness as he discussed these issues with the examiner.

School is clearly undesirable for Austin. He claims to like nothing about it, says he makes poor grades, and says he gets along terribly with his teachers. Austin says he has trouble concentrating on schoolwork because he wants to do things he likes better.

Classroom Observation

Observation within the school did not reveal significant information. The observer noted that there were many activities going on since the school year was nearing the end. Austin was observed briefly on the playground and in the class for gifted students. No unusual behavior was observed. The teacher acknowledged that he was having a "good day."

Summary and Conclusions

Austin is a 10-year, 7-month-old boy who was referred for evaluation by his mother because of lack of motivation. He began participation last fall in the program for the gifted. Both at home and at school Austin is defiant toward authority, engages in power struggles, and has trouble with temper flare-ups. The teachers and Mrs. Mason are concerned about possible attention-deficit/hyperactivity disorder and emotional problems. The question is raised about a learning disorder in reading and writing. Austin has had increasing difficulties at school over the last several months, resulting in in-school suspension and one day of home suspension. Mrs. Mason indicated that there have been problems with misbehavior going back to the early elementary school years.

Results of this evaluation must be viewed with caution because of Austin's resistance to working appropriately with the examiner. This fact, and his well-above-average level of intellectual performance documented by the school system, renders highly suspect the results of the differential ability scale administered on the first day of the evaluation. The validity of the achievement assessment on the Kaufman Test of Academic Achievement is also of questionable validity, though Austin seemed to perform better on this task. Results on both the intellectual and achievement assessments varied considerably, from well-below, to well-above-average levels. It is clear that his

FIGURE 4–3, *continued*

verbal skills and math reasoning are excellent. This evaluation does not provide a basis for determining the presence of a learning disorder due to Austin's lack of effort.

There is abundant evidence in teacher and parent reports, and in Austin's behavior during this evaluation, of the strength of his oppositional behavior when he is in a situation he has not chosen or is unhappy for some reason. He can then be verbally aggressive and controlling. Yet, when things go his way, he can be equally appealing and enjoyable.

Diagnoses

314.01 Attention-deficit/hyperactivity disorder, combined type

Recommendations

1. It is recommended that a child psychiatrist be seen for a second opinion on the diagnosis of attention-deficit/hyperactivity disorder, given Austin's history of underachievement and behavior difficulties often associated with ADHD.
2. Family-oriented psychotherapy is strongly recommended to address unresolved issues and help develop new patterns of behavior among family members.
3. In addition to family therapy, it is suggested that Mrs. Mason consider participation in a parenting class at some point. This, along with psychotherapy, could give her ongoing support she needs to meet the challenges of Austin's parenting.
4. Reevaluation of Austin's academic skills may be useful for educational planning once he is willing to cooperate with an examiner.
5. Austin's resistance to homework completion is a long-term concern of Mrs. Mason, and this is an area of frequent conflict between them. A variety of books are available that provide helpful information on this topic. They include John Rosemond's *Ending the Homework Hassle* and Lee Carter's *Homework without Tears.*

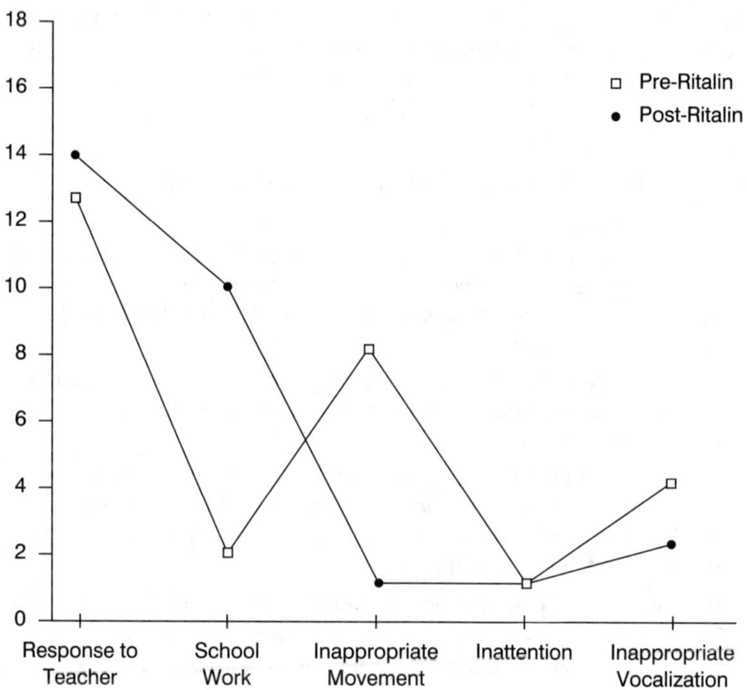

FIGURE 4–4
Momentary Time Sampling Categories from the Behavior Assessment System for Children—Student Observation Scale (BASC—SOS)

REFERENCES

Abikoff, H., & Klein, R. G. (1992). Attention-deficit hyperactivity and conduct disorder: Comorbidity and implications for treatment. *Journal of Consulting and Clinical Psychology, 60*(6), 881–892.

Achenbach, T. M. (1991). *Child behavior checklist, teacher's report form.* Burlington, VT: Author.

American Psychiatric Association. (1968). *Diagnostic and statistical manual of mental disorders* (2nd ed.). Washington, DC: Author.

American Psychiatric Association. (1980). *Diagnostic and statistical manual of mental disorders* (3rd ed.). Washington, DC: Author.

American Psychiatric Association. (1987). *Diagnostic and statistical manual of mental disorders* (3rd ed., rev.). Washington, DC: Author.

American Psychiatric Association. (1994). *Diagnostic and statistical manual of mental disorders* (4th ed.). Washington, DC: Author.

Barkley, R. A. (1990). *Attention deficit hyperactivity disorder: A handbook for diagnosis and treatment.* New York: Guilford Press.

Conners, C. K. (1985). The computerized continuous performance test. *Psychopharmacology Bulletin, 21,* 891–892.

Conners, C. K. (1989). *Conners' teacher rating scales–39.* Toronto, Canada: Multi-Health Systems, Inc.

DuPaul, G. J. (1991). Parent and teacher ratings of ADHD symptoms: Psychometric properties in a community-based sample. *Journal of Clinical Child Psychology, 20*(3), 245–253.

DuPaul, G. J. (1992). How to assess attention-deficit hyperactivity disorder within school settings. *School Psychology Quarterly, 7*(1), 60–74.

DuPaul, G. J., Anastopoulos, A. D., Shelton, T. L., Guevremont, D. C., & Metevia, L. (1992). Multimethod assessment of attention-deficit hyperactivity disorder: The diagnostic utility of clinic-based tests. *Journal of Clinical Child Psychology, 21,* 394–402.

Frick, P. J., Kamphaus, R. W., Lahey, B. B., Loeber, R., Christ, M. G., Hart, E. L., & L. E. Tannenbaum (1991). Academic underachievement and the disruptive behavior disorders. *Journal of Consulting and Clinical Psychology, 59*(2), 289–294.

Frick, P. J., & Lahey, B. B. (1991). The nature and characteristics of attention-deficit hyperactivity disorder. *School Psychology Review, 20*(2), 163–173.

Goldstein, M., & Goldstein, S. (1990). *Managing attention disorders in children.* New York: John Wiley & Sons Inc.

Henker, B., & Whalen, C. K. (1989). Hyperactivity and attention deficits. *American Psychologist, 44,* 216–222.

Hinshaw, S. P. (1987). On the distinction between attentional deficits, hyperactivity, and conduct problems/aggression in child psychopathology. *Psychological Bulletin, 101*(3), 443–463.

Hinshaw, S. P. (1992). Academic underachievement, attention deficits, and aggression: Comorbidity and implications for intervention. *Journal of Consulting and Clinical Psychology, 60*(6), 893–903.

Kamphaus, R. W., & Frick, P. J. (in press). *Clinical assessment of children's personality and behavior.* Needham Heights, MA: Allyn & Bacon.

McCarney, S. B. (1989). *Attention deficit disorder evaluation scale—School version.* Columbia, MO: Hawthorne Educational Services.

Mash, E. J., & Barkley, R. A. (1989). *Treatmer' of childhood disorders.* New York: Guilford Press.

Naglieri, J. A., LeBuffe, P. A., & Pfeiffer, S. I. (1994). *Devereux behavior rating scales—School form.* New York: The Psychological Corporation.

Neeper, R., Lahey, B. B., & Frick, P. J. (1990). *Comprehensive behavior rating scales for children.* New York: The Psychological Corporation.

Piacentini, J. (1993). Checklists and rating scales. In T. H. Ollendick & M. Hensen (Eds.), *Handbook of child and adolescent assessment* (pp. 82–97). Needham Heights, MA: Allyn and Bacon.

Reynolds, C. R., & Kamphaus, R. W. (1992a). *Behavior assessment system for children—Student observation scale.* Circle Pines, MN: American Guidance Services, Inc.

Reynolds, C. R., & Kamphaus, R. W. (1992b). *Behavior assessment system for children—Teacher rating scales.* Circle Pines, MN: American Guidance Services, Inc.

Schachar, R., Rutter, M., & Smith, A. (1981). The characteristics of situationally and pervasively hyperactive children: Implications for syndrome definition. *Journal of Child Psychology and Psychiatry, 22,* 375–392.

Swift, M. (1982). *Devereux elementary school behavior rating scale II.* Devon, PA: Devereux Foundation Press.

Weiss, G., Hechtman, C., & Perlman, T. (1978). Hyperactives as young adults: School, employer, and self-rating scales obtained during a ten-year follow-up evaluation. *American Journal of Orthopsychiatry, 48,* 538–545.

Whalen, C. K., Henker, B., & Dotemoto, S. (1980). Methylphenidate and hyperactivity: Effects on teacher behaviors. *Science, 208,* 1280–1282.

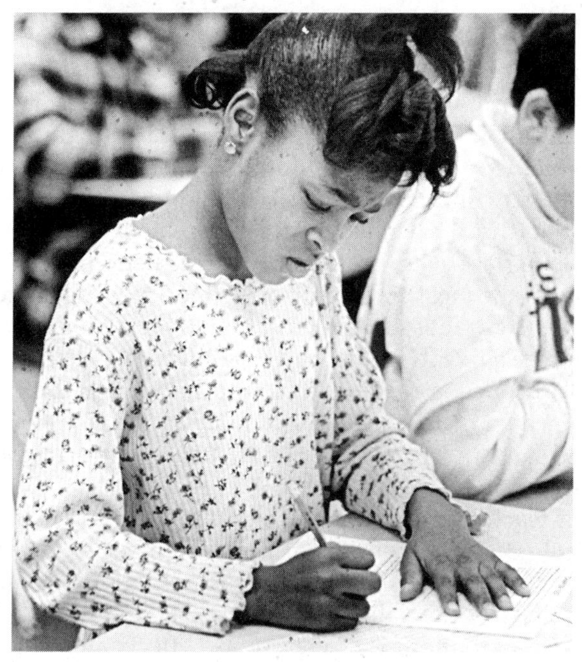

CHAPTER 5

Medical Interventions and School Monitoring

William N. Bender, Ph.D.
University of Georgia

One of the most common interventions for children with ADHD is the use of medication to assist the child in maintaining concentration. Various reports have indicated that the vast majority of students diagnosed with ADHD are receiving some type of medication for that condition. Between 2% and 6% of all elementary-age children in schools in the United States are treated with psychostimulant medications alone (Jacobvitz, Sroufe, Stewart, & Leffert, 1990), making this medical treatment the most common intervention for school-age children.

In addition to administering medication to their children at home, parents must also play a role in medication monitoring to assist the physician in determining appropriate medications and dosages (Fell & Pierce, 1995). Thus, parents need a complete understanding of the common medications and side effects, and they must know how to assist the doctor in selecting the appropriate treatment plan.

Although teachers generally do not administer the medications, and certainly cannot prescribe them, they have a number of medication monitoring responsibilities (Fell & Pierce, 1995). These include documentation of behavioral manifestations of the problem prior to and during the diagnosis process, as well as monitoring of medication effects after a prescription is made. Teachers may be asked to complete periodic behavioral rating questionnaires, such as those discussed in Chapter 4, or make other types of observations to provide the attending physician with the data necessary to adjust the medical treatment program.

Further, when a student is involved in a medically prescribed drug treatment program, many teachers find that their role for providing educational interventions during the medical treatment phase is somewhat expanded. Only with expanded teacher involvement can the appropriate combination of medication and educational interventions be identified for a particular child.

Clearly, parents and teachers need a good understanding of the major aspects of medical intervention programs. Such an understanding can assist them in interacting with the physician and with each other. This chapter presents suggestions about management of medical interventions for parents and teachers.

A TEAM-BASED APPROACH

Numerous researchers and practitioners have recommended a team-based approach to the treatment of individuals with ADHD who are receiving medical interventions (Fell & Pierce, 1995; Parker, 1995). Fell and Pierce (1995), for example, recommend an approach in which a physician, the parents, the teachers, and the child (when appropriate, according to the child's age and maturity level) collaborate to determine the most appropriate treatment for the child. In this model, each individual has a defined role and responsibility to determine the best combination of intervention options. Fell and Pierce's team-based model is presented in Figure 5–1.

In Fell and Pierce's model, each person other than the child has some type of monitoring role. The parent typically will become an expert observer, whereas the teacher must continually evaluate the behavioral progress of the child during school hours and help relate that progress (or lack of it) to the medication plan in effect. The teacher must implement educational interventions at all times to assist the child in academic areas. The physician must constantly monitor the effects of the prescription medication in relation to the needs of the child and the demands of the student's home and academic environment.

With this team approach in mind, it should be clear that parents, teachers, and children must all be involved. Only when these individuals are working together can reasonable expectations for the child's success be met (Fell & Pierce, 1995).

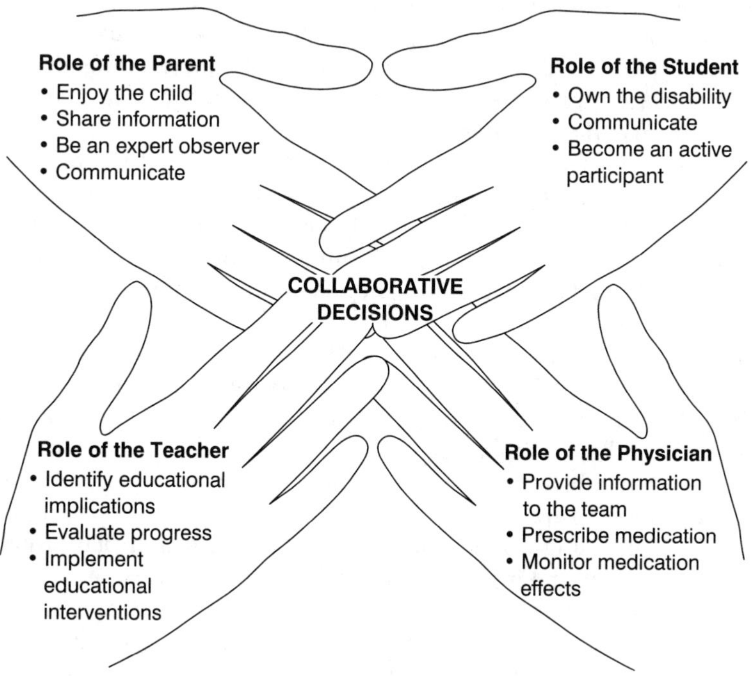

FIGURE 5–1

Diagram of a Team-Based Approach to ADHD Intervention

From "Meeting the ADD challenge: A multimodal plan for parents, students, teachers, and physicians" by B. Fell and K. Pierce, 1995, *Intervention in School and Clinic*, *30(4)*, 198–202. Copyright (1995) by PRO-ED, Inc. Reprinted by permission.

STIMULANT MEDICATIONS

While the team-based approach is crucial for successful intervention, some understanding of the medications typically utilized for students with ADHD is also essential to facilitate effective communication among members of the team. It is unfortunate that many teachers are not provided with information on these medications as part of their preservice and/or inservice preparation. Also, because the vast majority of students with ADHD are on only one type of medication (stimulants), many teachers may incorrectly assume that if they have knowledge about the stimulants they understand the diverse array of medication treatments. To be effective team members, teachers must have some understanding of the classes of drugs described here.

Medications Used

Bradley (1937) was the first practitioner to use stimulant medication to treat behavior problem children, and experimentation with medical treatments has continued ever since. Stimulant medication treatment became very popular in the 1960s, and today this type of treatment is widely used because of the popularity of Ritalin (generic name methylphenidate). This drug alone is responsible for approximately 90% of the stimulant medication market for ADHD (DuPaul & Barkley, 1990).

While dosages vary considerably, the recommended initial dosage of this medication is 0.3 mg/kg (milligrams of medication per kilogram of the child's body weight), usually twice daily (see DuPaul & Stoner, 1994, for a comprehensive review of dosage recommendations). This dosage can be increased to 0.6 mg/kg twice daily. The maximum recommended dosage is 0.8 mg/kg.

The effects of Ritalin are noticeable 30 minutes after ingestion, the first time it is used, and the peak efficacy occurs between one and three hours after ingestion (DuPaul & Stoner, 1994, p. 139). Ritalin metabolizes in the body quickly and loses its efficacy after four to six hours. During the early 1980s, Ritalin was distributed in fast, longer-acting, sustained-release form (Ritalin-SR); the typical effects of this form of the medication last up to eight hours. With a morning dosage included in the medication plan, Ritalin-SR obviated the need for taking a pill during the school hours.

There is some question concerning the relative effects of the short-acting versus the sustained-release form. Some research argues that the shorter-acting original form is more effective, and other research suggests that no differences in efficacy exist (DuPaul & Stoner, 1994, p. 139). Certainly, more information on this question will soon be forthcoming in the research literature, and teachers and parents will want to keep abreast of the latest research.

Another medication similar to Ritalin is Dexedrine (dextroamphetamine), a stimulant that works in much the same manner as Ritalin. Dexedrine should be dispensed in about half the quantity as Ritalin. Like Ritalin, Dexedrine is available in a sustained-release form (DuPaul & Stoner, 1994, p. 139).

The effects of Cylert (pemoline), another stimulant medication used recently, have not been studied as thoroughly as those of the other stimulants (DuPaul & Stoner, 1994, p. 137). A typical dosage is 2.25 mg/kg, usually given once in the morning. This medication takes up to three to four weeks to achieve appropriate clinical effect. Peak effects seem to occur two to three hours after oral ingestion and last up to six hours. Adverse effects of Cylert may include hypersensitivity and, more significant, abnormal liver function.

The psychostimulants are by far the most commonly used medical-based treatments for students with ADHD (Barkley, 1990). However, these medications may not be appropriate for some students. Students who demonstrate motor tics and/or anxiety disorders are not good candidates for psychostimulant treatments; antidepressant drugs (described briefly later) would typically be utilized for such students.

Efficacy of Stimulants

There is wide general agreement in the research literature that stimulant medications help alleviate the problematic symptoms associated with ADHD in the short term for approximately 70% of the children with ADHD (Barkley, 1990; Hinshaw, 1995; Swanson, 1993). Results were initially documented in terms of improved attention behavior and improved social behavior, as well as decreased impulsive responding among students with ADHD (DuPaul & Stoner, 1994, p. 142; Hinshaw, 1995). Students' impulse control and attention to task seem to improve with the regular use of stimulant medication. Hinshaw (1995) studied the effects of Ritalin in a summer camp program and indicated that this medication brought under control both aggressive behaviors and noncompliant behaviors. In fact, the medication effectively brought those problem behaviors into the range of functioning of normal children in that study.

Many parents feel that not only are the behaviors of the child with ADHD enhanced, but also the child's relationship to everyone else in the family is enhanced. This is quite understandable, since decreased aggression and noncompliant behaviors result from stimulant treatment for most children, as noted. Thus, the overall quality of family life can be positively affected by this medical treatment.

While many in the popular press have challenged the use (some would say the abuse) of stimulant medications in treating children and youth with ADHD, few parents and teachers who work with these individuals on a daily basis would issue such a challenge. There is also some support for the proposition that stimulant medications enhance the academic performance of individuals with ADHD (DuPaul & Stoner, 1994, p. 143; Swanson, 1993). Initially, the research on this question indicated no direct benefits on academic achievement resulting from stimulant medications. However, recent research, using more sophisticated measures of academic achievement (which may be more sensitive to change than standardized achievement tests), seems to indicate improved academic functioning as a result of stimulant medical treatment (DuPaul & Stoner, 1994, p. 139).

Finally, there is growing recognition of the efficacy of stimulant medication for adults with ADHD (Murphy, 1992; Wender, 1994). Murphy (1992) indicates that the same medications used for children are also useful for adults and may lead to not only improved behavior but also a greater sense of overall organization in the life of the adult with ADHD.

Unanswered Questions

In spite of these findings, there is considerable controversy regarding the use of stimulant medications as treatments for children. First, the long-term effects of such medications have not been adequately demonstrated (Swanson, 1993; Wender, 1994). Swanson (1993), in his review of a massive body of available research literature (over 3,000 studies), indicated that very few studies on the use of stimulant drugs for children and youth with ADHD indicate any significant long-term effects. However, many of these studies did not include measurement and research design features that would have indicated long-term positive results, had such results existed. Other studies may have included measures of increased attention to task, improved behavioral performance, and so on but may have not looked at a wider array of variables that may indicate other, more significant, long-term effects.

In contrast to the earlier research, Wender (1994) has described an ongoing research effort with adults with ADHD that seems to document positive long-term effects of medication treatments. In this research effort, Wender and his colleagues studied the behavior of 125 individuals administered either a stimulant medication or a placebo, for a three-year period. The purpose of the study has been to look at long-term effects in a more appropriate fashion for an adult population. Whereas attention to task and academic and behavioral achievement are appropriate long-term measures of success for school-age children, in an adult population, questions concerning improvement in marriages and other relationships and improved functioning in the workplace would be more appropriate measures of long-term success. Wender (1994) suggests that his results (as yet unpublished) have demonstrated such long-term improvement for subjects who continued to take their medication, resulting in improved relationships both at home and at work.

A second unanswered question concerns the possible overuse of the stimulant medications. There has been considerable controversy in the public press concerning stimulant medications and the growing number of children on such medication. In the context of the overuse of these medications, some journalists have challenged the existence and/or nature of ADHD itself (Merrow, 1995). It had been suggested that stimulant medication leads to stunted growth and may not be entirely safe if taken on a year-round basis. However, we now know a great deal about the effects of stimulants, and while some side effects (described next) are present in some children, these medications are widely regarded as safe, even if taken year-round (Mandelkorn, 1995). Further, there is no evidence that even long-term use of stimulant medications leads to addiction of these medications or any other drugs (Mandelkorn, 1995). The unresolved questions on the possible overuse and overdependence on medication treatments concern the parents and professionals involved, rather than any danger of addiction on the part of the clients themselves.

Side Effects of Medications

The negative side effects of these stimulant medications can be a major factor in determining what medication plan is right for a particular student. The side effects should be thoroughly discussed with the attending physician, and parents and teachers should watch closely for any of these side effects. Figure 5–2 is a chart of the most commonly used medications and the side effects associated with each.

The most common adverse effects of stimulant medications include insomnia and loss of appetite resulting in concern for growth retardation.

FIGURE 5–2
Commonly Used ADHD Medications and Their Side Effects

Medication Type	Side Effects
Psychostimulants	
Ritalin, Dexedrine, Cylert	Decreasing appetite, weight loss, irritability, headaches, abdominal pain, increase in nervous tics
Antidepressants	
Norpramin, Tofranil	Increased blood pressure, increased heart rate
Antihypertensives	
Clonidine	Sedation, sleepiness

Several good reviews present information on side effects. See Barkley (1990, p. 585) and DuPaul and Stoner (1994).

The latter difficulty, however, has largely been discounted by recent research indicating that growth suppression is not a major concern except with high dosage levels (Mandelkorn, 1995). More severe but infrequent effects include abnormal involuntary motor movements (tics) and the possibility of depression. Barkley (1990, p. 587) mentions that around 90% of the available studies indicate that side effects were observed in the subject population but that in the vast majority of these studies that showed side effects, the side effects were noted as mild. Perhaps more important from the teacher's and parent's perspective is the number of children actually affected by any side effects. Barkley, McMurray, Edelbrock, and Robbins (1990) studied parents' and teachers' reports of side effects of stimulant medication and demonstrated that slightly more than half the children had some side effects; again, the vast majority of reported side effects (typically, 90%–95% of all side effects noted) were reported as mild.

OTHER MEDICATIONS UTILIZED

Antidepressants

Two antidepressant medications, Norpramin (desipramine) and Tofranil (imipramine), are frequently used with children with ADHD (Barkley, 1990, p. 607). Typically these medications are tried with children who have not responded positively to the psychostimulant medications described earlier (DuPaul & Stoner, 1994, p. 140). Biederman, Baldessarini, Wright, Knee, and Harmatz (1989) demonstrated that, among the 30% of children with ADHD who do not respond favorably to stimulant medications, approximately 70% will respond favorably to treatment with Tofranil. Also, Tofranil may be used when indications of ADHD and depression coexist. Dosage levels range up to 2.5 mg/kg per day, and one to three weeks of administration is typically required before an optimal therapeutic level is achieved.

These medications are not typically a first-choice medication treatment, since their side effects may be more serious than the side effects associated with stimulants. Increases in blood pressure and possible adverse effects on heart action result in the need for much closer monitoring of these medication treatments (DuPaul & Stoner, 1994, p. 140).

Clonidine

Other medications are also used with students with ADHD. One of the most common is clonidine, which is typically used with students who display, in addition to the ADHD symptoms, extreme hyperactivity and/or highly aggressive behaviors (DuPaul & Stoner, 1994, p. 141). This medication, like the antidepressants, may be used when students have shown a poor response or no response to stimulant treatment. Alternatively, sometimes clonidine is prescribed along with Ritalin if a student responds to a Ritalin prescription treatment with increased insomnia (DuPaul & Stoner, 1994, p. 141) (this type of medical drug combination is sometimes referred to as a medication "cocktail").

THE TEACHER'S ROLE IN MEDICATION TREATMENTS

When a medication treatment plan is in effect, the role of the teacher must be that of both intervention specialist and monitor. Bender and Mathes (1995) described this role as a three-factor set of responsibilities involving, first, the assessment of behavior and support of the parents and child during the identification process; second, the implementation of educational interventions; and third, the monitoring of the efficacy of all interventions. Each of these responsibilities involves some commitment of time and effort, and each is critical to the overall success of the intervention effort.

The Assessment and Identification Process

The major issues of ADHD assessment are discussed in Chapter 4. Here we deal with critical concerns regarding assessment and identification involved with medical treatments. First, under federal law, assessment for at-risk students suspected of having disabilities involves identification of conditions that may affect learning; some of these conditions may be medical in nature. Historically, only physicians have identified individuals who suffered from medical conditions, and school personnel typically do not have access to a physician or physician's report when they first suspect that a child may suffer from ADHD.

Further, as the team emphasis in this chapter makes clear, teachers alone should not typically formulate a diagnosis or even a suspected diagnosis. The teacher is well advised to remember that the term *ADHD* is a medical term, and most states do not recognize it as a disability within the special education laws and regulations. Consequently, teachers should not suggest to a parent that their child seems to have or may have ADHD, since such a suggestion implies that the teacher can make such a diagnosis.

Rather, the teacher's role in the identification process is to document the child's behavioral and/or academic problems, as well as the educational interventions that have been attempted previously. If academic and behavioral problems persist in spite of educational modifications and implementation of educational treatments (as described in Chapter 7), the teacher can confidently state that some problem seems to exist that has a noneducational basis and that further assessment to discover the potential problem is necessary.

Two messages herein must be made clear because of their potential implications. First, teachers absolutely must provide some documentation of some type of unsuccessful intervention that they have attempted with the child to the team during the identification process. For example, if, in the face of Billy's consistent misbehavior (e.g., impulsive answering, out-of-seat behavior), the teacher attempts a behavioral contract intervention such as that described in Chapter 7 and that intervention results in little or no improvement, that teacher would be correct in seeking additional assessment from a broad team of educational and medical practitioners. However, prior to implementation of any medical treatment, some educational intervention (preferably several types) must have been attempted and documented. Typically this documentation would be presented in terms of a behavioral chart involving baseline count and intervention results, but some data on attempted educational interventions above and beyond the instructional strategies used for everyone in the class must be presented (Bender & Mathes, 1995).

The second message is more subtle and involves legal issues for which no clear-cut answer is presently available. If a teacher suspects that a problem such as ADHD may exist and recommends that the parents take the child to a doctor who is known to specialize in ADHD, there is an open debate concerning who pays for that medical examination. Federal law stipulates that medical examinations be provided free, as part of the diagnostic process, when a learning problem based on a medical problem is suspected. However, many school districts balk at paying for outside medical examinations during the identification process. In fact, some school districts have specifically instructed teachers not to suggest to parents that they get a medical examination for the child, since such a suggestion may open the school district to a responsibility to pay the bill for that medical examination. Clearly, every teacher should check with his or her school district to establish beforehand what specific policies are utilized in that district.

Because such care is necessary in terms of what teachers may say to parents, communication must be thoughtfully considered. Figure 5–3 presents a sample letter used to assist a teacher in communicating with the parents and other members of the collaborative team.

Educational Intervention Responsibilities

Many chapters in this book focus on educational interventions for children and youth with ADHD, and the array of such interventions is quite broad. For our purposes in this chapter, we need only note that the teacher's responsibility for providing appropriate educational interventions does not end when the assessment process ends with a diagnosis of ADHD, nor does the need for individual interventions cease when medication is prescribed

Ms. Joanna Ellrott
1287 Riverside Rd.
Bishop, CA 93768

Dear Ms. Ellrott:

I have had the pleasure of teaching your daughter Debbie for the last two months in the second grade, and she has been both a joy and a challenge. I can assure you that she will often see connections between ideas that are exciting and quite unusual for a child her age, and I have learned a great deal from the pleasurable experience of having her in my class this year.

However, I do have a concern with some of the behaviors Debbie has demonstrated. She is off-task a higher percentage of the time than some of the other children in the class, particularly on seatwork papers and similar assignments. Also, she seems to answer impulsively when a question is asked in class, often without raising her hand.

I have implemented a reward system exclusively for her to help her finish her work. She can now earn three minutes of computer time each day for appropriate behaviors (and I'm sure you realize how much she enjoys computer time). This has helped some, as the enclosed behavioral chart indicates.

Still, I think it would be appropriate for a team of experts to meet and assess Debbie to increase my understanding of how to help her. These persons will include a psychologist, a master teacher, and an educational diagnostician. We may also want to speak with your family physician, but that has not yet been determined. Also, we would very much appreciate your involvement with this team.

Please call me and help me schedule a time for a brief meeting for the two of us. Bring any educational and/or medical records you have, which may help us understand Debbie and her learning styles. I look forward to working with you.

Yours,

Ms. René Dubois

FIGURE 5–3
Sample Letter for Communicating Behavioral Concerns

(Bender & Mathes, 1995). In fact, there is some evidence that the efficacy of medical treatments can be enhanced considerably when an educational intervention such as any of the behavioral interventions and perhaps the self-monitoring interventions is utilized (Fiore, Becker, & Nero, 1993). In short, individual interventions must be coupled with the medical treatment and planned with that joint intervention in mind.

Monitoring the Treatment

Medication

Monitoring of the treatment involves several responsibilities, which may be as simple as keeping a medications log and as involved as implementing a behavioral intervention charting process to document minute changes in behavior over time. Clearly, with numerous children using medication at school, the school personnel have a responsibility to monitor the medications given to children during the school day. Gone are the days when a secretary pulled out an unmarked envelope from the office desk and administered medication to a child. At a minimum, the most qualified medical person in the school should administer the medication that is to be taken during the school day. Often, this will be a school nurse or nurse practitioner. In schools that do not have a full-time nurse, others may be expected to administer the medications, but a set of procedures should certainly be followed to ensure that medication administration takes place in an appropriate fashion. Figure 5–4 presents a set of considerations that should be attended to. Again, these considerations should be addressed in a set of written procedures that stipulate specifically how medication is to be monitored.

Figure 5–5 is a sample form for a medications log, which can be used by the school person administering the medication for numerous children each day. As these are completed, they should be kept for at least four years, in an orderly fashion in the principal's office. Note that some person must sign for

- Make sure that appropriate security for the medications is provided. Medications should be kept under lock and key.
- Medications should be administered only from clearly and correctly labeled medication bottles, not from, for example, envelopes from parents. The bottles should clearly state the type of medication, the appropriate dosage, and the time of administration.
- A medications log should be kept by the school persons administering the medication to ensure that the right child receives the right medication at the right time. Each medication administration should include a signature of the person responsible for that drug administration, to be kept on file.
- The person administering the medication should watch the child take the medication to ensure that the child actually swallows the medication, rather than spits it out.
- Phone numbers for the child's parents, as well as of the physician who prescribed the medication, should be available in each child's records.

FIGURE 5–4
Considerations for Medication Treatment Monitoring

each medication administration for each child. This is intended to ensure that a responsible person has administered the medication in a fashion consistent with the approved procedures stipulated by the school district.

Effects of Medications

Typically, medication treatments will result in a much higher success rate on classroom work, as well as improved behavior within the class. The monitoring of such effects is predominantly the role of the teacher. Monitoring the effects of medication may be completed by the teacher in one of two ways. First, teachers are frequently asked by the physician to complete behavioral ratings (such as those discussed in Chapter 4). Many physicians have particular behavioral ratings they prefer, and sometimes school districts have chosen to adopt particular rating forms for this purpose. The teacher should use the behavioral rating form preferred by the school district and/or the attending physician. It is not uncommon for a physician to request that a behavioral rating form be completed every few months during medication treatment.

Child's Name	Date	Medication	Dosage	Time Required	Time Given	Person Responsible

FIGURE 5–5
Sample Medications Log

However, many behavioral ratings are not terribly sensitive to minute changes in behavior, nor are ratings that are completed several months apart accurate in depicting when the behavioral improvement actually took place. For this reason, many practitioners prefer a second, more sensitive method for behavioral monitoring—the behavioral chart. As mentioned previously, the teacher will continually conduct various interventions with the child with ADHD, and many of these interventions will result in behavioral charts or graphs that depict, across a fairly large time span, how a child is doing in class.

As one example, Figure 5–6 presents the data for Tyrone, a fourth-grade male student with ADHD. Because the most important behavioral concerns for the teacher were Tyrone's tendencies to blurt out answers inappropriately and to get out of his seat, the teacher decided to keep a daily count of these behaviors. However, the teacher realized that Tyrone was interested in curbing these behaviors only during the morning language arts instructional period prior to recess, since most of the afternoon activities in the class were group projects, and physically active instructional periods anyway. For this reason, the teacher kept data on the two behaviors only for the morning instructional period.

The teacher noticed improvement in the two chosen behaviors within two weeks after school began, which is when Tyrone began to take Ritalin. The teacher confirmed the improvement in Tyrone's behavior with the parents and the physician. Notice the high indicators of problem behaviors on Monday and Wednesday of the third week. These types of "peaks" are not uncommon and frequently indicate days when the child forgot to take his medication. Notice the sensitivity of this type of behavioral charting in terms of identification of the specific days when the child was not taking medication.

Of course, there may have been other problem behaviors the child demonstrated that were not included on the chart; for this reason, the chart may not represent every single instance of misbehavior. However, charting problematic behaviors such as these can give the team a great deal of information on the efficacy of the medications utilized. Every teacher should be prepared to keep data of this nature for students on medication and to freely share these data with the other members of the team. Only in this fashion can the efficacy of the medication treatment plan be gauged.

CONCLUSION

The medical interventions used by many children with ADHD present new and different responsibilities for educators. Not only do educators now need to have a broader grasp of medications used for hyperactivity, but they must also recognize their responsibilities for implementation of the medica-

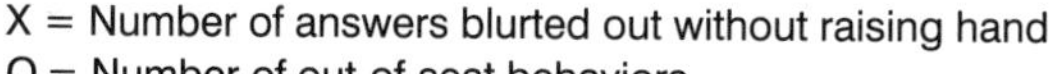

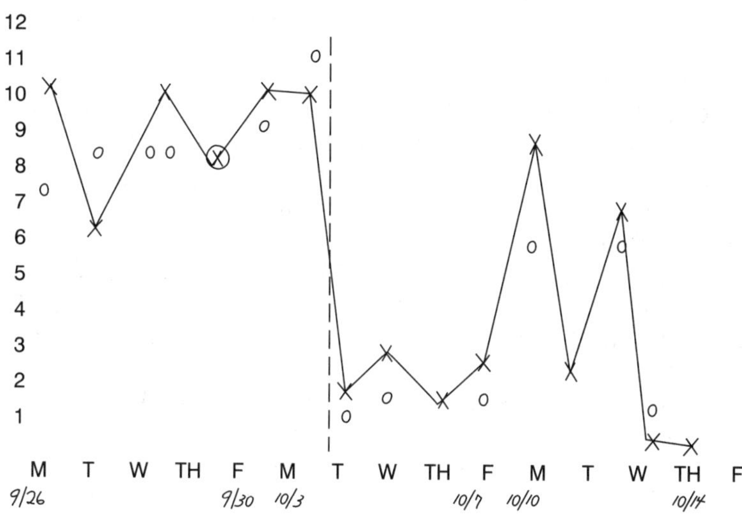

Note: Student began using Ritalin on 10/4.

FIGURE 5–6
Chart of Behavioral Progress for Tyrone
Note: Student began using Ritalin on 10/4.

tion plans. These concepts, while brief, will give the educator a preliminary understanding of the responsibilities in working with the team to ensure success of the medication monitoring program.

REFERENCES

Barkley, R. A. (Ed.) (1990). *Attention deficit hyperactivity disorder: A handbook for diagnosis and treatment.* New York: Guilford Press.

Barkley, R. A., McMurray, M. B., Edelbrock, C. S., & Robbins, K. (1990). The side effects of Ritalin in ADHD children: A systematic placebo-controlled evaluation of two doses. *Pediatrics, 86,* 184–192.

Bender, W. N., & Mathes, M. O. (1995). Students with ADHD in the inclusive classroom: A hierarchical approach to strategy selection. *Intervention in School and Clinic, 30,* 226–234.

Biederman, J., Baldessarini, R. J., Wright, V., Knee, D., & Harmatz, J. S. (1989). A double-blind placebo controlled study of desipramine in the treatment of ADD: 1. Efficacy. *Journal of the American Academy of Child and Adolescent Psychiatry, 28,* 7770–7784.

Bradley, W. (1937). The behavior of children receiving benzedrine. *American Journal of Psychiatry, 94,* 577–585.

DuPaul, G. J., & Barkley, R. A. (1990). Medication therapy. In R. A. Barkley (Ed.), *Attention-Deficit Hyperactivity Disorder: A handbook for diagnosis and treatment* (pp. 573–612). New York: Guilford Press.

DuPaul, G. J., & Stoner, G. (1994). *ADHD in the schools: Assessment and intervention strategies.* New York: Guilford Press.

Fell, B., & Pierce, K. (1995). Meeting the ADD challenge: A multimodal plan for parents, students, teachers, and physicians. *Intervention in School and Clinic, 30,* 198–202.

Fiore, T. A., Becker, E. A., & Nero, R. C. (1993). *Research synthesis on education interventions for students with attention deficit disorders.* Research Triangle Park, NC: ADD Intervention Center at the Center for Research in Education.

Hinshaw, S. (1995). An interview with Stephen Hinshaw. *Attention! 1*(4), 9.

Jacobvitz, D., Sroufe, L. A., Stewart, M., & Leffert, N. (1990). Treatment of attentional and hyperactivity problems in children with sympathomimetic drugs: A comprehensive review. *Journal of the American Academy of Child and Adolescent Psychiatry, 29,* 677–688.

Mandelkorn, T. (1995). Summertime medication? *Attention! 1*(4), 24–29.

Merrow, J. (1995). *Attention deficit disorder: A dubious diagnosis? The Merrow Report.* New York: The Merrow Report.

Murphy, K. R. (1992). Coping strategies for ADHD adults. *CHADDER, 6*(2), 10–11.

Parker, H. C. (1995). Assessment of ADD: A team approach. *CHADDER: Special International Issue.* Plantation, FL: CH.A.D.D.

Swanson, J. M. (1993). *The effect of stimulant medication on children with attention deficit disorder: A review of reviews.* Irvine: University of California–Irvine ADD Center.

Wender, P. H. (1994). An interview with Paul H. Wender. *Attention! 1*(1), 1.

CHAPTER 6

Intervention Strategies for Preschool Children with ADHD

Josh Hall
University of Georgia

Richard Marshall
University of Texas

Melanie Vaughn
University of Georgia

George W. Hynd
University of Georgia

Cynthia Riccio
University of Alabama

Preschool children with attention-deficit/hyperactivity disorder (ADHD) present behavioral management considerations that are both common to older children with ADHD and singularly unique to this younger population of children. Preschool children with ADHD present much of the same behavioral symptomatology as do their older counterparts. As such, they are overly inattentive, impulsive, and hyperactive. Coupled with the preschoolers' typical penchant for exploration and inquisitiveness, as well as temper tantrums and moodiness, ADHD preschoolers put challenging demands on their parents and teachers (Barkley, 1990). In this chapter we review current intervention methodologies for preschool children with ADHD that may be of assistance with their families as well as teachers.

ECOLOGICAL STRESS IN THE FAMILY

Many factors exacerbate the capacity of parents and teachers of preschool children with ADHD to appropriately respond to the behavior management needs of their children and students. Mash and Johnston (1983a) studied four groups of students—ADHD and normal subjects of 3–6 and 7–10 years old. Mothers of preschool children with ADHD initially reported that they were more competent in their capacity to manage the maladaptive behavior of their children than mothers of older children with ADHD. However, this competency effect progressively declines as these children grow older, their maladaptive behavior becomes more entrenched, and parents acknowledge that behavior management strategies typically utilized with normal children are not as effective with children with ADHD. In the same study, these authors report that mothers of children with ADHD in both age groups rated themselves on assessment measures as significantly depressed, socially isolated, and lacking in self-esteem. These findings are supported by other studies, such as Befera and Barkley (1985) and Cunningham, Benness, and Siegel (1988), which indicate that parents of children with ADHD are more depressed and feel more socially isolated in their contact with extended relatives than do parents of normal children. In addition, Mash and Johnston (1983a) found that parenting stress was significantly higher in the mothers of the younger children with ADHD and, not unexpectedly, these stress levels increased as the mother's rating of her child's maladaptive ADHD behavior increased.

Thus, it appears that children with ADHD cause significant social/emotional difficulties within the family structure. Further, the degree of these problems is related to the severity of the child's maladaptive behaviors, such that the worse the child's behavior, the more chronic the mother's affective concerns. Mash and Johnston (1983b) suggest that a result of these concerns may be that some parents of children with ADHD overreact to their children's behavior, even when the infraction is of a relatively minor nature.

In other studies, Barkley (1988) and, later, Campbell (1990) found that mothers of children with ADHD tend to report giving more frequent commands, directions, supervision, criticism, and punishment to their children than do parents of non-ADHD preschoolers. Further, Heffron, Martin, Welsh, and Perry (1987) examined in a retrospective analysis the records of 124 children ranging from 2 to 17 years of age who were referred to a university clinic for ADHD. They found that children with ADHD are more likely to experience a higher frequency of physical abuse and subsequently require attention from hospital emergency rooms on a more frequent basis than children from the general population. The authors suggest that ADHD may either contribute to or result from physical abuse. These findings indicate that many parents of children with ADHD not only react in an internalizing manner (e.g., show symptoms of depression) but also demonstrate an exceptionally low frustration tolerance in association with externalizing behaviors (e.g., aggression) toward their children. Given this overall aversive reaction to children with ADHD, it is not surprising that long-term outcome studies suggest that these children also display a much higher rate than non-ADHD children of psychiatric disorders, including conduct disorders and antisocial behavior (25%–28%), alcoholism (14%–25%), hysteria or affective disorder (10%–27%), and learning disabilities (30%–70%) (Cantwell, 1972; Morrison, 1980; Singer, Stewart, & Pulaski, 1981; Gittelman, 1985; McGee, Partridge, Williams, & Silva, 1991).

These difficulties were more recently examined by Barkley, Fischer, Edelbrock, and Smallish (1991) in an eight-year longitudinal study. The subject population consisted of 158 children ages 4 to 12 years originally referred to a clinic for ADHD and 66 normal children within the same age range. Follow-up assessment in adolescence was conducted for 78% of the original sample of these children. Findings indicated that children who were considered hyperactive tended to experience more automobile accidents than the normal subjects. The ADHD population also exhibited a significantly higher rate of oppositional-defiant disorder (ODD) and conduct disorder (CD) than expected in the normal population. ODD is a disorder involving such behaviors as arguing with adults, defying adult requests, deliberately annoying others, and blaming others for their mistakes. CD is characterized by those who have initiated physical fights, stolen, run away from home, are truant from school, and so on. In addition, this latter group was found to be significantly more likely than normal subjects to abuse substances such as cigarettes, alcohol, and marijuana. Academically, hyperactive students were much more likely to have been suspended or expelled from school and at least three times more likely to have failed a grade. Also, as might be expected, the subjects with ADHD were significantly more likely to have been enrolled in special education classes (Barkley, 1990).

Additional factors that exacerbate the stress level of families of preschoolers with ADHD include school participation and corresponding complaints from teachers. Campbell, Schleifer, and Weiss (1978) report that preschool children with ADHD are more likely to be out of their seats, talk and verbalize excessively, disrupt play activities, wander the classroom at inappropriate times, and exhibit more frequent episodes of aggression than their peers. The authors suggest that these behaviors produce generally negative feedback from the school and can result in aversive communication between school and home. Further, several studies (Campbell, Endman, & Bernfeld, 1977; Palfrey, Levine, Walker, & Sullivan, 1985; Blackman & Levine, 1987) suggest that follow-up with preschool children with ADHD in elementary school indicates that the ADHD symptomatology continues to persist and children with ADHD are clearly differentiated from normal children when judged on the basis of externalizing behaviors and low self-esteem.

When these difficulties are integrated with normal child-rearing demands, it is not surprising that parents of preschool children with ADHD are significantly stressed within their parenting role and often actively seek remedies to alleviate their difficulties. In addition, preschool teachers of children with ADHD often become easily frustrated when typical behavior management contingency strategies that are successful with non-ADHD children suddenly become ineffective with this population of children. As such, the need for behavioral intervention strategies at the preschool age is imperative in order to appropriately enhance the quality of childhood, the socialization and academic experiences of school, and later adult life for these individuals.

The issues associated with ADHD and family interactions and school performance are varied but must be understood and addressed by all adults working with preschoolers with ADHD. Typical family interaction issues are summarized in Figure 6–1.

INTERVENTION STRATEGIES

Behavior Management

In terms of behavior management, initial intervention strategies should be limited to two to three main areas of dysfunction, with identification of target behaviors accomplished through functional analysis. First, the primary offending behavior should be delineated and described in specific, quantifiable terminology. For example, the broad goal of "Improving Johnny's behavior in group settings" should be more specific, such as "Johnny will remain seated with his learning group for the first 5 minutes of the instructional session." As such, the latter goal can be accurately and reliably assessed.

- Mothers of preschool children with ADHD initially report that they are competent in their capacity to manage their children's maladaptive behavior. This competency effect progressively diminishes as the children become older and their maladaptive behavior becomes more entrenched.
- Mothers of children with ADHD are significantly limited on measures of self-esteem. In addition, they tend to be more depressed and feel more socially isolated in their contact with relatives than do mothers of non-ADHD children.
- Parenting stress is found to be significantly higher in mothers of younger children with ADHD. Further, the mothers' stress levels increase proportionally with the degree of problematic behavior reported.
- Parents of children with ADHD may overreact to their child's behavior, even if the infraction is relatively minor.
- Mothers of children with ADHD tend to report giving more frequent commands, directions, supervision, criticism, and punishment to their children than do mothers of non-ADHD children.
- Children with ADHD are more likely to experience physical abuse than do mothers of non-ADHD children.
- Long-term outcome studies of children with ADHD indicate that they experience a significantly high rate of psychiatric disorders, alcoholism, hysteria or affective disorder, and learning disabilities than do mothers of non-ADHD children.
- Children with ADHD experience significantly high rates of oppositional-defiant disorder and conduct disorder. Children who exhibit features of ADHD as well as conduct disorder are more likely to abuse substances such as cigarettes (nicotine), alcohol, and marijuana.
- Children who are hyperactive are much more likely than nonhyperactive children to have been suspended or expelled from school at some point in their school careers.
- Preschool children with ADHD are likely to be out of their seats often, talk excessively, disrupt play activities, wander the classroom, and exhibit more frequent episodes of aggression. As a result, aversive communication between home and school is often encountered.
- Preschool children who are diagnosed with ADHD are likely to persist in their presentation of ADHD behaviors in elementary school.
- Significant family difficulties are encountered when children with ADHD concurrently exhibit the typical problems of most preschoolers.

FIGURE 6–1
The ADHD Preschooler and Family Interaction Issues

The antecedents and the consequences of the behavior within the specific setting should then be identified. The antecedents may include such things as changing classrooms and sitting next to another child, or they may involve more extraneous events, such as prior arguments with parents, siblings, and other children. Consequences follow problematic events and may maintain inappropriate behavior, either advertently or inadvertently (such as providing attention to the behavior), despite the good intentions of parents and teachers.

In addition, positive behaviors must be taught and modeled, as well as consistently reinforced, so that such behaviors will be more likely to be demonstrated. For example, parents who encourage reading in their children should frequently read themselves. Parents who encourage their children to be organized could maintain a specific schedule themselves throughout the day and utilize organizational aids, such as a "time scheduler" in which to write appointments and "to-do" lists.

The underlying foundation of behavior management involves the timing and power of the antecedents and consequences. Hersher (1985), in a review of controlled studies published from 1965 to 1985, reported that children who were clinically diagnosed with ADHD responded in a less active manner when behavior therapy with an immediate reward was utilized. When the reward was delayed, however, behavior therapy made no positive contribution to the behavior of children with ADHD. In contrast, children who were moderately active responded equally well to both immediate and delayed rewards.

An issue of further concern and interest is whether there is a permanent change in the behavior of children with ADHD when utilizing behavior management techniques. Dubey, O'Leary, and Kaufman (1983) attempted to answer this question when they worked with a treatment-delayed control group and two experimental groups—one including children whose parents received behavior therapy training and one including parents who were taught Parent Effectiveness Training (PET). The main premise of PET is to teach parents to understand the underlying and unexpressed feelings of the child that lead to certain behavior. After nine months of intervention therapy, the respective groups of children were assessed, with indications that all children whose parents received training were less impulsive than those children who were included in the treatment-delayed group. Nevertheless, children who received behavior modification were no less impulsive than those whose parents received PET. Thus, both therapies were considered equally effective, and the authors concluded that behavior therapy, just as medication therapy, must continue at least into adolescence to be effective.

In a later study, Pelham (1992) noted that the use of rewards is especially beneficial in modifying the behavior of children who have ADHD. Further, Barkley (1990) commented that, based on the inattentive and overactive behavior they present, children with ADHD often appear insensitive to their environment because of the overwhelming frequency of negative feedback (such as reprimands and complaints). As such, children with ADHD often require more frequent and powerful rewards than do other children.

While behavior management therapy has many benefits, it also presents the possibility of negative or aversive effects. This procedure can be extremely time-consuming for the classroom teacher or parent, so it may result in non-ADHD siblings being ignored or getting less attention than they formerly received. These children may become overactive or inattentive just to obtain some of the attention that is now directed toward the child with ADHD.

Social Skills Training

Social competence, as noted by Hartup (1986) and Rubin (1982), involves mainly the appropriate regulation of disruptive behavior and control of attention. Alessandri and Schramm (1991) present a detailed case study of a four-year-old child, Derric. Among their findings were indications that Derric presented deficits in sustained attention in free play as well as in structured group activities. The authors concluded that these difficulties were associated with developmental delays in Derric's ability to play and interact with his peers. More expansive studies, such as Campbell (1990), Campbell and Cluss (1982), and Rubin and Clark (1982), suggest that hyperactive behavior and aggression toward peers are associated with social skills deficits.

Recently, Alessandri (1992) investigated attention, play, and nonplay behavior in 20 four- to five-year-old children with ADHD and 20 children without ADHD. He notes that by investigating ADHD in preschool children, variables that influence co-occurring behavior disorders at later ages are not a factor. Specifically, he found that preschoolers with ADHD play patterns were not as mature as non-ADHD preschoolers and that their cognitive play was primarily sensorimotor in function and principally characterized by repetitive motor movements. Further, the normal subjects demonstrated a routine and stereotyped use of materials evidenced by increased touching of the materials and more pounding activities than their non-ADHD counterparts. Preschoolers with ADHD also engaged in less parallel and group play as well as fewer peer conversations. In contrast, non-ADHD children engaged in more constructive and purposeful play activities. There was no significant evidence of more aggressive behavior in the preschool ADHD children than in the non-ADHD children. These factors obviously are of critical importance in the development of the preschooler with ADHD. Further, social skills deficits of this nature may result in rejection by peers and the shattering of self-esteem, further exacerbating the ADHD concerns and contributing to social and behavioral difficulties (Campbell & Paulauskas, 1979).

There are many instructional packages with the sole aim of promoting social skills development in children. Most have a goal of increasing the student's social knowledge (sensitivity and awareness of how their behavior affects others) and skill acquisition—that is, to have the child acquire new and improved social interaction skills. However, at this point, little research has been conducted with preschool children to establish the efficacy of these programs. Moreover, available research suggests that when such a program is successful, the behavior skills learned within a specific environment often do not generalize to new social settings (Barkley, 1990).

Instructional strategies that teachers should employ to increase social skills development include the suggestions listed in Figure 6–2. These strategies are also appropriate for use at home.

- In group settings, give the student a responsible role, such as that of group leader or teacher assistant.
- Model appropriate social behavior for the child at all times.
- Assist the student in identifying inappropriate behaviors presented within social interaction settings.
- Assist the student in developing friendships by pairing him or her with other children who model appropriate behavior.
- Reinforce other students for responding in an appropriate manner with the student with ADHD.
- Vary social groupings to find the groups in which the student successfully interacts.
- Provide opportunities for appropriate interaction within the classroom.
- Intervene in the social setting before the student loses control of his or her behavior.
- Limit interaction with inappropriate peer models.
- Teach the student social interaction skills (e.g., appropriate manners, friendly and complimentary words)

FIGURE 6–2
Social Skills Strategies for Preschoolers with ADHD
From *The Pre-referral Intervention Manual: The Most Common Learning and Behavior Problems Encountered in the Educational Environment,* by S. B. McCarney and K. K. Cummins, 1988, Columbia, MO: Hawthorne Educational Services; and *How To Reach and Teach ADD/ADHD Children,* by S. F. Rief, 1992, West Nyack, NY: Center for Applied Research in Education.

Cognitive-Behavioral Techniques

Most cognitive-behavioral programs involve teaching the students to self-monitor and self-regulate their behavior, as well as providing instruction in problem-solving strategies. Training usually consists of instructing the students how to monitor their own behavior and determine when self-reinforcement is appropriate. These techniques have proven to be useful with older students with ADHD. (The self-monitoring approach is discussed in detail in Chapter 8.)

In general, cognitive-based therapies have not proven to be effective with preschoolers with ADHD (Barkley, 1981). This appears largely because of the limited level of cognitive development and insight regarding decision-making processes that is inherent with children of this young age (Barkley, 1981; Cohen, Sullivan, Minde, Novak, & Helwig, 1981). Cognitive therapy may be successful, however, in restructuring parents' behavioral expectations of preschool children with ADHD (Barkley, 1990).

PARENT–CHILD INTERACTION STRATEGIES

Just as with school-based intervention strategies for preschoolers with ADHD, relatively minimal research has concentrated on parent intervention strategy effectiveness. With older ADHD populations, therapy efforts have focused on family education and training, behavior modification, cognitive-behavioral therapy, and family therapy. Within the preschool population, however, behavior modification (previously noted) and family education and training have been most frequently and effectively employed (Erhardt & Baker, 1990).

The importance of treating the whole family when providing intervention for preschoolers with ADHD is underscored by several researchers. Cohen and Minde (1981), Mash and Johnston (1983a), and Szumowski, Ewing, and Campbell (1986) indicate that parents of hyperactive children report more marital discord than parents of nonhyperactive children, higher rates of psychiatric illness, lower levels of self-esteem, and greater stress, and they perceive themselves as less effective in their child-rearing practices than other parents.

In an especially well constructed investigation of parent–child interaction training with preschoolers, Strayhorn and Weidman (1989) utilized a relatively large sample of 89 low-income parents of 96 preschool children with ADHD (ages two to five). They divided these parents into two groups: a minimal-treatment control group and an extensive-treatment experimental group. Utilizing the treatment program manual *Training Exercises for Parents of Preschoolers,* trainers incorporated such concepts as reinforcement of positive behaviors, communication techniques with children, modeling of appropriate attention, timeout strategies, and effective reprimands. Their findings demonstrated that the extensive-treatment group produced significantly more improvement in parents' ratings of children's behaviors (specifically, fewer episodes of hostility, fearfulness, and attention-deficit symptomatology) than did the control group. Moreover, from the extensive intervention treatment, a blindly rated measure of videotaped interaction similarly produced significant improvement. However, the question of which portion of the intervention treatment strategies was most successful was unanswered by this study. As a result, a follow-up investigation was conducted by Strayhorn and Weidman (1991) of these same parents one year after the last intervention strategy session was conducted. Questionnaires were then mailed to the parents as well as to the current teachers of their children. Findings from this survey revealed that parent ratings and child achievement test scores from school indicated no difference between the minimal- and extensive-treatment groups. However, when blindly rated by teachers in regard to the condition of the intervention, children of the parents of the extensive-treatment group were noted to be significantly superior to the children of the parents of the minimal-treatment group on the basis of attention-deficit and hyperactivity concerns. Moreover, children's improvement in their classroom behavior was significantly correlated with advances that parents had achieved within the extensive-treatment strategies training sessions. One explanation offered by the authors was that either the parents had forgotten their skills or their parenting skills had deteriorated, but the children still retained some positive habits, which were tapped within the structured environment of school (Strayhorn & Weidman, 1991).

These findings are consistent with an earlier study by Pisterman et al.(1989), in which improved compliance was found with hyperactive preschoolers at a three-month follow-up interval following parent training. Also, these results are supported by Kazdin's (1987) earlier work with older students (ages 7 to 12), in which positive effects were found at one year following the end of training for both parents and children in problem-solving skills.

In another study of the role of parent training with preschoolers with ADHD Pisterman et al. (1992) studied 57 families with children with ADHD ranging in age from three to six years. These families were divided into the following groups: 23 treatment-group families (i.e., with training) and 22 control-group families (i.e., with no training), with 12 dropout families also included. During 12 sessions, parents were instructed on appropriate methodologies for effective treatment of their children's attention problems. These included instruction in reinforcing appropriate behaviors, implementing timeout procedures (such as sitting in a neutral corner for a specific period of time following inappropriate behaviors), and applying overall behavior management strategies. A parent manual with guided readings, instructions, and homework assignments was provided. Integral to this training process were parent instructions to issue a "refocusing" command to resume the task, usually a nonverbal reminder such as tapping the child's shoulder, whenever the child was off-task. A second strategy involved instruction in shaping behavior; parents were given specific criteria for progressively increasing the period of time a child spent on-task before providing appropriate reinforcement. Control-group parents were provided with no parent training strategies. The results of this investigation indicated that the treatment group of preschool students with ADHD demonstrated a significant increase in the percentage of appropriate behaviors and a significant decrease in the time taken to complete a list of commands. Parent behavior was also modified, such that parents issued more appropriate commands and displayed a higher rate of reinforcement when appropriate behaviors were observed. Moreover, parents issued proportionally fewer commands demanding on-task behaviors and provided more positive feedback to their children. It is suggested by the authors of the study that the parents established a better parenting style, which may have enhanced their self-esteem and sense of adequacy related to effective parenting skills.

Another study, by Erhardt and Baker (1990), addressed the same issue of the effectiveness of parent training in two case studies involving preschool children with ADHD. Employing a 10-week parent training program, the researchers sought to teach parents to implement effective behavior management strategies, as well as to alleviate some of the aversive parent comments directed to their children after their disruptive behavior. The investigators used a social learning model of behavior emphasizing to the parents how to recognize a behavior problem, take data, identify relevant antecedents and consequences, and develop and critique their own behavior management programs. As a result of this training, the parents demonstrated improvements in effectiveness-interaction skills with their children; the parents' confidence in appropriately coping with their children's behavior dramatically increased; and the parents appeared to have a greater appreciation of the positive qualities of their children. Nonetheless, the children's noncompliant behavior remained unacceptably high, and the authors concluded that brief parent training of this nature was insufficient to completely improve the behavior of preschool children with ADHD.

Another program of note is Barkley's (1987) parent training program for children with ADHD of ages 2 to 11 years. This program involves a nine-unit sequence of instruction that focuses on establishing positive incentives prior to the utilization of punishment. The initial emphasis centers on the need for positive parental attention to appropriate behaviors. Later units emphasize increasing compliance to parents' requests and during independent play, decreasing disruptiveness, and parent training in the effective utilization of timeout procedures. Barkley stresses that the goal of this methodology is not to "cure" the child with ADHD but to provide coping mechanisms for both parents and child such that the quality of their interaction is enhanced. Support for the efficacy of this program is suggested by Anastopoulos and Barkley (1990) when employing this treatment design with 50 preschoolers and their families.

While techniques that involve teachers sending notes to parents have been used successfully for many years with older students, especially to sustain on-task behaviors (McCain & Kelley, 1992), research regarding this methodology with preschool children with ADHD is sparse. However, in a one-student case study, McCain and Kelley (1993) report many advantages for this intervention design. These include the inherent need for both parents and teachers to combine their efforts in modifying the student's behavior, as well as the capacity to tap powerful consequences controlled by the parents at home. In addition, they mention that notes sent from school to home often replace intermittent negative feedback with consistent and positive teacher–parent communication. Utilizing a note with drawings of faces and the four items "Played Well with Others," "Followed Directions," "Picked Up Toys," and "Used Class Time Well," the authors provided ratings for both morning and afternoon performance in class for the student. Feedback was provided by the teacher in the form of circling either the happy, so-so, or sad face to indicate performance for that time period. For the last behavior, "Used Class Time Well," the student was required to stay with an activity for at least five minutes to earn an appropriate face. A timer was utilized, and when the buzzer went off, the student could color in a smiley face. The length of the interval was gradually increased, and eventually the student began to set the timer himself. The note was subsequently taken home and the student was reinforced for a satisfactory rating. Both parents and teachers report that this technique was easy to use and could easily be integrated in their respective routines. As a result, the student increased attentiveness and decreased disruptive behaviors. Further, the investigators suggest that this technique allows for increased flexibility to tailor feedback in a developmentally appropriate manner (smiley faces) for the student. Other strategies for parents of preschoolers are presented in Chapter 7.

STRATEGIES FOR THE PRESCHOOL CLASS TEACHER

Factors in Preschool Class Interventions

In light of indications that ADHD begins in the preschool years or earlier (American Psychiatric Association [APA], 1994) it is surprising that little research has been conducted regarding the academic and behavioral functioning of preschool children with ADHD within school settings. Moreover, little is known regarding the efficacy of interventions with preschoolers that have proven successful with older children (Abramowitz & O'Leary, 1991). As such, the utility of many intervention treatment strategies remains rather unclear. Nonetheless, the importance of intervention capabilities within this type of setting is suggested by numerous investigations with older students.

Weiss and Hechtman (1986) report in a study of adults with ADHD that positive teacher attitude was an important step in helping these individuals with their academic problems. In terms of problematic behavior, Hinshaw (1987) found that approximately 50% of all children with ADHD develop behavioral problems of an oppositional nature. These difficulties include temper tantrums, defiance to teacher instructions, and refusal to follow rules. In addition, social interaction skills are often impaired, resulting in difficulty establishing interpersonal relationships, as well as generally intrusive and negative interaction when attempted (Milich & Landau, 1982). Also, while little research has been performed, especially with preschoolers, it is presumed that when teachers encounter difficult children they first become more interactive and directive in their attempts to counter this disorder. When unsuccessful and frustrated, over time, teacher interactions with children with ADHD become more unproductive and negative, further promoting and escalating the student's academic and behavioral difficulties (Barkley, 1990).

Within the preschool academic setting, most goals involve resolution of disruptive actions, hyperactivity, and, to a lesser degree, social interaction problems. It is important for the classroom teacher to note that improvement in these areas of functioning does not guarantee scholastic improvement; further intervention strategies may be needed to address academic enhancement. Moreover, Whalen and Henker (1991) suggest that treatment of ADHD children must involve a multidimensional-multimodality approach. This has been further substantiated by other findings (Pollack & Gittelman, 1981; Gittelman, 1983; Satterfield, Cantwell, & Satterfield, 1979; Cantwell, 1980; Sprague, 1983) that therapies focusing on one method of intervention with children with ADHD have a poorer degree of success than when multiple-treatment approaches are employed.

Many variables compromise the efficacy of intervention strategies. Teacher education about the disorder is paramount to the establishment of productive corrective techniques. As such, a schoolwide or districtwide continuing professional development program is important for enlightening all teachers about this relatively high-incidence disorder. Also, in most settings, training in behavior management procedures should be required. Consultation can be sought for this purpose from school psychologists, school counselors, and other types of consultation service providers.

Teacher orientation also varies considerably. Instructors with a nondirective approach toward learning may feel that behavior management procedures rob the individual of creativity and the joy of learning. Often this attitude is in conflict with most classroom management programs, especially those for preschool children with ADHD. Although teachers may change their stance after successful utilization of behavior management strategies, assisting teachers to modify these attitudes may be an equally important treatment option.

Other important variables include class size and direct instructional assistance for the teacher within the classroom. Implementation of behavioral management programs requires an initial time investment from the teacher to keep track of rewards/consequences, records, and monitoring of children's behavior. It is apparent that these procedures are difficult to implement if the teacher is responsible for the instructional and disciplinary needs of a large class of children. Last, most projects of this nature should be completed through the auspices of a building-level interdisciplinary team, minimally comprising the classroom teacher, school psychologist, and principal.

Classroom Strategies

Primary methods of direct classroom intervention with preschool children include behavioral interventions, teacher-implemented consequences, modification of academic tasks, and environmental strategies. Through and in conjunction with these methodologies, teachers (as well as parents and children) should seek to gain an understanding of the effects of ADHD on the child's ability to maintain an appropriate attention span and limit impulsivity and hyperactivity. As such, the goal, beginning in the preschool years, should be to instruct the individual to make special adjustments regarding how to compensate for their disability (Nathan, 1992). In other words, one major goal of the preschool class is to get the child ready for mainstream and/or inclusive instruction in the regular education program during kindergarten and the early years of school. Further, young children with ADHD should ultimately learn to self-monitor their behavior within both academic and social settings.

Behavior Management

Many behavior management strategies have been demonstrated as effective with young children with ADHD. These strategies should form the basis of the preschool teacher's approach. Figure 6–3 lists several areas of behavioral management intervention strategies for preschool children with ADHD that may be employed in the preschool class.

Classroom Structure

In addition to behavioral management strategies, the organizational structure of the classroom can assist the young child with ADHD to modify his or her behavior positively. For example, many practitioners suggest preferential seating for children with ADHD, and most attempt to limit the number

- Design a behavior management program to reinforce the student for desired behaviors and to influence the student to change maladaptive behaviors.
- Establish specific classroom rules (e.g., stay in seat, work quietly, stay with your group, interact in a positive manner with other children). Rules should be repeated frequently.
- Provide reinforcement (e.g., praise) for the student when he or she is sitting appropriately and working steadily for the determined length of time. Progressively increase the length of time that behaviors are to be presented before providing reinforcement.
- Separate the student from others who model inappropriate behaviors. Instead, team the student with another pupil who demonstrates correct behavior.
- Communicate with the student's parents when the student exhibits positive behaviors. Suggest reinforcements that can be given at home, such as staying up late to watch a special television show or providing special time alone with a parent.
- Reinforce students who are modeling appropriate behavior, such as staying on-task.
- Clearly delineate the rules to be followed within the classroom. Make sure all teachers and teacher aides clearly and consistently reinforce classroom and school rules. Have the students verbalize the rules.
- Have the student carry a point card for a token system.

FIGURE 6–3
Behavior Management Strategies for the Preschool Class
From *The Pre-referral Intervention Manual: The Most Common Learning and Behavior Problems Encountered in the Educational Environment,* by S. B. McCarney and K. K. Cummins, 1988, Columbia, MO: Hawthorne Educational Services; and *How To Reach and Teach ADD/ADHD Children,* by S. F. Rief, 1992, West Nyack, NY: Center for Applied Research in Education.

of distractions within the class. Figure 6–4 is a list of these suggestions related to the structure of the classroom ar l classroom activities. Although all these suggestions may not be appropriate for every preschooler with ADHD, teachers who employ these structuring techniques will have fewer problems managing children with these problems.

Instructional Grouping

In addition to planning the overall structure of the classroom, preschool teachers must consider the instructional grouping arrangements for young

- Allow preferential seating in the front of the room or in close proximity to the teacher to permit frequent monitoring of off-task behavior. The student with ADHD should, when possible, be seated away from colorful bulletin boards, windows, and doorways.
- Desk or work area should be free from distraction, with only the materials needed for the task at hand.
- To the extent possible, limit distractions within the classroom.
- Keep the daily routine the same each day. ADHD children function better when they know what activities are to follow. Also, provide as pleasant and calm an atmosphere as possible.
- Maintain visibility of the student at all times.
- Allow the student to close doors or windows that might prove distracting.
- Instruct the student to appropriately respond to excessive stimuli, such as by moving to another part of the room or asking other people to be quiet.
- Schedule specific activities to be performed when the student is most likely to be successful (e.g., before recess rather than immediately after recess).
- Schedule more academic-intensive material during the morning hours and more social and play activities during the afternoon.
- Activities requiring an active response pattern may be more helpful than those requiring a passive response.
- Provide verbal reminders of needed materials for each exercise or play activity.
- Allow time at the beginning of the day for organizing materials to be used during the day.
- Make sure appropriate storage space is available.
- Chart the times the student was organized and ready to begin the exercise.
- Remind the student at the end of the day about materials needed for the next day.
- Establish with the student an individualized routine that he or she can follow each day (e.g., gather materials first thing in the morning).
- Try to provide the student with a container, such as a plastic bucket, in which to carry each activity.
- Provide an organizer for student's material inside his or her desk. Color-coded organizers are especially helpful.
- Make sure that the student is not inadvertently rewarded for not being organized. If materials are not available, make sure that they use used materials.

FIGURE 6–4

Classroom Structuring Suggestions for Preschool Classes

From *The Pre-referral Intervention Manual: The Most Common Learning and Behavior Problems Encountered in the Educational Environment,* by S. B. McCarney and K. K. Cummins, 1988, Columbia, MO: Hawthorne Educational Services.

children with ADHD. Because young children with ADHD manifest fairly obvious social skills deficits, the preschool teacher should give serious consideration to using a fairly wide array of instructional group activities. Further, experimentation with various instructional grouping arrangements can help the teacher understand what types of groupings seem to assist the young child with ADHD to modify his or her behavior. Figure 6–5 presents several suggestions for instructional group arrangements.

Teaching Tips

Most teachers with experience involving ADHD children will agree that identifying specific problems and presenting directions are factors in the overall success of programs for such children. If a child does not understand a set of instructions, then all possibility of compliance with those instructions is gone, and the child will experience yet another failure. Further, when teachers give multiple instructions at once (e.g., "Children, put away your drawing and your crayons and get out your calendar pictures"), children with ADHD (and with other disabilities) are often left in the dark. Presenting such multiple instructions should be avoided in the preschool class. Figure 6–6 presents some teaching tips for the preschool classroom where children with ADHD are involved.

- Be in close proximity to the student when oral directions are given, and check with the student often to ensure that he or she has understood the directions.
- For independent seat work, a quiet area (e.g., study carrel) may be helpful, particularly if other students are involved in more dynamic, interactive activities. Make sure the student understands that this is not a punishment.
- In the classroom, particularly in cooperative learning or other group activities, strive to surround the student with positive role models.
- Try various placements in instructional groups to determine in which group the student is most successful.
- Remove the child from group settings when he or she cannot control inappropriate behavior. Utilize timeout strategies.

FIGURE 6–5
Instructional Grouping for Preschoolers with ADHD
From *How To Reach and Teach ADD/ADHD Children,* by S. F. Rief, 1992, West Nyack, NY: Center for Applied Research in Education.

- Present directions that are clear and concise, and, to the extent possible, avoid complex syntactic or directional concepts. Repeat directions often, and maintain physical contact with the student (e.g., touch his or her shoulder) while talking with him or her. Require the student to establish eye contact with you while instructions are provided.
- Initially provide instructions in one-step format, and then gradually increase the complexity of the directions.
- Have a predetermined signal with the class (e.g., clapping hands or turning off/on lights) that precedes giving directions.
- Structure activities into small steps, with each step to be completed before attempting the next step.
- Provide as many opportunities as possible for demonstration, hands-on activities, and/or use of manipulatives to reinforce more abstract concepts.
- Provide the student with appropriate opportunities to move around the room (e.g., passing out papers, delivering attendance forms to the office, etc.).
- Structure instructional material such that more-desirable activities are followed by less-desirable activities. Make the next activity contingent upon completion of the previous activity.
- Keep a chart of the number of assignments the student completes each day.
- Provide the student with earphones if auditory stimuli appear to be especially problematic.
- Provide a timer by which the student can remain on-task until an alarm goes off.
- Call the student by name before giving instructions.
- Give directions that are made up of only one step. Progressively increase the introduction of new concepts as the student exhibits success. Have the student repeat the directions given. Allow access to pens, pencils, and other materials only after directions have been given. Collect materials after activity has been completed.
- Present one assignment at a time.
- Ask the student questions that can be answered simply yes or no.

FIGURE 6–6

Teaching Tips for the Preschool Classroom

From *The Pre-referral Intervention Manual: The Most Common Learning and Behavior Problems Encountered in the Educational Environment,* by S. B. McCarney and K. K. Cummins, 1988, Columbia, MO: Hawthorne Educational Services.

Assignment Modification

In spite of the best efforts of the preschool teacher, there will be times when the child with ADHD cannot meet the requirements of a particular assignment. The hyperactive and impulsive nature of many children with ADHD may preclude completion, and the preschool teacher, like other teachers, must be prepared to modify the assignments accordingly. Figure 6–7 presents suggestions for modifications of class assignments.

Teaching Pitfalls

Blackman, Westervelt, Stevenson, and Welch (1991) provided some specific suggestions concerning what to watch for in teaching preschoolers with ADHD. First, they recommend that teachers should recognize that children

- Allow the student with ADHD to perform alternative assignments. Progressively introduce components of the regular classroom curriculum.
- Allow additional time to complete assignments, especially when students are working in an independent manner.
- Model some of the work problems on a one-to-one basis before allowing independent work.
- Have the student keep a graph with the number of correct assignments completed.
- Assign shorter academic tasks to be completed, and provide reinforcement when finished (e.g., praise, smile, etc.). Progressively increase the complexity of tasks to be completed.
- Provide reinforcement at stages of completion (beginning, middle, and end) of assigned tasks.
- Teach appropriate task completion behaviors that the student can utilize before requesting assistance. Try doing the task or play activity for a second time if necessary.
- Reduce any emphasis on competitiveness that may cause the student to hurry in his or her activities.
- Use visual material, such as wall charts, to present new concepts.

FIGURE 6–7
Academic Modifications for Preschool ADHD Children
From *The Pre-referral Intervention Manual: The Most Common Learning and Behavior Problems Encountered in the Educational Environment,* by S. B. McCarney and K. K. Cummins, 1988, Columbia, MO: Hawthorne Educational Services.

with ADHD will not be like other children. The disciplinary focus should be on diminishing disruptive and aggressive behaviors while tolerating a higher activity level and shorter attention span than with normal children. Further, the teacher should not ask the child with ADHD to promise to behave. Children with ADHD usually break rules as a result of limited impulsive control and cannot decide when they are going to break or follow specific rules. The authors also note that teachers should not expect to "cure" the child with ADHD. Instead, they should provide the child with coping strategies that will assist in compliance within the classroom and at home. It is further suggested that instructors be alert to indications that the child with ADHD has tired of the rewards or punishments provided.

MEDICATION THERAPY WITH PRESCHOOLERS

Since the late 1950s, various types of medication have been utilized as a treatment option for children with ADHD. At present, it is estimated that approximately 1%–3% of the children in North America are administered psychostimulants (e.g., Ritalin) or other medications for this disorder (Pelham, Bender, Caddell, Booth, & Moorer, 1985; Barkley, 1990). The number of preschoolers with ADHD who utilize medication, however, is generally estimated to be less than 1% (Barkley, 1988). Physicians bear the professional responsibility of prescribing this medication, and teachers should steadfastly avoid making specific recommendations to parents that their children be administered medication. Rather, working with school-based special education instructors, the school psychologist, or other school personnel, these professionals and the teacher may make a recommendation for further consultation with the child's pediatrician or family practitioner so that the parents may make an informed decision whether medication is warranted. The classroom teacher's assistance, however, is especially important in collecting data of the child's behavior before medication is administered and then monitoring at periodic intervals behavioral changes while the child is being administered the medication. To perform these significant responsibilities, preschool teachers should educate themselves about ADHD through staff development workshops, college courses, and textbooks such as this.

Efficacy of Medication on Preschoolers

Studies of the efficacy of medications with preschool children with ADHD have been infrequent and variable. Cohen and Minde (1981) reported that stimulant medication demonstrated few positive effects on the behavior of preschool-age children. In contrast, Barkley (1988) administered two dosages (low and high) of Ritalin and a placebo to 27 preschool children with ADHD. He subsequently found that with the low dosage, a decrease in the mothers' use of commands was evidenced, while with the high dosage, there was a decrease in children's off-task and noncompliant behavior and a corresponding increase in sustained compliance with maternal commands. Further, Speltz, Varley, Peterson, and Beilks (1988) noted the successful use of Dexedrine in the treatment of a preschool child with ADHD and oppositional defiant disorder.

In a recent case study, Alessandri and Schramm (1991) studied the effects of Dexedrine on cognition and the social play of a four year old boy with ADHD. They concluded that positive benefits were observed, centering on a decline of off-task behaviors and improvement with sustained attention during play as well as in a structured group activity. Moreover, play behavior became more sequentially organized, symbolic, and developmentally appropriate while social behavior improved in the aspects of sharing more with peers and receiving increased positive feedback from teachers.

In spite of these results, some practitioners believe that medication should not typically be utilized with the preschool population under age six because of increased risk for aversive side effects and the absence of documentation of efficacy in this population (APA, 1994). In addition, stimulant medication is considered much less effective with the preschool child with ADHD than with the elementary school child (Barkley, 1990). Nonetheless, Barkley (1988) notes that 60% of 27 preschool children under four years of age exhibited a favorable compliance response to maternal instructions when administered low doses of Ritalin. However, current "best practices" dictate that behavioral intervention strategies should be attempted in school and home before consideration is given to the use of medication (National Association of School Psychologists, 1992; American Academy of Pediatricians, 1987).

CONCLUSIONS

Teaching preschoolers with ADHD is a challenge for even the most experienced preschool teacher, and there are numerous pitfalls to be avoided. However, the preschool teacher who utilizes certain recommendations will find that the children with ADHD in their charge will be more capable of entering the regular education program in later school years. Also, the preschool years will probably present the first opportunity for educators to establish good working relationships with parents (discussed in further detail in Chapter 7). With this in mind, the preschool teacher should make every effort to accommodate the needs of the preschool child with ADHD and to establish a working rapport with parents.

REFERENCES

Abramowitz, A. J., & O'Leary, S. G.(1991). Behavioral interventions for the classroom: Implications for students with ADHD. *School Psychology Review, 20*(2), 220–234.

Alessandri, S. M. (1992). Attention, play, and social behavior in ADHD preschoolers. *Journal of Abnormal Child Psychology, 20*(3), 289–301.

Alessandri, S. M., & Schramm, K. (1991). Effects of dextroamphetamine on the cognitive and social play of a preschooler with ADHD. *Journal of the American Academy of Child and Adolescent Psychiatry, 30*(5), 768–772.

American Academy of Pediatrics. (1987). Medication for children with an attention deficit disorder. *Pediatrics, 80*(5), 758–760.

American Psychiatric Association. (1994). *Diagnostic and statistical manual of mental disorders* (4th ed.). Washington, DC: Author.

Anastopoulos, A. D., & Barkley, R. A. (1990). Counseling and training parents. In R. A. Barkley (Ed.), *Attention-deficit hyperactivity disorder: A handbook for diagnosis and treatment.* New York: Guilford Press.

Barkley, R. A. (1981). *Hyperactive children: A handbook for diagnosis and treatment.* New York: Guilford Press.

Barkley, R. A. (1987). *Defiant children: A clinician's manual for parent training.* New York: Guilford Press.

Barkley, R. A. (1988). The effects of methylphenidate on the interactions of preschool ADHD children with their mothers. *Journal of the American Academy of Child and Adolescent Psychiatry, 27*(3), 336–341.

Barkley, R. A. (Ed.). (1990). *Attention-deficit hyperactivity disorder: A handbook for diagnosis and treatment.* New York: Guilford Press.

Barkley, R. A., Fischer, M., Edelbrock, C. S., & Smallish, L. (1991). The adolescent outcome of hyperactive children diagnosed by research criteria: 3. Mother–child interactions, family conflicts and maternal psychopathology. *Journal of Child Psychology and Psychiatry and Allied Disciplines, 32*(2), 233–255.

Befera, M., & Barkley, R. (1985). Hyperactive and normal boys and girls: Mother–child interaction, parent psychiatric status, and child psychopathology. *Journal of Child Psychology and Psychiatry, 26*, 439–452.

Blackman, J. A., & Levine, M. D. (1987). A follow-up study of preschooler children evaluated for developmental and behavioral problems. Special issue: developmental and behavioral disorders. *Clinical Pediatrics, 26*(5), 248–252.

Blackman, J. A., Westervelt, V. D., Stevenson, R., & Welch, A. (1991). Management of preschool children with attention deficit-hyperactivity disorder. *Topics in Early Childhood Special Education, 11*, 91–98.

Campbell, S. B. (1990). *Behavior problems in preschoolers: Clinical and developmental issues.* New York: Guilford Press.

Campbell, S. B., & Cluss, P. (1982). Peer relationships of young children with behavior problems. In K. Rubin & H. Ross (Eds.), *Peer relationships and social skills in childhood* (pp. 323–351). New York: Springer-Verlag.

Campbell, S. B., Endman, M., & Bernfeld, G. (1977). A three year follow-up of hyperactive preschoolers into elementary school. *Journal of Child Psychology and Psychiatry, 18*, 239–249.

Campbell, S. B., & Paulauskas, S. (1979). Peer relations in hyperactive children. *Journal of Child Psychology and Psychiatry, 20*, 233–246.

Campbell, S. B., Schleifer, M., & Weiss, G. (1978). Continuities in maternal reports and child behaviors over time in hyperactive and comparison groups. *Journal of Abnormal Child Psychology, 6*, 33–45.

Cantwell, D. P. (1972). Psychiatric illness in the families of hyperactive children. *Archives of General Psychiatry, 27*, 414–427.

Cantwell, D. P.(1980). A clinician's guide to the use of stimulant medication for the psychiatric disorders of children. *Journal of Developmental and Behavioral Pediatrics, 1*(3), 133–140.

Cohen, N. J., & Minde, K. (1981). The "hyperactive syndrome" in kindergarten children: Comparison of children with pervasive and situational symptoms. *Journal of Child Psychology and Psychiatry, 24*, 443–445.

Cohen, N. J., Sullivan, J., Minde, K., Novak, C., & Helwig, C. (1981). Evaluation of the relative effectiveness of methylphenidate and cognitive behavior modification in the treatment of kindergarten-aged hyperactive children. *Journal of Abnormal Child Psychology, 9*, 43–54.

Cunningham, C. E., Benness, B. B., & Siegel, L. S. (1988). Family functioning, time allocation, and parental depression in the families of normal and ADHD children. *Journal of Clinical Child Psychology, 17*, 169–177.

Dubey, D. R., O'Leary, S. G., & Kaufman, K. F. (1983). Training parents of hyperactive children in child management: A comparative outcome study. *Journal of Abnormal Child Psychology, 11*, 229–246.

Erhardt, D., & Baker, B. L. (1990). The effects of behavioral parent training on families with young hyperactive children. *Journal of Behavior and Experimental Psychiatry, 21*(2), 121–132.

Gittelman, R.(1983). Hyperkinetic syndrome: treatment issues and principles. In M. Rutter (Ed.), *Developmental neuropsychiatry* (pp. 437–452). New York: Guilford Press.

Gittelman, R. (1985). Parent questionnaire of teenage behavior (modified Conners). *Psychopharmacology Bulletin, 21*, 923–924.

Hartup, W. W. (1986). On relationships and development. In W. W. Hartup & K. H. Rubin (Eds.), *Relationships and development* (pp. 1–27). Hillsdale, NJ: Erlbaum.

Heffron, W. A., Martin, C. A., Welsh, R. J., & Perry, P. (1987). Hyperactivity and child abuse. *Canadian Journal of Psychiatry, 32*(5), 384–386.

Hersher, L. (1985). The effectiveness of behavior modification on hyperkinesis. *Child Psychiatry and Human Development, 16*(2), 88–96.

Hinshaw, S. P. (1987). On the distinction between attentional deficits/hyperactivity and conduct problems/aggression in child psychopathology. *Psychological Bulletin, 101*, 443–463.

Kazdin, A. E. (1987). *Conduct disorders in childhood and adolescence.* Newbury Park, CA: Sage Publications.

Mash, E. J., & Johnston, C. (1983a). Parental perceptions of child behavior problems, parenting self-esteem, and mothers' reported stress in younger and older hyperactive and normal children. *Journal of Consulting and Clinical Psychology, 51*, 68–99.

Mash, E. J., & Johnston, C. (1983b). Sibling interactions of hyperactive and normal children and their relationship to reports of maternal stress and self-esteem. *Journal of Clinical Child Psychology, 12*, 91–99.

McCain, A. P., & Kelley, M. L. (1992). Promoting academic performance in inattentive children: The relative efficacy of school-home notes with and without response cost. Unpublished manuscript.

McCain, A. P., & Kelley, M. L. (1993). Managing the classroom behavior of an ADHD preschooler: The efficacy of a school-home note intervention. *Child and Family Behavior Therapy, 15*(3), 33–43.

McCarney, S. B., & Cummins, K. K. (1988). *The pre-referral intervention manual: The most common learning and behavior problems encountered in the educational environment.* Columbia, MO: Hawthorne Educational Services.

McGee, R., Partridge, F., Williams, S., & Silva, P. A. (1991). A twelve-year follow-up of preschool hyperactive children. *Journal of the American Academy of Child and Adolescent Psychiatry, 30*(2), 224–232.

Milich, R., & Landau, S.(1982). Socialization and peer relations in the hyperactive child. In K. Gadow & I. Bialer (Eds.), *Advances in learning and behavioral disabilities* (Vol. 1, pp. 283–339). Greenwich, CT: JAI Press.

Morrison, J. (1980). Adult psychiatric disorders in parents of hyperactive children. *American Journal of Psychiatry, 137*, 825–827.

Nathan, W. A. (1992). Integrated multimodal therapy of children with attention-deficit hyperactivity disorder. *Bulletin of the Menninger Clinic, 56*(3), 283–312.

National Association of School Psychologists. (1992, May). Position statement on students with attention deficits. *Communiqué, 20*, 5.

Palfrey, J. S., Levine, M. D., Walker, D. K., & Sullivan, M. (1985). The emergence of attention deficits in early childhood: A prospectus study. *Journal of Developmental and Behavioral Pediatrics, 6*(6), 339–348.

Pelham, W. E. (1992). Children summer day treatment program: 1992 program manual. Unpublished manuscript, University of Pittsburgh School of Medicine, Western Psychiatric Institute and Clinic, Pittsburgh, PA.

Pelham, W. E., Bender, M. E., Caddell, J., Booth, S., & Moorer, S. H. (1985). Methylphenidate and children with attention deficit disorder. *Archives of General Psychiatry, 42*, 948–952.

Pisterman, S., Firestone, P., McGrath, P., Goodman, J. T., Webster, I., Mallory, R., & Goffin, B. (1992). The role of parent training in treatment of preschoolers with ADHD. *American Journal of Orthopsychiatry, 62*(3), 397–408.

Pisterman, S., McGrath, P., Firestone, P., Goodman, J. T., Webster, I., & Mallory, R. (1989). Outcome of parent-mediated treatment of preschoolers with attention deficit disorder with hyperactivity. *Journal of Consulting and Clinical Psychology, 57*, 628–635.

Pollack, E., & Gittelman, R. (1981). Practical problems encountered in behavioral treatment with hyperactive children. In M. Gittelman (Ed.), *Strategic intervention for hyperactive children* (pp. 160–177). Armonk, NY: Sharpe.

Rief, S. F. (1992). *How to reach and teach ADD/ADHD children.* West Nyack, NY: Center for Applied Research in Education.

Rubin, K. H. (1982). Social and social-cognitive developmental characteristics of young isolate, normal, and sociable children. In K. H. Rubin & H. S. Ross (Eds.), *Peer relationships and social skills in childhood.* New York: Springer-Verlag.

Rubin, K. H., & Clark, M. L. (1982). Preschool teacher ratings of behavioral problems: Observational, sociometric, and social-cognitive correlates. *Journal of Abnormal Child Psychology, 11*, 273–285.

Satterfield, J. H., Cantwell, D. P., & Satterfield, B. T. (1979). Multimodality treatment: A one-year follow-up of 84 hyperactive boys. *Archives of General Psychiatry, 36*, 965–974.

Singer, S. M., Stewart, M. A., & Pulaski, L. (1981). Minimal brain dysfunction: Differences in cognitive organization in two groups of index cases and their relatives. *Journal of Learning Disabilities, 14*, 470–473.

Speltz, M. L., Varley, C. K., Peterson, K., & Beilks, R. L. (1988). Effects of dextroamphetamine and contingency management on a preschooler with ADHD and oppositional defiant disorder. *Journal of the American Academy of Child and Adolescent Psychiatry, 27*, 175–178.

Sprague, R. L.(1983). Behavior modification and educational techniques. In M. Rutter (Ed.), *Developmental neuropsychiatry* (pp. 404–421). New York: Guilford Press.

Strayhorn, J. M., & Weidman, C. S. (1989). Reduction of attention deficit and internalizing symptoms in preschoolers through parent-child interaction training. *Journal of the American Academy of Child and Adolescent Psychiatry, 28*(6), 888–896.

Strayhorn, J. M., & Weidman, C. S. (1991). Follow-up one year after parent-child interaction training: Effects on behavior of preschool children.

Journal of the American Academy of Child and Adolescent Psychiatry, 30(1), 138–143.

Szumowski, E. K., Ewing, L. J., & Campbell, S. B. (1986). What happens to "hyperactive" preschoolers? *Journal of Children in Contemporary Society, 19*(1–2), 75–88.

Weiss, G., & Hechtman, L. (1986). *Hyperactive children grown up.* New York: Guilford Press.

Whalen, C. K., & Henker, B. (1991). Therapies for hyperactive children: Comparisons, combinations, and compromises. *Journal of Consulting and Clinical Psychology, 59*, 126–137.

CHAPTER 7

Teaching Students with ADHD in the Elementary Classroom

A Hierarchical Approach to Strategy Selection

Mickie Y. Mathes, M.Ed.
University of Georgia

William N. Bender, Ph.D.
University of Georgia

Recently, numerous school districts have begun to serve students with ADHD and students with other disabilities in inclusive classrooms, and this has raised a number of concerns. In such settings, educational modifications for these students are often provided by regular classroom teachers as required by Section 504 of the Rehabilitation Act of 1973. Alternatively, they may receive services through special education placement under the Individuals with Disabilities Act as having other health impairments (Davila, Williams, & MacDonald, 1991).

Also, some evidence indicates that the number of children and youth with ADHD has increased in recent years (Barkley, 1990; McBurnett, Lahey, & Pfiffner, 1993). One parent advocacy organization, Children and Adults with Attention Deficit Disorders (CH.A.D.D.), states that 3.5 million children and 2–5 million adults have some type of attention deficit disorder (Children and Adults with Attention Deficit Disorders, 1993). Thus, the number of students with ADHD who are receiving services in regular education classes is increasing. As a result of these factors, regular education teachers must frequently deal with students' attention problems. A regular education class may have several students with ADHD besides the 15–20 other students in the class. Further, the students with ADHD may set an inappropriate model for classroom behavior, and the teachers sometimes spend extra time dealing with such behavior. Many of these students require behavioral intervention and/or closer supervision than do other students (Mathes & Bender, in press).

In addition to these concerns, the stimulant medications that are typically used in the treatment of ADHD are not always effective. Research has shown that stimulant medication is effective with approximately 70% of the students identified as having ADHD (Barkley, 1990). Consequently, the remaining 30% of students with ADHD require other forms of medication or educational intervention in their regular classrooms. For this reason, many researchers suggest a combination of treatments in which behavior modification, or cognitive-behavioral intervention, is coupled with medication treatments (Chase & Clement, 1985; Hinshaw, Henker, & Whalen, 1984; Hinshaw & Melnick, 1992; Horn, Chatoor, & Conners, 1983; Mathes & Bender, in press).

However, Swanson (1993) argues that there is not enough empirical evidence to support combination treatments. Further, Swanson (1993) pointed out that medication treatment may show immediate short-term effects but not positively affect the learning or complex cognitive skills of children with ADHD. They also indicated that medication treatment has no positive residual effects once the pharmacological effects dissipate.

For all these reasons, implementation of structured intervention strategies, which are not dependent on medication, become crucial for many students with ADHD. Regular and special education teachers must be able to identify the needs of students with ADHD and implement structured interventions effectively if these children are to succeed in the academic environment.

This chapter reviews the various types of strategies available within the context of a hierarchical intervention plan (Bender & Mathes, in press). The three levels of intervention strategies discussed in the chapter include unstructured, moderately structured, and highly structured strategies that are helpful to teachers in working with students with ADHD in regular and special education classroom settings. Depending on individual students' characteristics and their need for more or less structure, the regular education teacher should choose a strategy from the appropriate level of hierarchy to facilitate effective inclusive instruction for the student. While hundreds of specific tactics are available to the teacher, a hierarchical approach to strategy selection seems most appropriate because it offers an opportunity to match instructional strategies to the needs of particular students (Bender & Mathes, in press). It also offers teachers a rough guideline for selecting from the wide array of available strategies in working with children with ADHD and other disabilities.

First we discuss the teacher's responsibilities for students with ADHD. Then the hierarchical intervention plan is presented.

ADHD CRITERIA AND TEACHERS' OBSERVATIONS

Regular classroom teachers are responsible for assessing students' behaviors for identification purposes. It has often been noted that teachers may recognize possible behavioral problems in children before other professionals recognize them. Likewise, a regular classroom teacher may be the first individual to identify symptoms of ADHD in particular children.

As mentioned in earlier chapters, the American Psychiatric Association has identified four ADHD subtypes in the fourth edition (DSM-IV) of its *Diagnostic and Statistical Manual of Mental Disorders* (American Psychiatric Association [APA], 1994). Teachers should become familiar with the ADHD characteristics for the first three subtypes to pinpoint symptoms that are related to inattention, hyperactivity/impulsivity, and combinations of these symptoms. For example, Johnny may be exhibiting behaviors such as fidgeting with his hands or feet and getting out of his seat during seat work. However, according to the DSM-IV, at least four of the symptoms listed in the "hyperactivity-impulsivity" category need to be exhibited by Johnny to a degree that is maladaptive and inconsistent with developmental level for him to be identified as ADHD in that particular subtype (APA, 1994).

Documenting the behaviors associated with ADHD symptoms is crucial for both identification and intervention planning. Teachers may be consulted by physicians and other professionals to assist in identifying students with ADHD. Teachers should have data to show what the maladaptive behaviors are, rather than presenting merely subjective thoughts and opinions. The two documentation tools discussed next, the Critical Incidents Log and the Daily Checklist of Behaviors, are easy for regular classroom teachers to implement—teachers do not have to stop teaching to collect data. It is crucial for teachers, as professionals and advocates, to be able to show the daily data to the students' parents, physicians, and others.

Critical Incidents Log

Teachers use a Critical Incidents Log (Sugai, 1986) to record brief descriptions of antecedents, behaviors, and consequences. It should be used by teachers immediately after a problem behavior occurs.

A simple Critical Incidents Log can be easily adapted by Johnny's teacher to get an overall picture of his behaviors, including how and when the behaviors are exhibited and antecedents that may be common (Sugai, 1986). The teacher keeps the log on the desk and writes a brief description of any behavior or problematic event immediately after the behavior occurs. For example, Johnny's teacher asks the class to answer a question (antecedent), Johnny blurts out an answer (behavior), and the teacher ignores Johnny (consequence). This process helps the teacher to see Johnny's impulsive answering behaviors and get an overall picture of the event in an objective way.

Daily Checklist of Behaviors

If Johnny exhibits numerous ADHD-type symptoms, they may become too frequent for the teacher to keep track of using a Critical Incidents Log. The next step is to review the log to find a pattern of frequently exhibited behaviors and to list each behavior on a Daily Checklist of Behaviors, as shown in Figure 7–2. The record provides some indication of how frequently the maladaptive behaviors occur.

For example, from reviewing the Critical Incidents Log, Johnny's teacher identified several frequent behaviors exhibited by the student: fidgeting, getting out of his seat without permission, running in the classroom, becoming loud and boisterous during activity periods, blurting out answers

Date	Time	Antecedents	Behavior	Consequences
9/16	2:05	Student told to take out history book.	Student blurted out "I hate history."	Teacher ignored student's behavior.

FIGURE 7–1
Critical Incidents Log

Student: ____________________

Behavior \ Date															

FIGURE 7–2
Daily Checklist of Frequently Exhibited Behaviors

before the teacher calls a student's name, and showing frustration when he has to wait for turns in group activities. The teacher listed these on the Daily Checklist of Behaviors and kept the list available. Then, during instruction, she marked a check next to the behavior that was demonstrated by Johnny. A simple data collection tool such as this is easy and practical for teachers to use while engaging in lessons and activities.

HIERARCHICAL APPROACH TO STRATEGY SELECTION

Because regular education teachers have multiple role responsibilities in the assessment, intervention, and monitoring of students with ADHD, they must have a clear understanding of the array of strategies available to them. In this section we discuss unstructured, moderately structured, and structured intervention strategies.

Figure 7–3 is a checklist for the hierarchical strategy plan for teachers as they choose appropriate types of interventions. With adequate support and effective instructional and behavioral interventions, students with ADHD can succeed in mainstreamed activities. This concept also may be expanded and introduced to paraprofessionals who are working with students with ADHD.

Unstructured Interventions

Unstructured intervention strategies involve practical techniques that can be implemented relatively easily by regular education teachers. Many of these ideas stem from the research on effective teaching behaviors (Evertson, Emmer, Clements, Sanford, & Worsham, 1984) and may be thought of as efficient habits teachers should develop. Typically, unstructured interventions do not require collecting daily performance data nor preparing any additional work on the part of the teacher, other than practicing the habits that are identified as effective teaching behaviors.

Scholars have identified a number of unstructured practical strategies for teachers in inclusive classrooms (Hale, 1994; Bender & Mathes, in press; Vail & Huntington, 1993; Rooney, in press). These simple techniques can be easily used by teachers for working with students with ADHD and others to prevent inattentive, impulsive, and hyperactive behaviors. They can be categorized into three general areas: structuring the lesson, organizing the classroom, and monitoring the student's behavior (Bender & Mathes, in press).

Structuring the Lesson

Structuring lessons is one way to direct students with ADHD to function adequately in the classroom. Appropriate assistance needs to be provided so the students with ADHD can follow academic directions and accomplish the tasks given to them.

Provide Outline of Lesson. Children with ADHD often have difficulty focusing their attention when teachers lecture for a long period of time. Having an outline of the lesson helps some of these students to follow as teachers present topics to the class. An outline may consist of segments and a summary of major points for each segment.

Provide Clear Directions. Many of the behavioral problems associated with students with ADHD occur during transitional periods when the class moves from one activity to another. Teachers can prevent many of these problems by providing clear directions during transitions between subjects and avoiding multiple commands and multistep directions. They should take the last two minutes of the lesson to draw closure, prepare for the next set of activities, and make certain that all the children understand what they are expected to do.

Train to Recognize Cues. Students with ADHD often fail to recognize cues and may get behind on activities. They may be looking somewhere else when the teacher has already started the next subject or activity. It is important to train students with ADHD to recognize "time to begin" cues. A brief organizational period at the beginning of each class session can serve as a cue for the student. The teacher closes the door, faces the students, and checks for proper materials and books. The student should be listening as the teacher reviews goals and objectives for the period.

Plan for Frequent Breaks. It is often difficult for students with ADHD to sit and work for a long period of time. Note-taking sessions that last 20–25 minutes can be especially challenging for students with ADHD. Perhaps teachers in the elementary grades should assign some physical activity every 15 minutes or so to allow the student to use excess energy. Frequent breaks allow the students an opportunity to move around and stretch.

Use Physical Activities in Instruction. Another way to handle the problem of students with ADHD not being able to stay in their seats for long periods is to utilize physical activities in instruction. The students with ADHD function better if physical activities are incorporated into the lesson. For example, the teacher may divide the class into four groups and tell the students to make a straight line per group. When the teacher asks a question, the four students in the front row (one student from each group) compete to answer it by hitting a buzzer in front of them. The four front-row students

Student ________________ Teacher(s) ____________________ Date ____________

I. Description of Frequently Observed Behaviors

1. ______________________________
2. ______________________________
3. ______________________________
4. ______________________________

II. Intervention

Level 1: Unstructured

Checking the modifications might be helpful for the student to function in the inclusive classroom.

A. Structuring the Lesson

( ) Provide outline of lesson.
( ) Provide clear directions.
( ) Train to recognize cues.
( ) Plan for frequent breaks.
( ) Use physical activities in instruction.
( ) Use high-interest activities.
( ) Use clear, uncluttered worksheets.
( ) Decrease the length of the task.
( ) Teach organizational and study skills.
( ) Teach outlining skills.
( ) Assign a notebook in which to write daily homework.

B. Organizing the Classroom

( ) Use a physically structured classroom.
( ) Display classroom rules.
( ) Post daily schedule and assignments.
( ) Seat students away from noise.
( ) Place desks away from each other.
( ) Assign two desks.
( ) Provide alternate activities.

C. Monitoring the Student's Behavior

( ) Visually monitor and chart behavior.
( ) Discuss consequences of behavior.
( ) Use self-monitoring strategies.

FIGURE 7–3
Hierarchical Intervention Strategies for Teaching Students with ADHD

Level 2: Moderately Structured Interventions

A.( ) Token Economy (describe)

Assessment:____________________

Intervention:____________________

Monitoring:____________________

B.( ) Response Cost

Assessment:____________________

Intervention:____________________

Monitoring:____________________

C.( ) Self-Monitoring

Assessment:____________________

Intervention:____________________

Monitoring:____________________

D.( ) Hero Procedure

Assessment:____________________

Intervention:____________________

Monitoring:____________________

E.( ) Other Behavioral Interventions

Assessment:____________________

Intervention:____________________

Monitoring:____________________

Level 3: Structured Interventions

Describe the highly structured interventions used in your school.

A.____________________

B.____________________

C.____________________

FIGURE 7–3, *continued*

move to the back after their turn, thus allowing the next students to move to the front. This type of activity provides the students an opportunity to move around and yet contribute to their team performance.

Use High-Interest Activities. Students with ADHD often lose interest quickly and move on to other activities. However, many children are accustomed to playing with computer games at home and can focus on that type of activity for a long period of time. In recent years, a number of computer-facilitated academic activities has become available to classroom teachers. Such computer activities allow immediate feedback and are highly motivational to many students with ADHD. In addition, because writing tasks are often exhausting to children with ADHD, these children should be encouraged to use a computer for writing activities. Computers are also helpful in correcting spelling and grammatical errors.

Use Clear, Uncluttered Worksheets. Students with ADHD are easily distracted by decorative figures on worksheets. Teachers should thus avoid using unrelated drawings, such as flowers and animals, on worksheets. If a drawing illustrates a point, the teachers should discuss the drawing with the class. The use of graph paper is helpful for the students to organize long division and multiplication problems. Underlining or highlighting directions and math process signs may also help the students to focus on the core of the problems.

Decrease the Length of the Task. Students with ADHD are often frustrated and discouraged when they are unable to complete assignments. Some feel that they can never finish a task. Teachers should give assignments that are brief enough for the student to accomplish. This may require that teachers reduce the number of problems, words, and sentences and give fewer math problems to these students. For example, if a student is given 30 math problems, he or she may be assigned to answer only 15 problems first. Once the student learns to complete 15 problems, the teacher may increase the assignment to 17 problems, then to 20, and so on.

Teach Organizational and Study Skills. Students with ADHD often lack study skills and adequate work habits. They need to be taught how to number pages, how to make space between lines, how to erase thoroughly, and so on. Teachers may assist the students by dividing tasks into parts and estimating the amount of time needed to complete each part of the task. Also, the students must learn to clear their desks before beginning the next task. It is important for ADHD students to put away the books and assignments from the previous period so that clutter does not become distracting. For example, a teacher should routinely give 3–4 minutes to all the students for organizing and clearing their desks every Friday afternoon. The students can then return to school the following Monday and start the week in an organized environment.

Teach Outlining Skills. Students with ADHD may not be paying attention when a teacher is discussing key issues or moving to another section during a lesson. Teachers should direct students to write headings and key phrases from a discussion or class lesson and should repeat major points whenever possible. Learning outlining skills will help the students with ADHD to organize their notes and to prepare for exams. Students who are considered visual learners should be taught to draw a chart or write down key issues and words; auditory learners may use a tape recorder to record the key points. It is especially useful for many middle school and high school students to listen to their own voices to review lessons. In addition, students with ADHD need to be aware of words that give cues to take notes in order (e.g., "first," "second," "next," and "finally"). Also, teachers should repeat or verbally emphasize major points in each lesson.

Assign a Notebook in Which to Write Daily Homework. Students with ADHD often forget about homework. They should have a notebook to keep up with daily assignments. The parents can review the notebook daily to check the homework assignment. If the child has no homework, the teacher should sign his or her name in the notebook to let the parents know. Since the child is expected to bring the notebook home daily, it can also serve as a communication tool between the parents and the teacher.

Organizing the Classroom

Organizing the classroom helps to provide an adequate environment for students with ADHD to be involved in academic tasks. There are numerous ways to prevent distractions from external forces that may influence the students in negative ways. These strategies can be initiated easily by regular education teachers.

Use a Physically Structured Classroom. Students with ADHD can be easily distracted by an unstructured physical environment. Teaching such students in a physically structured classroom is more effective than teaching them in an "open" classroom. Having walls and a door will block out visual and auditory distractions in the hallway. In addition, some students with ADHD function better when they work in study carrels than when seated in the middle of the class. The study carrels provide three walls around the desks and may prevent the students from looking around and being distracted by others. Therefore, a teacher should have a few study carrels available for any student to use. Of course, students should not be singled out for the use of the study carrels; students without disabilities should also use them to avoid any possibility of stigma being associated with the carrels.

Display Classroom Rules. Students with ADHD may fail to remember classroom rules, or they may act impulsively in certain situations. Having a large visual display of classroom rules works as a reminder for students with ADHD. Teachers should review the rules with the students frequently. The students should be encouraged to role play both appropriate and inappropriate behaviors. Teachers should appoint the students with ADHD to roles that demonstrate appropriate behaviors.

Post Daily Schedule and Assignments. Students with ADHD often have difficulty organizing and preparing for the next period. They also need a reminder of daily assignments. A daily schedule should be posted in the corner of the chalkboard for easy reference. Teachers may refer to the daily schedule each period during the first two weeks of school to help the students become familiar with the schedule. During these early weeks, at the end of each period the teacher should ask the students to state which subject comes next. Also, daily assignments need to be posted on the board for the students to copy.

Seat Students Away from Noise. Students with ADHD are often affected by auditory and visual distractions and thus lose concentration. Items such as air conditioners, heating vents, doors, windows, and electric pencil sharpeners can distract these students. When another student sharpens a pencil, for example, a student with ADHD may stop paying attention to the lesson. Therefore, students with ADHD need to be away from auditory distractions and high-traffic areas of the classroom.

Place Desks Away from Each Other. Students with ADHD can be easily distracted by peers. Teachers should space desks at least one arm's length away from each other. It is important not to seat students with ADHD in the back of the room, where the teacher may not be able to provide close supervision. Students with ADHD should be seated in the middle of the room surrounded by positive role models (Hale, 1994). Students with ADHD can learn from the positive influence of these students and model their behaviors appropriately.

Assign Two Desks. As mentioned already, ADHD students have difficulty sitting still for a long period of time. Students with ADHD will, on occasion, stand up and move out of their desks without realizing why. If teachers are not able to provide for enough breaks in the lesson, they may allow the students with ADHD to move to a second desk. The teachers must acknowledge to the class that the student has a right to change desks when he or she wishes.

Provide Alternate Activities. Students with ADHD may become inattentive after a repetition of similar activities. Teachers should assist these students by providing alternate activities to eliminate desk fatigue. If a teacher assigns the students to work on seat assignments for 20 minutes, the teacher should use activities that encourage active responding for the next lesson. Such activities may include asking for volunteers or appointing someone to work at the board. Also, a question-and-answer time could be made into an active game. The game "Simon Says" and having students stand or sit to indicate a "Yes" or "No" answer are examples of such activities.

Monitoring the Student's Behavior

It is crucial for a teacher to monitor students' behaviors. Students with ADHD, in particular, need to be monitored closely so that appropriate modifications can be made for them. Also, teachers must monitor students who are receiving medical treatment because teachers are often able to observe changes in behavior that might suggest medication problems. The teachers may then contact the parents to communicate the observations. Monitoring is also important in evaluating behavioral and academic interventions the teacher has employed with the student.

Visually Monitor and Chart Behavior. Because of the frequent distractible behaviors exhibited by children with ADHD, teachers need to keep a record of the increase or decrease of these behaviors. These data may be useful to the students' physicians in determining the effectiveness of medication. The chart can also be shown to the student to review his or her behavior. In addition, using the chart can provide an opportunity for the teacher to talk with the student about establishing reasonable goals for future behavior. The information collected on the Daily Checklist of Behaviors, described earlier, should be charted in the same way to determine frequencies of particular behaviors.

Discuss Consequences of Behavior. Students with ADHD sometimes do not realize what they are doing wrong. It is important for teachers to encourage students to consider the consequences of their behaviors. For example, if the student with ADHD blurts out an answer without raising his or her hand, the teacher should institute a negative consequence for the student, such as losing a minute of recess. The teacher should stress student awareness of behavioral consequences by having the student repeat the phrase, "If I blurt out answers, I will lose some recess time." If the student then exhibits inappropriate behaviors, the teacher must follow through with the specified consequences.

Use Self-Monitoring Strategies. Children with ADHD often become inattentive when they work on seat assignments. Self-monitoring is an effective technique for students to use to monitor their own behavior and record the results. A teacher can show the student, via modeling, what effective attention behaviors look like and then help the student imitate these behaviors. (The details of a self-monitoring strategy are discussed in a later section.)

Moderately Structured Interventions

Moderately structured interventions administered by regular classroom teachers typically include pre- and postobservations of behavior. This level of hierarchy involves three important components, identified as *AIM*: assessment, intervention, and monitoring.

First, teachers must conduct an assessment of the student's behaviors. Identifying the target behavior of a particular student is necessary for electing an appropriate intervention. Some type of data collection should be applied before, during, and/or after the intervention to determine the effects of the strategy employed.

Regular education teachers often believe that they have to stop instruction to observe one student for data collection purposes. However, there are ways to observe and collect data on intervention without interfering with the ongoing instruction. For example, as mentioned earlier, the Critical Incidents Log and the Daily Checklist of Behaviors are simple tools to use, and teachers can employ these systems while conducting ongoing instruction. Teachers can also collect data while the students work on seat assignments, interact while waiting in line, or play during recess.

Next, an intervention should be applied for a specific target behavior. The assessment conducted prior to an intervention is essential in determining an appropriate intervention strategy for a student with ADHD. The behavioral management techniques introduced in this section provide strategies that can be implemented in regular education, special education, and inclusive classrooms.

Finally, monitoring the efficacy of medical treatment and observing the effects of other interventions are important practices for regular education teachers. These teachers must work closely with the students' parents and physicians in updating the effectiveness of the medical treatment program. Close supervision helps the teacher see how well the student is responding to the medication. By monitoring closely, teachers can observe behavior changes that could help predict when the medication will wear off and provide an alternative strategy to assist the student during the transitional period.

Overall, AIM identifies the important teacher responsibilities in conducting moderately structured interventions. Assessment, intervention, and monitoring are necessary for effective implementation.

Next we introduce several intervention strategies, including the token economy, response cost strategies, self-monitoring, and the hero procedure. Each scenario provides an example of the three AIM responsibilities.

Token Economy

Assessment. First, a teacher must assess the frequently exhibited behavior of a student with ADHD. A target behavior, such as out-of-seat behavior, can be easily counted by using a wrist counter (golf counters) or moving pennies or paper clips from one pocket to another. The following example will help clarify the technique (Bender, 1992; Lewis & Doorlag, 1983).

Ms. Lee, a special education teacher in a third-grade class, was concerned that Sam was very fidgety and frequently out of his seat during the reading class. His behavior interrupted his learning, and it also interrupted the class. Other students were disrupted by Sam's behavior every time he was out of his seat.

A specific definition is needed to facilitate an accurate frequency count for any behavior (Bender, 1992). Ms. Lee defined inappropriate out-of-seat behavior as occurring any time both buttocks were not in contact with the seat of the desk. By this definition, standing up and putting one leg on the chair was counted as out-of-seat behavior. However, if Sam requested permission to leave his seat for an appropriate reason (e.g., to sharpen a pencil), that was not counted as inappropriate out-of-seat behavior.

Once a behavior is clearly defined in measurable terms, baseline data are collected. To collect the data, Ms. Lee moved a paper clip from her right pocket to her left pocket every time Sam was inappropriately out of his seat during the morning reading period. This frequency count measurement technique did not take time from Ms. Lee's teaching. Figure 7–4 indicates that Sam exhibited an average of 20 out-of-seat behaviors per reading class during the first five days of the baseline phase.

Intervention. After Ms. Lee studied the frequency of Sam's out-of-seat behavior, she decided to implement a token economy as an intervention. The teacher first met with Sam and discussed the out-of-seat behavior problem. She told him of the reinforcement he could earn by staying in his seat. Ms. Lee used a token economy to reinforce Sam for remaining in his seat during the intervention. For every 5-minute period in which Sam remained in his seat, he received 20 cents (of play money) in the token economy. A timer was placed on his desk, and he was told to use the timer to remind himself to stay in his seat during each 5-minute interval. If he left his seat inappropriately, he was told to return to his seat and start the timer again.

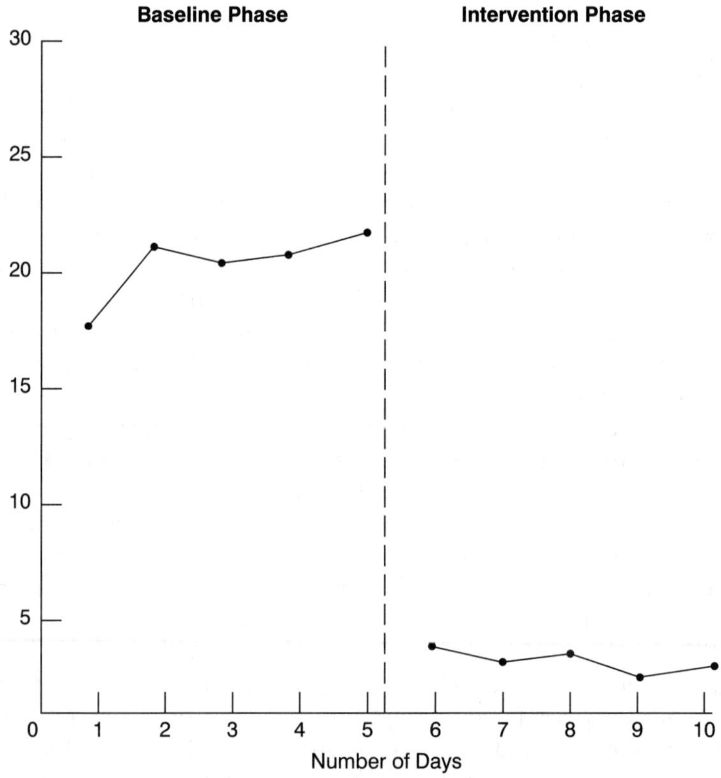

FIGURE 7–4
Sample Token Economy Graph

Monitoring. Sam responded positively to the intervention, as shown in Figure 7–4. As a result, he exchanged his earned tokens for pencils, stickers, or computer time every Friday. Meanwhile, Ms. Lee continued to monitor his behaviors using her paper clips.

Summary. The results of monitoring the intervention indicated that the procedure was effective in reducing Sam's out-of-seat behaviors. The number of out-of-seat behaviors during the intervention phase was reduced to an average of one out-of-seat behavior per period. The frequency count was helpful in collecting data during both baseline and intervention periods. Most important, Ms. Lee's teaching was not disturbed by the implementation of the technique. She was able to both collect data and continue her lessons as usual. Finally, when the teacher showed this simple chart to the parents, they immediately saw the advantages of such a structured reinforcement approach.

Response Cost Strategies

Assessment. A response cost strategy may be used to decrease inappropriate behavior. Like the token economy, this strategy is dependent upon a frequency count of behavior. For example, Juanita often blurts out answers in class. This impulsive type of behavior is one of the characteristics of students with ADHD. Mr. Wong, a fourth-grade regular classroom teacher, told Juanita a number of times to raise her hand instead of blurting out, but Juanita continued to blurt out answers. Mr. Wong decided to assess how often Juanita actually blurts out in class.

Mr. Wong first defined blurting-out behaviors and collected the baseline data during the first period each day using a frequency count. Figure 7–5 shows that Juanita blurted out an average of 10 times per period during the baseline phase.

Intervention. Mr. Wong decided to use response cost to modify Juanita's inappropriate behavior. First, Mr. Wong introduced an intervention program to Juanita. He listed the numbers 20 through 0 on the board and explained that they indicated the number of minutes that she would be allowed to have as her recess period. He crossed out the highest number each time Juanita blurted out an answer, thus reducing her recess for each inappropriate response. If she blurted out five times, she had 15 minutes left for recess for that day.

Monitoring. Mr. Wong continued to monitor Juanita's behavior throughout the intervention phase. The results indicated that Juanita's blurting-out behavior significantly decreased. During the intervention phase, the average number of Juanita's blurting-out behavior was reduced to two.

Summary. This type of intervention holds several advantages. First, this procedure can be easily implemented by regular classroom teachers without interfering with their lessons. Also, interventions with demonstrated effectiveness such as this please the parents of many students with ADHD. Many parents are concerned about the teachers' ability to deal with their child's disorder, and this type of strategy demonstrates the teacher's skills in intervening in the child's problem behaviors.

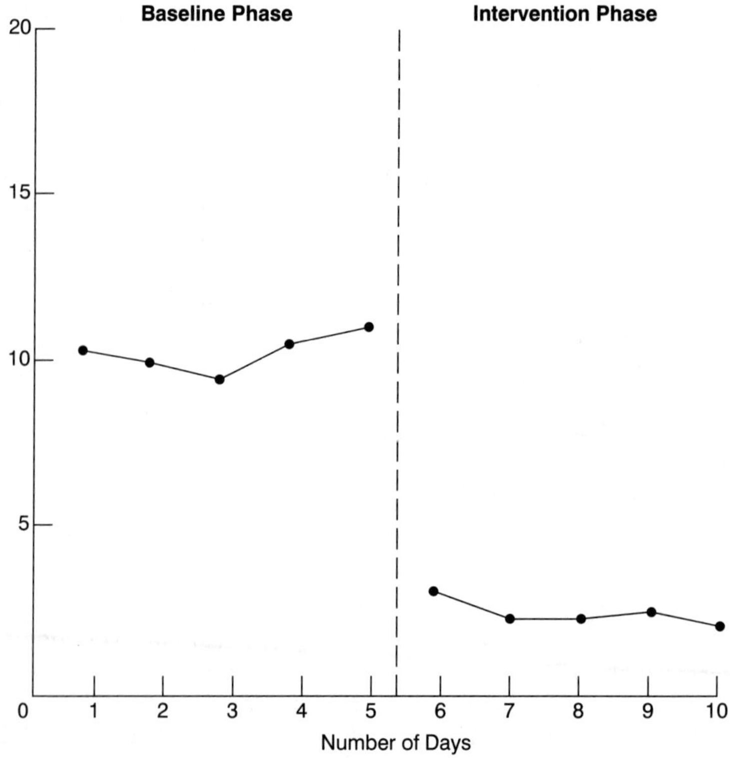

FIGURE 7–5
Sample Response Cost Graph

Self-Monitoring

Self-monitoring is an intervention strategy that requires a student to record the occurrences of his or her own target behavior (Hallahan, Lloyd, & Stolley, 1982). There are several advantages to having students self-monitor their own behaviors. First, self-monitoring procedures free teachers to focus on academic instruction rather than spend time managing inappropriate behaviors. Second, self-monitoring can be an effective tool for students with ADHD to increase the frequency of appropriate behaviors, even for students who are already receiving medication to enhance their successful experiences (Mathes & Bender, in press).

Assessment. This example comes from a typical fifth-grade classroom. David is a student with ADHD in Ms. VanderVeen's class. Ms. VanderVeen has been concerned about David's inattentive behavior. He often stays off-task when individual seat assignments are given.

During the language arts period, Ms. VanderVeen decided to collect data using a momentary time-sampling procedure. She developed a recording sheet and defined on-task behaviors as eye contact with the appropriate educational task. Each observation session was divided into 60 intervals of 10 seconds each. This procedure requires an observer to look for the occurrence or nonoccurrence of the target behavior at the end of each interval. The observer records a "+" if on-task behavior is observed at the end of each interval or a "–" if off-task behavior has been observed. In this example, the percentage of on-task behavior was calculated by dividing the number of observed on-task behaviors by the total number of observed behaviors and multiplying by 100 (Cooper, Heron, & Heward, 1987). Ms. VanderVeen was the observer of David's behavior during seat work in the language arts class.

Intervention. Ms. VanderVeen decided that the self-monitoring procedures introduced by Hallahan and his colleagues (1982) would be an appropriate intervention for David. First, she made a cueing tape by recording tones from an electric keyboard by hitting a particular key. This tape was used to cue David to consider his behavior. As recommended by Hallahan and his colleagues, the tones should be unexpected; therefore, the interval between each tone varied from 10 to 90 seconds over a 20-minute time period. Next, the teacher constructed a self-monitoring sheet, which is presented in Figure 7–6. Also, a tape recorder and headphones were needed for the intervention.

On the first day of intervention, Ms. VanderVeen took David to a conference room before class for a training session on self-monitoring. She indicated that she wanted to assist David in improving his attentive behavior; she talked about how beneficial self-monitoring was. Ms. VanderVeen then presented a tape recorder, a tape, and a self-monitoring sheet. David was told to ask himself the question, "Was I paying attention when I heard the tone?" He was then instructed to check the self-monitoring sheet under "Yes" or "No" each time. Next, on-task and off-task behaviors were defined, and Ms. VanderVeen modeled examples of such behaviors. Then David was asked to give examples of attentive behaviors and to demonstrate the self-monitoring procedure by listening to the tones on the tape recorder. After they returned to the classroom, David was directed to a particular desk to sit and self-monitor during a seat assignment. David continued to self-monitor himself everyday when the class was assigned to work on review questions for 15–20 minutes for 10 days. He made significant improvements on his on-task behavior during this time, as shown in Figure 7–7.

FIGURE 7–6
Sample Self-Monitoring Chart

Date:________ Name:________________

Was I paying attention?

	Yes	No
1		
2		
3		
4		
5		
6		
7		
8		
9		
10		
11		
12		
13		
14		
15		
16		
17		
18		
19		
20		

Monitoring. Ms. VanderVeen continued to collect data on David's on-task behavior. The data showed a significant improvement on his target behavior during the intervention phase. Therefore, weaning phases were considered (following the procedures presented by Hallahan and colleagues). The first weaning phase involved taking the tape recorder away from the student. Ms. VanderVeen told David that he was doing so well that he did not need to use the tape recorder anymore. David was instructed to ask himself the question, "Was I paying attention?" whenever he thought about it and to praise himself if the answer was "Yes." Then he marked the sheet and returned to his work. David continued to keep a high percentage of on-task behavior during each observation during this three-day weaning phase.

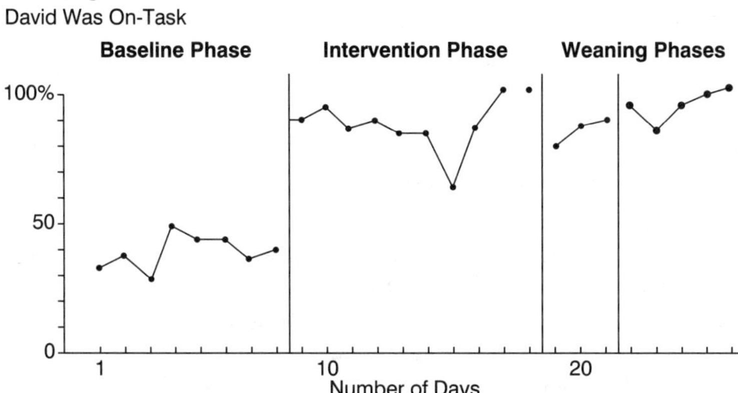

FIGURE 7–7
Sample Self-Monitoring Graph

The second weaning phase was implemented after stable data were established for the first weaning phase. David was congratulated on his ability to stay on-task without using the tape-recorded tones. He was weaned from using the self-monitoring sheet. During this period, David was guided to ask himself the question, "Was I paying attention?" whenever he thought about it. Ms. VanderVeen encouraged him to give himself a pat on the shoulder and/or to say to himself, "Yes, I'm paying attention and doing great!" David continued to stay on-task during this phase, as shown in Figure 7–7.

Summary. The data presented in Figure 7–7 represent the observations that the teacher noted, and not David's own self-monitoring record. A self-monitoring procedure such as this is very effective even if the teacher does not record data to actually measure the student's change in behavior (Snider, 1987).

There are a number of advantages in utilizing the self-monitoring strategy. First, it is a student-directed procedure instead of teacher-directed. Students are responsible for monitoring themselves and rating their own behavior. Second, self-monitoring frees teachers from constantly intervening in students' inappropriate behaviors. Thus, self-monitoring is a practical and effective tool for teaching students with ADHD.

The Hero Procedure

The hero procedure (Cooper et al., 1987) refers to a teacher administering one consequence to all members of the group based on the behavior of one person. The procedure can be used for a student with a specific target behavior such as the impulsive or disruptive behaviors that characterize students with ADHD. Contingent upon the performance of the student, the entire class receives a reward (Cooper et al., 1987). This method thus can produce positive interaction among students. The following is an example of how a teacher uses the hero procedure and measures the results by using simultaneous behavioral observation.

Assessment. Mr. Alexander, a fifth-grade teacher, was concerned that Bill, who had ADHD, was frequently exhibiting inappropriate behaviors while standing in line. Although the student was taking medication, he frequently bothered others by pushing and kicking while the class waited in line in the cafeteria. First, the teacher decided to collect baseline data by using simultaneous observation on Bill and another student who did not have ADHD as a comparison. Ken was chosen to be observed simultaneously with Bill since he was the same race and sex as Bill and had no disability. The data collection chart is shown in Figure 7–8.

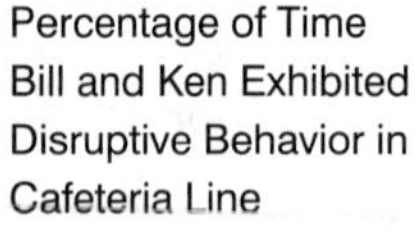

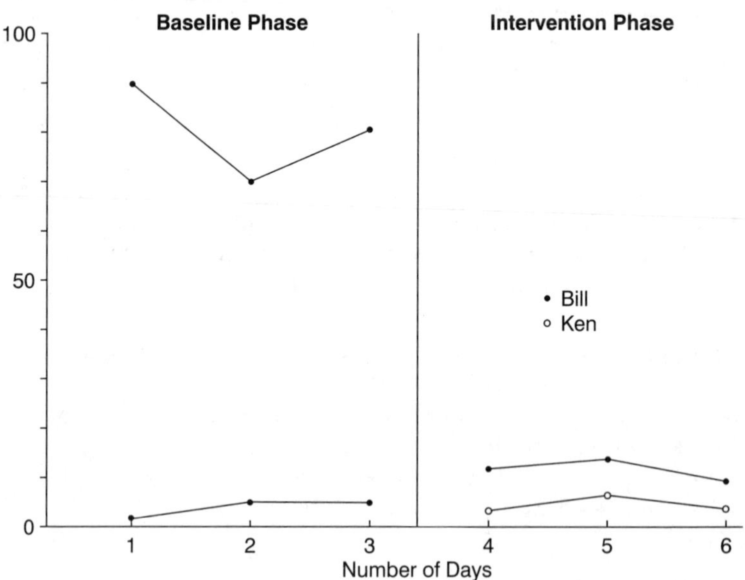

FIGURE 7–8
Sample Hero Procedure Chart

Mr. Alexander used a momentary time sampling to conduct simultaneous observations. Figure 7–9 shows the recording sheet the teacher used. While the class was in line in the cafeteria, Mr. Alexander looked at Bill every five seconds and recorded his behavior at the end of the interval. For the next interval, he observed Ken and recorded his behavior. Mr. Alexander repeated the procedure for a total of five minutes for three days. During the baseline phase, Bill bothered others an average of 80% of the time, while Ken did so only 5% of the time.

Intervention. Mr. Alexander decided to implement the hero procedure. Many of his students complained to Mr. Alexander that Bill was bothering them while they waited in the lunch line. The teacher told the class that they would have an extra five minutes for recess if Bill did not touch anyone in an aggressive way while waiting in line.

Monitoring. Both Bill and the class responded to the intervention very well. Other students in the class reminded Bill by shaking their heads when Bill was about to bother someone. On the other hand, they smiled at Bill when he stayed in line quietly. Other students thanked Bill for getting an extra five minutes for recess. That made Bill feel proud and accepted.

Summary. The hero procedure was very effective in decreasing Bill's inappropriate behavior, as shown in Figure 7–8. The intervention was responsible for decreasing his disruptive behavior to 10%. Since other students in the class were affected by Bill's performance, they became supportive and reminded him to do well. Based on the behavior of one student, the whole class received a reward. One of the advantages of the hero procedure is that other students can provide positive influence to a student with a specific target behavior.

Structured Interventions

The final level of the hierarchical plan involves structured interventions. These strategies involve more than one teacher or professional. Students with ADHD in departmentalized schools may require a coordinated intervention to reduce behavior problems. Students may change classes and receive instruction from various teachers everyday. In such a case, structured intervention strategies that are uniform across teachers and classrooms need to be practiced, and this type of intervention is usually implemented at the schoolwide level. Programs involving such tools and methods as multiteacher behavioral contracts, assertive discipline, Project RIDE, and paraprofessionals are intended for use by the entire faculty of the school.

	1	2	3	4	5	6	7	8	9	10	11	12	13	14	15
Bill															
Ken															
	16	17	18	19	20	21	22	23	24	25	26	27	28	29	30
Bill															
Ken															

FIGURE 7–9
Sample Recording Sheet for Simultaneous Observation

Multiteacher Behavioral Contracts

Joan Cunningham (1994) developed a fairly involved procedure for academic and behavioral contracts to facilitate effective communication among the student's parents, the various teachers, and the doctors regarding the student's on-task behavior and assignment completion. The purposes of the contracts include setting academic expectations, fostering communication, providing an ongoing record, and tracking the impact of medical intervention.

The multiteacher contract, like all behavioral contracts, states conditions and expectations concerning behavior to which a student must agree. This type of contract also includes a communication mechanism to solicit each teacher's input on a daily basis. The student takes a Homework/On-Task Sheet (see Figure 7–10) to every class and presents it to the teachers to sign at the end of each class period. The teachers rate the student's on-task behavior, check the written homework assignment, verify homework completion, and sign the sheet. Students are rewarded by the lead teacher for having each classroom teacher complete the form.

At the conclusion of the school day, the student presents the completed Homework/On-Task Sheet to the teacher in charge of the intervention. The student also takes the Homework//On-Task Sheet home to have it signed by one of the parents. Finally, the student brings the signed Homework/On-Task Sheet to the managing teacher at the beginning of the next day to check for the parental signature.

Advantages of this strategy include developing close communication with all teachers who work with the student, providing effective communication with the parents, and monitoring medical effects across periods during the school day. The contract and the Homework/On-Task Sheet provide an overall picture of the student's behavior in each class each day. If the parent reads about the child's excessive behaviors throughout the day, he or she may realize that the child did not receive medication every morning. Also, if problems arise during a particular period each day, the time of medical administration may need to be modified to increase the efficacy of medication during that period.

Assertive Discipline

Research has indicated that using an assertive discipline technique is quite effective in improving behavior (Mandlebaum, Russell, Krouse, & Gunter, 1983). The philosophy behind the system indicates that teachers must get their needs met in the classroom, that no child should ever be allowed to prevent a teacher from teaching, that no child should ever be allowed to prevent another child from learning, and that teachers should determine the behaviors that are in the children's best interests (Canter, 1979).

Student's Name_______________ Date_______________

CLASS	Was last night's homework completed? Y or N	Tonight's homework assignment	Was student on-task in class today? 1. Good 2. Fair 3. Needs improvement	Teacher's initials and comments
Math				
English				
Social Science				
Science				

Parent's Signature_______________ Date_______________

FIGURE 7–10
Daily Homework/On-Task Sheet

When a student shows inappropriate behavior, the teacher writes the student's name on a piece of paper on the student's desk as a warning. This is the student's first offense, and no consequence is given to the student. Next, if the student misbehaves again, a check mark is placed by the name for the second offense, indicating that the student must serve 15 minutes of detention after school. The teacher adds a second check if the student does it again, indicating that the student must stay in detention after school for

30 minutes. The teacher adds a third check for the fourth offense if the student continues to demonstrate inappropriate behaviors. The consequences for this offense are that the student must stay 30 minutes in detention after school and the parents receive a phone call concerning the disciplinary problems. Finally, the fifth offense involves removing the student from the classroom.

The directions for this intervention specify four basic competencies for teachers to achieve to be effective behavior managers (Canter, 1979). First, a teacher must know at all times what he or she wants the students to do and must communicate these expectations to the students. Teachers typically expect behaviors such as following directions, staying in seats, raising hands, and being prepared for class. In assertive discipline plans, a rule system that emphasizes these behaviors should be developed and reviewed with the student. Typically, these rules for appropriate behavior are posted in the classroom.

Second, teachers must possess the ability to respond consistently to appropriate student behaviors (Canter, 1979). Positive reinforcement should be given to the students to increase desirable behavior. Verbal praise to the student, positive notes sent home to the parents, and group rewards such as class parties or extended recess time are examples of reinforcement options.

Third, teachers must know how to systematically set limits when a student does not behave properly (Canter, 1979). Warning a student verbally and writing his or her name on a list on the teacher's or student's desk can be a calm and nondegrading strategy (Hill, 1990). This serves as a warning to the student. It also provides a record-keeping system for the teacher. If the student misbehaves again, a check is placed by the name. The teacher must be consistent and provide a negative consequence every time a student exhibits inappropriate behavior. Discipline plans need to be applied consistently throughout the school.

Fourth, teachers need to know how to elicit the cooperation of the student's principal and parents for their disciplinary efforts (Canter, 1979). Parents should accept that the teacher has a right to their help, and teachers should reinforce parents who are supportive by doing such things as sending home positive notes. Also, teachers need to share a discipline plan with the principal and inform the principal when modifications are made (Canter, 1979).

While assertive discipline can be implemented by a single teacher, Canter (1979) encourages the entire faculty to be involved. There are advantages of implementing a schoolwide assertive discipline plan. For example, some students with ADHD also exhibit conduct disorders, oppositional-defiant disorders, mood disorders, and anxiety disorders (McKinney, Montague, & Hocutt, 1993), and these may occur at any time of the day in any class. Under a schoolwide assertive discipline plan, when a student demonstrates these inappropriate behaviors, a consequence is given to the student in a systematic fashion; such a consequence would not vary from one class to the next.

The assertive discipline program provides teachers with an effective model for employing basic behavioral principles. It is consistent in dealing with both in-class and out-of-class behavior throughout the school, which helps students with ADHD to understand the structure of behavioral expectations.

Project RIDE

Project RIDE (Responding to Individual Differences in Education) was developed by the Great Falls (Montana) public schools to assist regular classroom teachers in dealing with at-risk learners (Beck & Weast, 1990). Many of the strategies are also effective in working with students with ADHD. The project was developed out of the need to provide teachers with research-based ideas explained in laypersons' terms. If the plan is used among the entire school faculty in a collaborative fashion with teacher support, teachers develop an inclusive attitude ("Not *your* kid, but *our* kid") in dealing with the problem behaviors of students with ADHD.

The Project RIDE program provides a support system for the regular classroom teachers. It is based on the assumption that no matter what kind of problem a student may have, it is a shared responsibility of the building faculty. The program consists of three major components: teachers' self-evaluation based on "effective schools" practices, a schoolwide assistance team (SWAT), and a "tactics bank" and video library (Beck, 1991). The teachers go through the RIDE process and implement strategies before a student is referred for special education placement.

Twelve teacher behaviors were identified from the "effective schools" literature (see Figure 7–11). These are included on a simple checklist to enable a teacher to conduct self-evaluation and to ensure compliance with effective teaching behavior.

The schoolwide assistance team (SWAT) is created as a systematic, building-based, problem-solving entity to provide support to teachers. The RIDE project emphasizes the collaborative approach to problems, involving the entire school faculty. The team consists of a building-level group of teachers and provides expertise and experience to assist teachers with problems before they make a referral to special education. This team assists the teacher in identifying strategies for particular problem behaviors. To facilitate this process, the teachers and SWAT team use a behavioral reporting form to describe in detail the specific problem behaviors.

The team uses a computer tactics bank to find research-proven strategies to alleviate students' behavior problems. For each type of problem, the tactics bank includes four to six research-proven strategies and specific steps to implement each. The teacher and SWAT team may also explore the video library to review examples of selected intervention strategies for the prob-

1. Instruction is guided by a preplanned curriculum.
2. High expectations are established for student learning.
3. Students are carefully oriented to lessons.
4. Instruction is clear and focused.
5. Learning progress is closely monitored.
6. When students don't understand, they are retaught.
7. Class time is used for learning.
8. There are smooth, efficient classroom routines.
9. Instructional groups fit instructional needs.
10. Standards for classroom behavior are explicit.
11. Personal interactions between teachers and students are positive.
12. Incentives and rewards for students are used to promote excellence.

FIGURE 7–11
Twelve Teacher Behaviors Identified for Project RIDE

lem behavior. Each video clip lasts about five to eight minutes and depicts actual classroom situations, demonstrating examples of interventions for particular behavior problems. The strategies in the tactics bank and videotapes are meant to be utilized by all the faculty in the building.

There are several advantages to using Project RIDE strategies for students with ADHD (Beck, 1991). When a teacher has difficulty dealing with a particular student, he or she can come to the SWAT team to address the problem. The repertoires of the experienced practitioners on the team are collectively and systematically used to deal with problem behaviors. The process can also serve as a prescreening procedure for special education services. One study involved six pilot elementary schools using RIDE in the Great Falls public schools from 1986 to 1989. Beck and Weast (1990) indicated that, before the RIDE program was implemented, 54% of the students whom teachers referred to special education were not eligible for such education; after the RIDE program was implemented, the number of referred individuals who were not eligible decreased to only 20%. Thus, more regular education teachers were dealing with minor behavior problems rather than constantly referring children to special education.

Project RIDE can be a powerful tool for teachers in dealing with many overt behavioral problems associated with ADHD. Teachers are able to direct and control the students' behaviors and to match them with a wide array of strategies in the tactics bank. Also, as demonstrated by the use of the program in the Great Falls schools, the accuracy of referrals can be increased considerably.

Irvine Paraprofessional Program

Kotkin (in press) developed a model using paraprofessionals in regular education classrooms to meet the needs of students with ADHD. These students often exhibit difficulty producing quality academic work despite having normal intelligence. Many of these students also have difficulty relating to others and demonstrate a lack of social skills. Kotkin argued that regular classroom teachers, in general, do not have enough training in the use of behavioral interventions to address these needs. He developed the Irvine Paraprofessional (IPP) model to directly intervene with students with ADHD in the regular classroom by using specially trained paraprofessionals as interim instructional aids.

The IPP model works in the following fashion. Once a student is identified as having ADHD, a school study team (consisting of a psychologist, a special education teacher, and a referring teacher) considers that student's needs. The classroom teacher reports on the student's problem behaviors, the desired alternative behaviors, and modifications and interventions that may have been attempted. The psychologist then observes the student. Next, the team meets to construct a behavioral intervention for the classroom teacher to implement. If the student does not show improvement, a trained paraprofessional is assigned to work with the student in the regular classroom for 12 weeks on the behavioral plan. The paraprofessional serves as an instructional aide to the classroom teacher, and the school psychologist provides periodic supervision of the paraprofessional. The teacher indirectly receives training in behavioral interventions by watching the trained paraprofessional.

The paraprofessionals for this model may be undergraduate students or selected instructional aides. They receive extensive training to work with students with ADHD on behavioral modification programs. The training includes a 30-hour course covering the characteristics of children with ADHD, behavior modification strategies, and the role of paraprofessionals in the school. Then the trainees undertake 200 hours of supervised fieldwork as paraprofessionals in the regular classrooms. Once the paraprofessionals complete the training, they conduct two types of interventions: token systems and social skills training.

Token System. A paraprofessional is assigned to work in a regular classroom for one-half of the day to implement a token reinforcement system for 12 weeks. The paraprofessional gives the targeted students feedback every 15 minutes on whether they earned stamps on their daily report card. They earn the stamps by performing the behaviors listed on each contract.

A reinforcement center provides a place where the students exchange tokens for activities each day. For example, if a student earned 90%–100% of stamps for the day, he or she could play Gameboy, LEGOS, and other games. If the student earned 80%–89%, then he or she could read, work on the computer, and do art activities. If the student earned 79% or lower, the choices would be very limited, to an activity like drawing.

Social Skills Training. The paraprofessional also conducts skills training groups twice a week for one hour. Specific social skills (e.g., displaying good sportsmanship, ignoring provocations and disruptions, displaying acceptance) are introduced to the students in modules. The paraprofessional begins each session by asking the students to share their feelings and conducts lessons using group-based contingencies and other types of reinforcements.

One of the main goals for the IPP program is that a regular classroom teacher eventually be in charge of intervening for students with ADHD. A transition takes place from paraprofessional-directed interventions to teacher-directed interventions once the student reaches an average of 90% in earning stamps.

This model has a number of advantages. First, the regular classroom teachers learn intervention strategies in working with students with ADHD and by the effective modeling of the paraprofessional. Second, the teachers are expected to learn general classroom management strategies and to create a proper environment for learning. Third, the school can utilize a reinforcement center for other students who might benefit from the token program.

SUMMARY

With increasing numbers of students receiving services in inclusive classes, regular and special education teachers are frequently called upon to deal with students' attention problems. The teachers must be aware of the symptoms of students with ADHD for identification purposes. Documenting these behaviors is helpful for teachers to communicate with the student's parents, physician, and other professionals.

To intervene on problem behaviors exhibited by students with ADHD, a hierarchical intervention plan is necessary. The three levels of intervention strategies discussed here include unstructured, moderately structured, and highly structured strategies. Unstructured intervention strategies stem from effective teaching behaviors and may be thought of as effective habits teachers should develop. This level of intervention may be all that is required to facilitate effective instruction for some students with ADHD.

The second tier, moderately structured interventions, includes the AIM responsibility: assessment, intervention, and monitoring. Assessment is crucial for identifying problem behaviors. Many students with ADHD require intervention at this level to succeed in inclusive classes. At the very least, daily data-based instruction allows a teacher to monitor the effects of medication.

Finally, structured interventions involve more than one professional and are usually implemented at the schoolwide level. Programs such as those involving multiteacher behavioral contracts, assertive discipline, Project RIDE techniques, and the Irvine Paraprofessional model are intended for use by the entire faculty of the school. Students with ADHD in departmentalized schools may require a coordinated intervention of this type to attain success in inclusive classes.

Depending upon an individual student's characteristics and need for more or less structure, the regular and special education teachers should select a strategy from the appropriate level to facilitate effective instruction for that student. With this hierarchical approach to strategy selection, teachers will be able to manage the appropriate behaviors on an individual basis for most students with ADHD.

REFERENCES

American Psychiatric Association. (1994). *Diagnostic and statistical manual of mental disorders* (4th ed.). Washington, D.C.: Author.

Barkley, R. A. (1990). *Attention deficit hyperactivity disorder: A handbook for diagnosis and treatment.* New York: Guilford Press.

Beck, R. (1991). Project RIDE. *Teaching Exceptional Children*, 2, 60–61.

Beck, R., & Weast, J. (1990). Project RIDE: A staff development program for assisting "at risk" students in the regular classroom. *ERS Spectrum*, 3, 9–16.

Bender, W. N. (1992). *Learning disabilities: Characteristics, identification, and teaching strategies.* Boston: Allyn & Bacon.

Bender, W. N., & Mathes, M. Y. (in press). Teaching students with attention deficit hyperactivity disorder in the inclusive classroom: A hierarchical approach to strategy selection. *Intervention in School and Clinic.*

Canter, L. (1979). Competency-based approach to discipline—It's assertive. *Thrust*, *8*, 11–13.

Chase, S. N., & Clement, P. L. (1985). Effects of self-reinforcement and stimulants on academic performance in children with attention deficit disorder. *Journal of Clinical Psychology*, *14*, 323–333.

Children and Adults with Attention Deficit Disorders. (1993). *CH.A.D.D. Facts 8: The national organization working for children and adults with attention deficit disorders.* Washington, D.C.: Author.

Cooper, J. O., Heron, T. E., & Heward, W. L. (1987). *Applied behavior analysis.* Upper Saddle River, NJ: Merrill/Prentice Hall.

Cunningham, J. (1994). A videotape presentation in W. N. Bender & P. J. McLaughlin, *Behavioral contracting, program 2: Instructional strategies for ADD.* Athens: University of Georgia ADDNET Project.

Davila, R. R., Williams, M. L., & MacDonald, J. T. (1991). *Memorandum to chief state school officers re: Clarification of policy to address the needs of children with attention deficit disorders with general and/or special education.* Washington, D.C.: U.S. Department of Education.

Evertson, C. M., Emmer, E. T., Clements, B. S., Sanford, J. P., & Worsham, M. E. (1984). *Classroom management for elementary teachers.* Upper Saddle River, NJ: Merrill/Prentice Hall.

Hale, L. (1994). A videotape presentation in W. N. Bender & P. J. McLaughlin, *ADD from A to Z: Comprehensive guide to attention deficit disorder, program 2: Instructional strategies for ADD.* Athens: University of Georgia ADDNET Project.

Hallahan, D. P., Lloyd, J. W., & Stolley, L. (1982). *Improving attention with self-monitoring: A manual for teachers.* Charlottesville: University of Virginia.

Hill, D. (1990). Order in the classroom. *Teacher Magazine, 1,* 70–77.

Hinshaw, S. P., Henker, B., & Whalen, C. K. (1984). Self-control in hyperactive boys in anger-inducing situations: Effects of cognitive-behavioral training and of methylphenidate. *Journal of Abnormal Child Psychology, 12,* 55–77.

Hinshaw, S. P., & Melnick, S. (1992). Self-management therapies and attention-deficit hyperactivity disorder: Reinforced self-evaluation and anger control interventions. *Behavioral Modification, 16,* 253–273.

Horn, W. F., Chatoor, L., & Conners, C. K. (1983). Additive effects of dexedrine and self-control training: A multiple assessment. *Behavior Modification, 7,* 383–402.

Kotkin, R. A. (in press). The Irvine paraprofessional program: Using paraprofessionals in serving students with ADHD. *Intervention in School and Clinic.*

Lewis, R. B., & Doorlag, D. H. (1983). *Teaching special students in the mainstream.* Upper Saddle River, NJ: Merrill/Prentice Hall.

Mandlebaum, L. H., Russell, J. K., Krouse, J., & Gunter, M. (1983). Assertive discipline: An effective classwide behavior management program. *Behavioral Disorders, 8,* 258–264.

Mathes, M. Y., & Bender, W. N. (in press). Effects of self-monitoring on children with attention deficit disorder who are receiving medical interventions: Implications for inclusive instruction. *Remedial and Special Education.*

McBurnett, K., Lahey, B. B., & Pfiffner, L. J. (1993). Diagnosis of attention deficit disorders in DSM-IV: Scientific basis and implications for education. *Exceptional Children, 2,* 108–117.

McKinney, J. D., Montague, M., & Hocutt, A. M. (1993). *A synthesis of research literature on the assessment and identification of attention deficit disorder.*

Coral Gables, FL: Miami Center for Synthesis of Research on Attention Deficit Disorder, University of Miami.

Rooney, K. J. (in press). Working with students with attention disorders. *Intervention in School and Clinic.*

Snider, V. (1987). Use of self-monitoring of attention with LD students: Research and application. *Learning Disabilities Quarterly, 10,* 139–151.

Sugai, G. (1986). Recording classroom events: Maintaining a critical incidents log. *Teaching Exceptional Children, 18,* 98–102.

Swanson, J. M. (1993). *The effects of stimulant medication on children with attention deficit disorder: A review of reviews.* Irvine: University of California-Irvine ADD Center.

Vail, C. O., & Huntington, D. (1993). Behavioral Interventions. In W. N. Bender (Ed.), *Learning disabilities best practice for paraprofessionals.* Stoneham, MA: Butterworth-Heinemann.

CHAPTER 8

Teaching the Secondary Student with ADHD

Patricia Wallace Tilson, M.Ed.
University of Georgia

William N. Bender, Ph.D.
University of Georgia

ADHD IN THE PREADOLESCENT, ADOLESCENT, AND POSTADOLESCENT YEARS

Although attention-deficit/hyperactivity disorder (ADHD) was at one time thought to dissipate with age (Bradley, 1957; Eisenberg, 1966; Laufer & Denhoff, 1957), more recent studies discuss ADHD as a developmental disorder that crosses age spans (Minde, Lewin, Weiss, Lavigueru, Donglass, & Sybes, 1971; Mendelson, Johnson, & Stewart, 1971; Brown & Borden, 1986). Researchers have suggested that approximately 80% of the individuals who demonstrate ADHD behaviors as children begin to outgrow some of the overt symptoms, such as hyperactivity, during puberty (Hagerman, 1983; Jordan, 1988, 1989). However, while overt symptoms may appear to lessen in intensity as an individual moves through puberty and related changes, studies demonstrate that many other characteristics of ADHD (e.g., impulsivity, short attention to task, organizational deficits, poor social skills, and low self-esteem) remain and cause difficulty through adulthood (Barkley, Fischer, Edlebrock, & Smallish, 1990; Robin, 1990; Parker, 1992; Zentall, 1993; Weiss & Hechtman, 1986). Further studies suggest that students may have multiple behavioral and learning disorders coexisting with their ADHD that interact with and exacerbate each other, and these comorbid disorders need to be considered in the age span development of adolescents with ADHD (Barkley, 1990; Biederman, Newcorn, & Sprich, 1991).

The Preadolescent Years

As is typical of most preadolescents (i.e., ages 11–13), many students with ADHD in the late elementary grades demonstrate a desire for increased independence and a considerable resistance to conformity (Fowler, 1992; Barkley, 1990). The distinction between the "typical" preadolescent and the preadolescent with ADHD is that for the child with ADHD such behaviors are a continuation of long-standing difficulties that began as early as infancy and certainly by age four (Anderson, Williams, McGee, & Silva, 1987; Barkley, 1990; Fowler, 1992). Both the degree of ADHD symptoms and their duration seem to determine which children are likely to continue to demonstrate chronic problems with ADHD beyond early childhood and into adolescence (Barkley, 1990). By the time the child with ADHD reaches preadolescence, patterns of nonconstructive behavior (academic, familial, and social) are well established.

The social structure in most schools creates additional problems for the student with ADHD (Wender, 1987). The disorder does not affect intelligence as ordinarily defined and measured by intelligence tests and is not in any way related to mental retardation (Wender, 1987). However, the child with ADHD will fidget, look around, daydream, or act restless during academic endeavors. These behaviors will tend to cause uneven academic development (Wender, 1987; Fowler, 1992). When a student must continuously divert energy from learning to behavioral inhibition, the academic outcome is questionable (Zentall, 1993).

The preadolescent with ADHD may also perform erratically in the classroom—one day performing at near normal levels and completing all assignments, yet the next day failing assignments or not turning them in at all. Preadolescents with ADHD often do not repeat activity patterns long enough to establish routines. Therefore, because they do not have a routine place for books, notes, and so on, they may lose things at school, be unable to find homework that has been completed, or fail to complete tasks (Zentall, 1993). These students are likely to be much less organized than the typical preadolescent. Impulsive behaviors (i.e., reacting without thinking) often produce academic errors for these students. The student with ADHD will not wait long enough to consider alternative suggestions, other information, consequences, or responses. Failure to delay may also contribute to poor planning and organizational skills, trademarks of the preadolescent with ADHD (Wender, 1987; Zentall, 1993).

In addition to the difficulties with academics the preadolescent with ADHD encounters *because* of his ADHD behaviors, he or she may encounter additional academic learning difficulties (Barkley, 1990). Some of these learning difficulties may go undetected, masked by ADHD behaviors. These comorbid disorders begin a telling and destructive interaction that, for some children, becomes quite apparent during the preadolescent years. For example, 19%–26% of students with ADHD also have at least one type of learning disability in either math, reading, or spelling (Barkley, 1990). Children with ADHD who also have learning disabilities must not only overcome academic impairments (which afflict about one-half of all students with ADHD) but must also compensate for these specific learning disabilities. They underachieve because they do not understand or do not follow instructions and because they have difficulty storing and retrieving information once they have learned it (Taylor, 1990). They may never master the core academic skills, so they are increasingly impaired under the weight of the accelerated demands and expectations at the higher grade levels. Educationally, children with both ADHD and learning disabilities have more trouble than children with one disability or the other; this comorbidity is a double curse that is very difficult to overcome. These problems remain the most significant and unresolved in our educational system.

Also often comorbid with ADHD are social behavior problems. Socially, preadolescent students with ADHD display greater difficulties with oppositional and defiant behavior, aggressiveness and conduct problems, and even antisocial behavior than do normal children (Loney & Milich, 1982; Robin, 1990; Barkley, 1990; Biederman et al., 1991). Over 65% of clinically referred students with ADHD may show significant problems involving stubbornness, defiance, refusal to obey, temper tantrums, and verbal hostility toward others (Loney & Milich, 1982). The most common types of problems are lying, stealing, truancy, and aggression (i.e., oppositional, defiant, stubborn, explosive, hostile, verbally aggressive, and fighting behaviors) (Barkley, 1990). Some students strive to be leaders but with a marked tendency to be bossy. They may be socially aggressive but drive other children away with inappropriate behaviors. Further, the preadolescent with ADHD is unable to internalize the behaviors expected of him or her and transfer those behaviors across situations (Barkley, 1990). Emotionality, mood swings, exaggerated demands for independence, and poor judgment are all more common with preadolescent children with ADHD than with non-ADHD preadolescents (Robin, 1990). Children with ADHD have a lower tolerance for frustration and may have a more violent reaction to it. These students are subject to temper tantrums when things do not go as planned. Between 30% and 65% of children diagnosed as having ADHD are likely to develop symptoms of oppositional-defiant disorders or conduct disorders between 7 and 10 years of age, and these comorbid problems compound each other (Barkley et al., 1991; Barkley, DuPaul, & McMurray, 1991; Taylor, 1990). In general, children with ADHD and aggression display significantly greater levels of physical aggression, lying, and stealing, as well as more rejection by peers, than do children with only one of these disabilities. These disruptive behavior disorders affect the social conduct and activities of the student with ADHD, as well as interfere with the rights of others. These students are typically rated by teachers as more severely maladjusted and have a poorer adolescent and young adult outcome than children having either ADHD or behavioral disorders alone (Barkley, 1990; Taylor, 1990).

The Adolescent Years

Of children diagnosed with ADHD during preadolescence, 70%–80% continue to be impaired by ADHD symptoms during later adolescent years (ages 13–20) (Barkley, 1990). These deficits affect both behavioral and academic realms. Socially, the adolescent with ADHD, who tends to be socially immature, now has to deal with issues of identity, group acceptance, dating, and acceptance of physical development and appearance (Barkley, 1990). Academically, the adolescent with ADHD has not learned core skills, so the gap between potential and actual achievement gradually widens, and discouragement may set in (Taylor, 1990).

An emerging pattern of social isolation may have appeared by this age, if not earlier, in over half of all children with ADHD because of poor social skills (Goldstein & Goldstein, 1988; Bloomquist, August, & Ostrander, 1991; Robin, 1990; Guevremont, 1990). Research suggests that children with ADHD often have problems socially because of two very different sets of behaviors: high-frequency, low-impact behaviors and low-frequency, high-impact behaviors. High-frequency, low-impact behaviors are behaviors that are not physically threatening to others but are very irritating. Low-frequency, high-impact behaviors are those behaviors that are socially inappropriate or perhaps legally unacceptable (Goldstein & Goldstein, 1988). While adolescents with ADHD may not "tornado" through a classroom, they are often less popular or less accepted than others and may be socially isolated as a result of these behavior problems.

An example of a high-frequency, low-impact behavior is blurting out tangentially related thoughts. This can be quite distracting to teachers and other students in the room and is particularly disruptive when several adolescents with ADHD in the same room engage in such behavior. One adolescent described this behavior as "ping-ponging," which is described in the following vignette.

Ping-ponging: Impulsivity in the Classroom

We had a cricket stuck behind the file cabinet in our classroom. Every few minutes he would chirp. It was really bugging everybody. Even though the teacher was talking, a friend of mine yelled out, "I can get that cricket." A second student said, "Let's name him Chirpy!" A third student said, "Hey! That was my uncle's nickname." The next person said, "My uncle's nickname is Bingo." By that time everyone was talking about their uncles and vacations and had forgotten all about the cricket in the room. When my teacher asked a couple of the boys to move the file cabinet, they did and then sat back down. Nobody even remembered that the cabinet was being moved to get that stupid cricket until the teacher asked one of the boys to catch it and take it outside. What was so funny about it was that all those comments were ping-ponged in about 20 seconds. It looked really funny from where I was sitting—like people watching a tennis or ping-pong match. That is what I told the teacher. Now anytime we start blurting comments like that, the teacher says, "Ping-pong," and we know to stop and think.

As mentioned, low-frequency, high-impact behaviors are more severe and may place the adolescent with ADHD in socially inappropriate or legally unacceptable situations (Anderson et al., 1987; Barkley, 1990; Goldstein & Goldstein, 1988; Barkley et al., 1990; Weiss & Hechtmann, 1986). Barkley (1990) found that a significantly greater number of students with ADHD had smoked cigarettes or marijuana than did non-ADHD students. Weiss and Hechtmann (1986) suggested that hyperactive adolescents use more nonmedical drugs (particularly alcohol) and have a higher incidence of automobile accidents than do nonhyperactive adolescents.

In a recent study, Barkley, Fischer, Edlebrock, and Smallish (1990) followed a large sample of children with ADHD and normal children prospectively for eight years after initial evaluation. The results indicated that a great number of students had significant behavioral difficulties in conjunction with their ADHD. When involved in adolescent delinquency, adolescents with ADHD who also have learning disabilities are more likely to get caught than are their non-learning-disabled ADHD counterparts. For the same offenses, the students with ADHD and learning disabilities had higher rates of adjudication and were more than twice as likely as nonimpaired adolescents to be judged delinquent by the courts (Barkley et al., 1990). Academically, adolescents with ADHD continue to have difficulties (Barkley, 1990; Zentall, 1993; Hamlett, Pelligrini, & Conners, 1987; Tant & Douglas, 1982; Zentall, 1988; Voelker, Carter, Sprague, Gdowski, & Lachar, 1989). These students are over three times more likely to have failed a grade or have been suspended, and they are over eight times more likely to have been expelled or to have dropped out of school, than are non-ADHD adolescents (Barkley, 1990).

As a group, students with ADHD may be impulsive, poorly organized, and relatively inefficient in complex problem-solving strategies and organizational skills (Hamlett et al., 1987; Tant & Douglas, 1982; Zentall, 1988; Voelker et al., 1989). These difficulties seem to be due to lack of effective use of strategies during performance of the task itself (Voelker et al., 1989). The student may not have the skills necessary to begin a task, complete the task steps in the appropriate order, or know when to switch to another task. For example, an adolescent with ADHD who is attending a postsecondary cabinet-making class may have difficulty understanding the direction "Gather your materials." This information may need to be broken into several specific tasks (e.g., "Look in the top file cabinet drawer for the plans for a base cabinet. Get a piece of 24" × 30" oak from the storage cabinet. . . . Take these materials to your work area"). The use of a checklist will ensure that steps are completed in order and without omissions. Students with ADHD also show indication of significant deficits in executive processes or strategies or mechanisms needed to organize and monitor their own thoughts and behaviors (Gordon, Thomason, Cooper, & Ivers, 1991).

The Young Adult Years

Of children diagnosed with ADHD, 50%–65% will continue to have difficulties as adults (Barkley, 1990). While the majority of these adults will not demonstrate antisocial behaviors, a small percentage will display a persistent pattern of such conduct over time. Self-esteem problems, which have been compounding over the adolescent years, continue to cause problems for the adult with ADHD. These adults often have not experienced success in relationships and may be oversensitive emotionally. They may have a difficult time maintaining satisfactory relationships with others. They often have difficulty with conversation because thought patterns may be loose and poorly organized. The adult with ADHD may demonstrate immature social skills and may not successfully fit into typical social situations.

Adults with ADHD continue to be disorganized (Barkley, 1990), which may negatively affect job performance. The adult with ADHD may, for example, be late to meetings, lose or misplace items, miss deadlines, or scatter materials around his or her work area. Many adults place themselves in job situations that emulate the (unsuccessful) school setting—jobs where they must sit for long periods of time, deal with supervisors who give multistep directions, or work on projects that extend over long periods of time with little supervision—rather than look for jobs where their creativity and unending fountain of energy can be directed and channeled into successful endeavors. This type of adult tends to be dismissed from several jobs because of an inability to establish rapport with colleagues, take direction from a boss, arrive at work on time, or concentrate on the task at hand (Jordan, 1993).

Needless to say, these problems often result in a troubled home life. While research evidence on adults with ADHD is scarce, several researchers have suggested that adults with ADHD have more problematic relationships than do non-ADHD adults (Weiss & Hechtman, 1986). Some have suggested that a higher divorce rate may be anticipated among adults with ADHD.

EDUCATIONAL INTERVENTIONS

Given the range and significance of difficulties at school posed by students with ADHD, a great need exists for effective school interventions for adolescents with ADHD. The Chesapeake Institute for the Division of Innovation and Development conducted a study during the 1993–1994 school year documenting the effectiveness of promising practices of educating children and youth with ADHD (McInerney, 1994). Six school districts were visited in California, Florida, Maryland, North Carolina, and Wisconsin. Fifty-six children were identified with ADHD. Data were collected and analyzed on the frequency and effectiveness of practices used to educate these children. Figure 8–1 lists the target practices adapted from McInerney (1994) and discussed in this chapter.

These four target practices—effective teaching, behavior modification, ADHD-specific practices, and cooperative learning—demonstrate the areas of need for educational intervention strategies specifically designed for the adolescent student with ADHD. Interventions in these areas can have a powerful and positive impact on the lives of students with ADHD (Barkley, 1990; Parker, 1990; Fowler, 1990, Levine, 1994).

Effective Teaching	Behavior Modification Techniques	ADHD-Specific Practices	Cooperative Learning
Instructional environment	Cognitive behavior therapy	Study and organizational reading skills	Student team learning
Teacher behaviors	Social skills training	Handwriting	
Behavioral strategies		Work rate	
		Math	
		Spelling	
		Following directions	
		Memory	

FIGURE 8–1
Target Practices for Educating Children with ADHD

The teacher working with adolescents with ADHD needs an understanding of ADHD and its manifestations. While there is no special curriculum for such students, special accommodations or adaptations may be needed to enable success for this student. The case study in the following vignette describes an adolescent with ADHD with an unmet need.

Joseph: A Case Study

Joseph was a precocious preschooler. He was always curious about everything in the room, keeping his teacher and other adults constantly on watch to ensure that nothing was turned over, bothered, or eaten in an impulsive moment. His mother kept him in preschool an additional year at the recommendation of his teachers because he was "immature for his age and needed another year to catch up with his peers."

By kindergarten, Joseph had developed a reputation with mothers in the neighborhood and with his peers. He was avoided by many because he would pull hair, push, or otherwise annoy his fellow classmates. Joseph spent a great deal of time in "timeout" during kindergarten because of his behavior. Academically, Joseph seemed to know all the answers, constantly blurting them out before anyone else had a chance to answer. However, the teachers rarely got anything in writing from him.

In first and second grade, behaviors escalated to the point that Joseph was removed from the classroom on several occasions "in order that the other students could have the opportunity to learn." He was not able to remain on-task long enough to complete an assignment. His gross motor skills were poor, causing him to appear clumsy in the classroom and on the playground. Gaps in his learning were beginning to appear.

Frustrated by his inability to know all the answers (as he did earlier), Joseph would create diversions from the academic activity. These diversions were increasing in severity. By the time Joseph had reached fourth grade, he had set two fires in the trash can in his classroom, had opened the emergency door on the bus (while it was moving), attempted to shove a child out the back door of the bus, and had brought a knife to school to scare a child who had been "bugging" him.

In fifth grade, Joseph's truancy was a major concern of teachers. He frequently caused trouble in his community while truant from school. Juvenile Court Services and the Department of Family and Child Services were involved. Middle school, with its hourly changing schedule (and seven different academic teachers), increased the frustration felt by Joseph. Behaviors similar to those previously seen continued. In addition, Joseph threw the school walkie-talkies in the sewage treatment pond, earning a trip to tribunal and placement in an alternative school for conduct-disordered students. By sixth grade, Joseph was demonstrating behaviors that would label him as emotionally and behaviorally disordered.

Unfortunately for Joseph and many others like him, what began as attentional difficulties in preschool and kindergarten escalated far beyond this by adolescence. Studies suggest that early intervention is necessary for the student with ADHD to achieve success academically and socially (Barkley, 1990; Biederman et al., 1991). Students who receive early training and intervention have a better chance of completing school, maintaining relationships, and holding a job (Taylor, 1990). Based on this data, it is glaringly obvious that our job as educators is to stop the cycle of failure so that students with ADHD may become productive members of our society.

Effective Teaching

Instructional Environment

Structure, supervision, and support are three environmental necessities for adolescents with ADHD (Taylor, 1990). Structure, one of the most critical elements for success, should be provided through clear communication of expectations, rules, and consequences. Descriptions of rules, consequences, and rewards should be posted in the room and followed consistently. Lee Canter's (1986) assertive discipline plan provides an excellent reference for consistent, clear communication of expectations. Canter's workbook, available for both middle school and secondary school teachers, contains many ready-made forms, which facilitate record keeping (for both discipline and positive communication between school and home). Canter offers suggestions for dealing with discipline in large classes, in small groups, and with individuals.

Simple environmental modifications in the classroom make a significant difference for students with ADHD. Anything out of place can be distracting to the student with ADHD. Such students should be provided a space relatively free from distractions, where supervision is easy. Figure 8–2 offers suggestions for modification of the environment to ensure success for the adolescent with ADHD.

Teacher Behaviors

Supervision is a crucial environmental concern for adolescents with ADHD. Effective supervision of the learning task should be provided by teachers who are calm, who can deal with problems as they occur, and who will give quiet reminders or prearranged signals to alert students of a change in routine or a possible behaviorally difficult time approaching (Taylor, 1990). Rules and consequences should be provided by teachers who are consistent but positive in their disciplinary approach (Pfinner & Barkley, 1990). Instruction should be clear, brief, and delivered through multiple means of presentation.

- Arrange desks in straight rows, facing the front.
- Create an "office" space, where student may elect to go to work.
- Allow student to use earphones or earplugs to block distractions during seat work and test-taking times.
- Seat child near the teacher, surrounded by students who are calm. Also care to seat student away from the door, high-traffic areas, noisy heaters, air conditioners, etc.
- Create a special section in your room for supplies.
- Allow extra desktop space, if possible. Also allow extra room between desks to prevent an invasion of personal space.
- Do not place highly colored pictures on the wall nor hang mobiles from the ceiling.
- Clean the blackboard each day to start "with a clean slate."

FIGURE 8–2
Modifications of the Environment for the Student with ADHD

Because of motivational deficits, consequences used to manage the behavior of adolescents with ADHD must be delivered more swiftly and immediately than is needed for other students. These consequences must often be of a higher magnitude (i.e., more powerful) than those needed to manage the behavior of others. Teachers can avoid many behavioral problems by limiting the amount of instructional lag time when students are waiting for teacher direction. Teachers must be more mindful of planning ahead in managing students with ADHD during phases of transition between lessons (Pfinner & Barkley, 1990; Taylor, 1990). Transitional times can be eased by signaling (e.g., flashing the lights, ringing a bell, playing music) and rewarding smooth transitions. Some general rules of thumb for supervising the choices and transitional periods of students with ADHD (and thus preventing behavioral problems) are listed in Figure 8–3.

The supportive classroom offers an "I CARE" atmosphere to the student with ADHD (Taylor, 1990). This means that the teacher uses logical consequences firmly, quickly, and consistently to demonstrate to the student that he or she will not be given a chance to avoid facing the consequence at the time of the misbehavior. Figure 8–4 defines this "I CARE" philosophy, developed by Taylor (1994).

Signaling and redirecting are very effective techniques that help to head off trouble while allowing the student with ADHD to avoid embarrassment in front of peers. Signals can be hand signs or words that are agreed upon privately beforehand, between teacher and student (to warn or cue student to calm down, get up and stretch, stop talking, sit appropri-

- Use predetermined signals (such as dimming the lights) to warn of approaching transition.
- Warn students of approaching change in routine or task.
- Use proximity control.
- Review and practice rules and expectations frequently.
- Offer generous amounts of positive attention.
- Redirect inappropriate behavior.
- Use behavioral contracts that monitor and reinforce behaviors for short intervals of time.
- Remember the saying, "The bell does not dismiss the class, I do."
- Dismiss students in small groups, not all at once; wait until all are in control before dismissing.

FIGURE 8–3
Preparing for Transitional Periods

ately, etc.). An observant teacher can redirect students by asking them to do tasks such as straightening the bookshelf, running an errand to the office, and passing out papers.

Behavioral Strategies

Specific behavioral strategies that may effectively be used with adolescents with ADHD include positive attention, token economy systems, response cost systems, cognitive-behavioral intervention, contingency contracting, and self-monitoring (i.e., metacognitive) procedures (Brown, Wynne, &

I —Interrupt the inappropriate behavior.
C —Cool off (send the child to a timeout place).
A —Affirm (show empathy for student's feelings; express faith and confidence in student's judgment and ability to understand what you are saying and to cooperate with you).
R —Redirect.
E —Educate (explain the domino effect of student's behavior, and discuss better choices of behavior for next time).

FIGURE 8–4
"I CARE" Philosophy

Medenis, 1985; Copeland & Walker, 1989; Pfinner and Barkley, 1990; Sullivan & O'Leary, 1990; Barkley, 1994). Of course, many of these strategies are appropriate for students with ADHD across the age range and thus are discussed in other chapters. Here we discuss strategies that involve positive attention, token economies, and response cost systems. Cognitive-behavioral intervention will be discussed in a separate section.

Positive Attention. A positive teacher–student relationship may not only improve academic and social functioning in the short term but may also increase the likelihood of long-term success for many adolescents with ADHD (Pfinner & Barkley, 1990). Experience suggests that young adolescents will meet their attentional needs, regardless of whether the consequences of their behaviors are positive or negative. In the classroom, the teacher will determine whether these needs are fulfilled positively or negatively. A positive teacher attitude is critical for caring, sensitive, and responsible student behavior in the long term.

Most students, including adolescents with ADHD, thrive on positive attention from the teacher. One way to give this positive attention is to meet the student with ADHD at the door to the classroom with a smile and a welcoming comment. This positive attention, given before the student has had an opportunity to seek attention in negative ways, will help to establish rapport between the student and the teacher. This gives the teacher an opportunity to praise the student before being frustrated by inappropriate student behavior.

Learning is a trial-and-error process that is shaped by both positive and negative reinforcers that occur in the students' daily lives. Positive attention from the teacher meets the adolescents' attentional needs in an appropriate fashion and reinforces positive behavior. However, if positive attention is not forthcoming, the student may conclude that negative attention is the next best thing. Therefore, ignoring a student's inappropriate behavior or withdrawing attention tends to reduce positive attention and therefore reduce positive behaviors. However, when you ignore student behaviors, you must be sure not to acknowledge the student in any way (e.g., with a glance, a sigh, etc.), particularly if the behavior escalates. If the student's behavior is ignored only until it reaches a certain severity, the student has simply learned that escalated behavior will result in the attention he or she seeks. While this attention will no doubt be negative, it will meet the child's attentional needs. Many behaviors can be shaped through the use of positive attention alone. However, the student with ADHD may require more frequent and powerful reinforcement than praising and ignoring of behaviors allows.

Token Economies and Response Cost Systems. As discussed in Chapter 3, token economies and response cost systems are effective tools for improving behavior in the student with ADHD. A device that has been shown to be particularly effective for adolescents with ADHD involved in these types of systems is the Attention Trainer (Rapport & Gordon, 1987), which can sit on the student's desk. Each minute, a point is given to the student, with the assumption that the child is on-task. The teacher carries a remote control with her and can push a button that flashes a red light at the student's desk and deducts a point each time the child is off-task. Results of a study by Rapport and Gordon (1991) demonstrated that the Attention Trainer provided structure sufficient to allow the students with ADHD to improve their attention to schoolwork. Implementation of the Attention Trainer appeared to have an immediate and powerful effect on the students' sustained attention. However, during this short time period (13 sessions, 50 minutes each), the gains in attentiveness were not internalized. Consequently, improvements in on-task behavior appear to require ongoing use of the device, at least for a longer period than was the case for the Rapport and Gordon subjects.

A second, easy-to-implement reinforcement tool for use with the adolescent with ADHD is the token economy checkbook. Each student is assigned an account number and is issued "checks" and "deposit slips." Many area banks are willing to provide nonnegotiable blank checks and deposit slips for classroom use. Checks and deposit slips suitable for use can also be generated on the computer. Guidelines are established within the class for earning money and for bills payable. Attentional skills may be reinforced. Not only do students see the effect of their efforts both academically and behaviorally, they improve math skills while learning a valuable life skill. Figure 8–5 gives examples of guidelines established for a seventh-grade class using token economy checkbooks.

- Each child must open an account in the classroom as they would at the bank (i.e., complete an application form).
- Each child is issued a check register and a book of checks (student ID or locker number can be used as the checking account number).
- Each child is awarded a salary for the week (e.g., $10.00).
- Bonus deposits may be awarded for assignments completed at 80% or above accuracy.
- Bills are sent to individuals for lost or incomplete assignments, for absences, and for not following preestablished rules.
- Checks may be written for privileges throughout the week.
- If a child "goes broke" before the end of the week, he or she must go to "court," where a consequence will be decided on by a jury of peers.

FIGURE 8–5
Using Checking Accounts for Behavioral Intervention in Middle School

Behavior Modification

Cognitive Behavior Therapy

Waldander and Hubert (1985) state that students need to become more aware of the external reinforcement of desirable behavior and adopt internalized controls that allow them to self-monitor their actions to increase generalization of improved patterns of behavior. Many behavior therapists have moved from total reliance on outside control to a model that combines manipulation of environmental contingencies with self-control processes of the subject (Meichenbaum, 1977; Abikioff & Gittelman, 1984; Brown et al., 1985; Abikoff, 1987; Hinshaw & Erhardt, 1991; Copeland, 1993). The self-monitoring project discussed in Chapter 7 is one example of cognitive behavior therapy.

The goal of cognitive therapy is to help students utilize language for problem solving rather than continue their impulsive responding to various situations. Internalizing the rules for behavior, learning self-control, and using mental dialogue for problem solving are the foundations for emotional maturity, good judgment, and appropriate responding, and each of these is strengthened in cognitive behavior therapy (Copeland & Walker, 1989). This self-directed set of rules is our mind's voice and forms the basis for our self-control. Our development of an inner voice creates the most far-reaching differences between how humans and animals use language. Our language permits us to do four very important things: exchange messages with each other that can serve to guide and influence our own and others' behavior; pass our knowledge about the world on to others, especially the next generation; give messages to ourselves so that we control our own behavior (i.e., have will power, or self-control); and invent new rules to follow when we are facing problems (Barkley, 1994).

This emphasis on self-control strategies resulted in part from the influence of Luria (1966), who stated that a student assumes control over his or her own behavior through internalizing self-directed verbal commands. He proposed a three-stage model in which behavior is first directed by the speech of others, next by the child's overt speech, and finally by covert, or inner, speech. Building on the concept, Lloyd (1980) lists three characteristics of most cognitive behavior modification programs: students act as their own teachers (modeling is often useful in training students to use self-guiding instructions); students use verbalization; and a series of steps, or strategies, is identified through which children proceed in solving problems.

Cognitive behavior therapy programs used for students with ADHD are based on the notion that children with ADHD lack the ability to organize and regulate their behavior because, unlike their non-ADHD counterparts, they fail to "stop, look, listen, and think" before responding to a situation (Douglas, 1972). A cognitive behavior modification program that attempts to teach the child with ADHD to think about the steps necessary to perform a task successfully or respond appropriately to a situation makes good intuitive sense. This capacity to wait or delay a response to a situation allows evaluation of events more objectively, rationally, and logically. It allows the student a much greater likelihood of formulating a response that will be successful.

When adolescents set goals for themselves, develop plans for the future, and then carry out their behavior according to those plans and goals, they are using their inner voice and rule-governed behavior. The student is more likely to be prepared for the future and indeed can accurately create the future to some degree. This capacity to use language internally underlies the essence of free will. Through it we can bring behavior under the control of rules, instructions, plans, and goals so that it is directed toward the future (Barkley, 1994). For the adolescent to gain this concept of self-control, the training should include a number of tasks and should occur across situations. It should make use of modeling, role play, games in which self-control procedures promote winning, and vicarious experiences through stories, anecdotal reports, and imagery (Ross & Ross, 1976).

Several studies involving the use of cognitive behavior modification have reported significant differences on follow-up assessment on measures of oral reading, oral comprehension, handwriting skills, and word attack skills, as well as changes in social behaviors and attending-to-task behaviors (Douglas, Parry, Marton, & Garson, 1976; Abikoff & Gittelman, 1984; Brown et al., 1985). Thus, cognitive behavior modification, or programs designed to teach children internal strategies for coping with situations that require delay or self-control, should be considered as an intervention strategy for the student with ADHD (Meichenbaum, 1977; Kendall & Braswell, 1982).

The ability of students to understand and profit from cognitive behavior plans may depend in part on their developmental level at the time of treatment. Loper (1980) suggests that self-understanding increases as the student becomes older and more aware of his or her interactions with the environment. *Metacognition* is a term used to describe the individual's understanding of his own cognitive processes. For cognitive training to be effective, it should be matched to the metacognitive level of the student. Campione, Brown, and Ferrara (1982) suggest that students first experience problem-solving activities in the presence of others and slowly participate themselves. Their suggestions to teachers are relevant to anyone concerned with changing behaviors: the message must be appropriate to the student's level of understanding; the student must be reminded of related prior knowledge; attention should be focused on the important facts; and comprehension should be monitored. Campione et al. distinguish between *metacognition* and *executive control*, which includes the overseeing management functions that the learner uses when attempting to solve problems. The latter includes checking the outcome, planning the next move, and testing, revising, and evaluating one's strategies for learning. The authors suggest that using executive control seems to lead to increased transfer to more intelligent behavior.

Hinshaw and his co-workers developed explicit, script-guided training procedures, designed expressly for hyperactive children, to teach self-monitoring/self-evaluation. Hinshaw believed that young adolescents could use this training procedure to improve social interactions and to control impulsivity and anger (Hinshaw & Melnick, 1992). The intention was not to replace reinforcement-based social learning principles with exclusively cognitive procedures but rather to extend the use of behavioral approaches through mediation and problem solving. Students in Hinshaw's study were trained in metacognition (self-monitoring and self-evaluation) during small-group therapy sessions. The students learned to appraise, with accuracy, adult ratings of social behavior during cooperative projects. Modeling of both good and bad examples of behavior ensured the trainer that the students were aware of the content of the desired actions. During both academic and unstructured activities, the adult rated the students' behavior every few minutes. Each student's goal was to match (i.e., accurately evaluate) the ratings that were given by the adult evaluator. The most important aspect of this training occurred during the discussion that took place when the adult and the student compared their respective ratings. The student received extra reinforcement for accurately matching the adult ratings. The trainer encouraged the student to recall—with behavioral specificity—the positive and negative aspects of his or her behavior during the preceding few minutes and made clear to the student why the adult rating was given.

During the teaching of anger management skills, the students were presented with role-play situations similar to those they would encounter during the day. The children were taught to recognize internal cues of impending anger, generalize cognitive-behavioral strategies for redirecting their anger, and rehearse these procedures.

Although cognitive interventions based on self-instructional models are not recommended as a primary treatment for ADHD (Abikoff, 1987; Hinshaw & Erhardt, 1991), the integration of cognitive procedures with sound behavioral treatments may result in greater benefits than those that accrue to either strategy alone. Indeed, the most important use for cognitive procedures would seem to be the one that was originally intended for such mediational strategies—namely, to extend the benefits that accrue to more traditional behavioral treatments (Meichenbaum, 1977).

It is important to remember that each adolescent is unique. The focus should be on the particular problems and strengths of the individual student. Students with ADHD often have multiple problems that require a combination of treatments guided by individual assessment. Concerned adults *can* make a difference. The school community has a responsibility to appreciate differences in individual students while helping them gain maximum academic and social skills.

Social Skills Training

While a few adolescents with ADHD are very popular and may be class leaders, the majority have significant problems in social relationships (Taylor, 1990; Copeland, 1993; Bloomquist et al., 1991). They often appear insensitive to others' feelings and needs, and their impulsive responding creates ongoing social interaction problems. For this reason, social skills training, both in the classroom and as part of a psychotherapeutic intervention program, can be quite helpful (Copeland & Love, 1990).

However, there are several things, short of a social skills intervention, that teachers can do to enhance social skills. Some general suggestions teachers may wish to use include the ideas in Figure 8–6.

The entire school may be involved in social skills instruction. One school in Great Falls, Montana, uses a buildingwide approach to social skills instruction. Each spring the staff sets a monthly schedule for the following year based on the observed needs of the students. A theme, or common focus, is set for each month. For example, in September the focus may be to create a positive, nurturing classroom climate; in October the focus may be one of enhancing self-esteem. These themes are actually affective social skills. A variety of materials related to each general social skills theme is organized in a resource book given to each teacher. (Many of the activities used at the Great Falls school were drawn from the ASSIST Program, a program of specific behavioral intervention skills [Higgins, 1993].)

All teachers formally focus on the affective skill theme once during the week; some may choose to focus on the theme daily for a week or more. In addition, each month, one specific behavioral social skill is taught and prac-

- Post and discuss rules of effective social interaction.
- Utilize stories and essays that illustrate positive human characteristics and graphically depict what happens when one is rude, selfish, mean, etc.
- Encourage a sense of responsibility for others.
- Encourage individual differences.
- Improve writing skills and develop sensitivity by having students keep a daily diary that addresses incidents as they occur (questions such as: What happened? Why did it happen? What were the consequences? How did others feel? How could it have been prevented? How can I use that situation to learn?).

FIGURE 8–6
Social Skills Training Suggestions

ticed. Rather than simply disciplining students for misbehavior, students are taught what rules to follow and also how to appropriately do so. Throughout the year, specific components, or steps, are taught. For example, students are taught steps toward how to follow directions, how to accept feedback, how to accept "no" as an answer, how to make a request, how to give and receive compliments, and how to disagree (see Figure 8–7).

Many of these materials may be purchased commercially (e.g., "Social Skills Survival Kit," Fister & Kemp, 1994). The new behavioral social skill is formally taught during the first week of the month. During the second and third weeks of each month, brief practice, reinforcement, and application of the activities and discussions are integrated into the daily curriculum. Figure 8–8 gives a possible annual planning schedule for affective and behavioral skills to be taught schoolwide.

Four major social skill areas must be specifically taught to the adolescent with ADHD: social entry skills (i.e., the skills needed to successfully initiate or join the ongoing interactions of another child or group of children); conversation skills (i.e., the ability to talk with one or more than one person without dominating the conversation); conflict resolution and problem-solving skills (i.e., a systematic and reflective approach to considering behavioral alternatives); and anger control skills (i.e., a system to help break the cycle of aggressive, disruptive, or annoying behavior that causes the adolescent with ADHD to be shunned by others) (Guevremont, 1990).

Social Entry and Conversation Skills. Taylor (1990) suggests that specific guidelines for obtaining social entry and communicating effectively must be taught to the adolescent with ADHD. Although Taylor's guidelines were written for parents, they may be effectively modified for the classroom (see Figure 8–9).

FIGURE 8–7
How to Disagree Appropriately

How to Disagree Appropriately

1. Look at the person you disagree with.
2. Use a pleasant voice.
3. Say, "I have a problem."
4. Tell what you disagree with.
5. Tell why you disagree.
6. Say, "Thank you for listening."

Month	Affective Skills	Behavioral Skills
September	Creating a caring classroom	How to follow directions
October	Building self-esteem	How to accept criticism
November	Friendship skills	How to accept "no" for an answer
December	Friendship skills	How to make a request
January	Decision making/goal setting	How to greet someone
February	Teaching cooperation	How to give and accept a compliment
March	Teaching cooperation	How to apologize appropriately
April	Handling anger and conflicts	How to disagree appropriately
May	Handling anger and conflicts	How to report peer behavior

FIGURE 8–8
Sample Planning Schedule for Teaching Behavioral Skills

To make friends, the student with ADHD should think of the following guidelines:

- Smile.
- Walk to a potential friend or group of friends.
- Talk to potential friends (rather than remaining silent).
- Ask potential friends questions (to find out their interests).
- Talk about potential friends' interests (rather than your own).
- Get friends to talk about themselves.
- Share information about yourself (in small doses).
- Invite these friends to your house; then be a friendly host or hostess.
- Never betray a confidence told in friendship.

FIGURE 8–9
Social Entry Skills for Students with ADHD

These skills may be taught through modeling or role playing. A talk-show format is an excellent way to introduce adolescents to the concept of questioning others about their interests. A videotape of their "production" can be made for the teacher to lead the class in providing feedback on appropriateness of skills used during their talk show.

Conflict Resolution and Problem-Solving Strategies. Teaching conflict resolution and problem solving provides a systematic and reflective approach to considering behavioral alternatives; understanding of such an approach is often lacking in students with ADHD (Robin, 1990; Guevremont, 1990). The main objective of problem solving is to encourage a reflective style of thinking. Problem solving typically involves the following steps (Robin, 1990; Guevremont, 1990):

1. *Identify the problem.* Accurately identify the nature of the problem and break it into parts.
2. *Use alternative thinking.* Be creative and search for various possibilities; use similar experiences as a starting point.
3. *Use consequential thinking.* Try to see immediate and long-term consequences of a particular action (i.e., cause and effect: "If I do this, then . . . will happen").
4. *Monitor progress.* Try one of the approaches and monitor your progress; devise a timetable of expected results; decide on indicators of progress.
5. *Make an evaluation.* Evaluate the results and modify the approach until the situation has been resolved or the goal accomplished.

As discussed earlier, cognitive-behavioral training uses a metacognitive (i.e., self-talk) approach to teaching a systematic and reflective approach to problem solving. Bloomquist, August, and Ostrander (1991) conducted a study designed to evaluate the feasibility of implementing a school-based, metacognitive prevention program dealing with social issues for students with ADHD. Their study involved dividing students into three groups: a multicomponent treatment group in which the children, teachers, and parents received training in a cognitive-behavioral training program; a teacher-training group in which only the teachers received the cognitive-behavioral training; and a waiting list group, which acted as a control group. Results of this study indicated that the multicomponent, cognitive-behavioral-trained group, in which both the teachers and students studied problem-solving skills, showed a statistically significant improvement on off-task/disruptive behavior. This group also exhibited a tendency toward maintaining such improvements.

Talents Unlimited, developed originally in 1971 by Carol Schlichter in the Mobile County, Alabama, public school system, is an excellent tool for teaching adolescents problem-solving strategies. This program is divided into six talents: the academic, or the base, talent; productive thinking; forecasting; communicating; planning; and decision making. The academic talent is viewed as the traditional talent that children use to acquire information. This talent might be called the status quo talent because it focuses on the acquisition of knowledge in its present state without manipulation. Memorization of information and rote practice of skills are typical behaviors associated with the academic talent, and the "one right answer" is characteristic of the instructional outcome.

Although right answers might yield a good score on a school test, success in the real world of work demands a variety of abilities, including skills in generating numerous solutions to a problem, analyzing and evaluating alternatives, organizing and implementing plans of action, predicting causes and effects, and communicating ideas and feelings. Maintaining the status quo is incongruous in a world where new information and technology are escalating at mind-boggling rates.

For this reason, the Talents Unlimited model is designed to enhance the acquisition of basic knowledge and skills by training students to use their knowledge to create new solutions to problems. As students learn to use a variety of creative and critical thinking skills to help them accomplish academic objectives in science, math, language, social studies, and so on, they are also practicing the kinds of thinking that are highly related to success in their social environment and success in the career world. Decision making in this model is defined by four observable student behaviors: identification of many different alternatives to solving a problem; the use of criteria to evaluate each alternative; the selection of the best alternatives; and the formulation and statement of many different reasons for the final choice. The decision-making talent empowers children and teaches them that they are decision makers but that with that right comes the responsibility of being accountable for their decisions and the consequences of those decisions. Figure 8–10 gives examples of how both academic and social skills may be addressed through the Talents Unlimited program.

Anger Control. Anger control is necessary to break the cycle of aggressive, disruptive, or annoying behavior demonstrated by the student with ADHD (Guevremont, 1990). These behaviors cause the student with ADHD to be shunned by others or to become the butt of scapegoating, teasing, and provocations. This in turn leads to anger-induced retaliatory actions, which lead to further removal from the group.

Teaching anger control involves teaching relaxation techniques, or ways to remove stress, as well as cognitive-behavioral training. The student learns to identify common external events that cause emotions to rise; identify internal events that are associated with anger; use a variety of coping skills in the presence of the stressful event; and actively practice using the coping skills (see Figure 8–11).

Environmental support (i.e., rules, consequences, and possible cues posted around the room) is necessary if this anger control program is to be successful. For these skills to be generalized, role-play "scripts" should be provided that include every aspect of the student's day at school. Possible responses to peer pressure or provocation should be practiced. These responses should be written in the student's notebook or on a notecard for a purse or wallet so that they are easily accessible at all times of the day. Because parents, teachers, and peers do not always respond to a change in behavior, peer partners should be invited to provide positive experiences when the student with ADHD practices his or her improved social skills. Time will be needed for breaking into preexisting friendship networks and winning new friends. Unfortunately, the reputation the student with ADHD has earned may continue to plague the child long after the behavior has stopped (Taylor, 1990).

ADHD-Specific Practices

When discussing academic difficulties of adolescents with ADHD, one tends to find two loosely grouped categories—those with *behavioral difficulties* that create difficulties for the student academically, and those with *specific skill deficits* that cause academic difficulties (Copeland, 1994). When devising a plan of action for the student with ADHD, the teacher must think of the individual, not of the label *ADHD*. Behavioral intervention is generally necessary to help these students attend to the task at hand. However, specific skills or strategies may also need to be taught to alleviate the poor self-esteem accompanied by a poor academic record. Adolescents who can benefit from this specific academic skill intervention will find success working with programs similar to those followed by students with learning disabilities. Clearly, ADHD and learning disabilities interact, and care must be taken not to ignore one or the other (Barkley, 1994). The following section will deal with specific academic difficulties found in adolescents.

The ADAPT program (Parker, 1992) provides an "Academic Performance Inventory," which enables the teacher to pinpoint specific areas for intervention. The "Interest Inventory" addresses the areas of attention, impulsiveness, motor activity, organizational planning, compliance, mood, social interaction, and academic ability. Each of these areas is matched to specific intervention strategies, which should then be used to formulate an accommodation plan. Figure 8–12 gives an excerpt from the attention area of the "Academic Performance Inventory."

Study and Organizational Skills

By definition, students with ADHD are disorganized. It is imperative that teachers organize the physical and emotional environment of the room and teach the students to organize their personal space. Figure 8–13 offers suggestions on organizational and study skills necessary for academic success in any secondary academic area.

Talent Area	Definition	Sample Academic Activity	Sample Social Activity
Productive thinking	To generate many, varied, and unusual ideas of solutions and add detail to the ideas to improve them or make them more interesting	Students working in a math unit on surveying and graphing are asked to think of a variety of unusual topics for a survey they will conduct and graph.	Asked to cut class, the student is asked to think of a variety of unusual replies.
Decision making	To outline, weigh, make final judgments, and defend a decision on the many alternatives to a problem.	Students ordering materials for a school store make final selections by considering such criteria as cost, interest, and availability.	Students in a parenting class make final decisions concerning the responsibility of having children while still in school themselves.
Planning	To design a means for implementing an idea by describing what is to be done, identifying the resources needed, outlining a sequence of steps to take, and pinpointing possible problems in the plan.	Students conducting an experiment on the unusual characteristics of slime mold are asked to design experiments to answer questions they may have about the behavior of the mold.	Students having difficulty making new friends design a plan for introducing themselves to a new group.

Forecasting	To make a variety of predictions about the possible causes and/or effects of various phenomena.	Students conducting a parent poll on their school's dress code are encouraged to generate predictions about the possible causes for low returns of the surveys.	The impulsive student who constantly blurts answers is asked to generate predictions about the possible cause of social rejection because of his or her behavior.
Communication	To use and interpret both verbal and nonverbal forms of communication to express ideas, feelings, and needs to others.	In an attempt to describe the emotions of different groups of Georgians, eighth graders studying Georgia history role-play as they hear Lincoln's Emancipation Proclamation.	When learning social entry skills, the students will role play appropriate ways of questioning others about their interests through a talk show format.
Academic	To develop a base of knowledge and/or skill about a topic or issue through acquisition of information and concepts.	Students read from a variety of resources to gain information about the Impressionist period of art and then share the information in a discussion of a painting by Monet.	Students discussing *Hamlet* relate the feeling of being betrayed to personal experiences.

FIGURE 8–10
Talents Unlimited Suggestions

Students should be taught to follow these steps:

- Consider behavioral alternatives to use when angry.
- Identify common external events that cause emotions to rise.
- Identify internal cues associated with anger.
- Use coping self-statements to control anger.

FIGURE 8–11
Anger Control

Handwriting

Students with ADHD experience more difficulties in handwriting and proper completion of written work than in any other single academic area (Copeland, 1993). Many, perhaps even most, hyperactive children write rapidly with little attention or care given to the quality and legibility of their work. Their handwriting style is frequently a mixed cursive-print form with

For each of the below items please check (✓) only if the student has had a *significant* problem relative to most other students *in the class in the past two weeks.*

In the area of ATTENTION, this student:
_____is easily distracted by other students or events
_____has difficulty sustaining attention
_____has difficulty following directions
_____often does not seem to listen (pay attention)
_____is "spacey"; in own world; often daydreams

[The "Accommodation Plan" then shows the following accommodations under the area of attention.]

_____Seat student in quiet area
_____Seat student near good role model
_____Seat student near "study buddy"
_____Increase distance between desks
_____Seat student away from distracting stimuli
_____Allow extra time to complete assigned work
_____Shorten assignments/work periods; use timer
_____Break long assignments into smaller parts

FIGURE 8–12
Excerpts from the "Academic Performance Inventory"
Used by permission from Parker, H. C. (1992), *The ADAPT Program.* Plantation, FL: Specialty Press, Inc.

- Have students organize desk, papers, textbooks, notebook, etc., by color. They should use colored folders and dividers to match the colored book jackets.
- Students should use a loose-leaf, three-ring notebook. Put a pencil pouch in the front of the notebook. Put a full monthly calendar (or student agenda) in the front for recording short- and long-term assignments and important dates. Keep colored pencils for underlining and color-coding assignments. Mark everything on calendar for English in red. At a glance, student can see that he or she needs all Red material to go home. This will help organize lockers as well.
- Have frequent notebook checks, with positive reinforcement and periodic notebook/desk clean-outs.
- Make a habit of modeling and leading students in the skill of appropriately recording assignments on their calendar (even initialing the assignment after it is written, if needed). Study buddies/peer partners can assist students with ADHD with this task.
- Present assignments and due dates visually (written in the same place each day), as well as orally.
- Teach students to recognize preferred learning style and how to use this style to best advantage.

FIGURE 8–13
Enforcing Study and Organization Skills

variable slant and spacing. Letters may be written as rapidly as possible and, consequently, may be misformed; the looped letters are frequently made with straight-line strokes, and letters such as *e* and *i* are often indistinguishable. Other errors of visual detail are also frequently present, such as *t*'s that are not crossed and *i*'s left undotted. Rules of punctuation and capitalization may also be ignored in written work, even when the student can verbalize the correct usage rule (Goor, 1995).

Improving Written Expression Skills

The inability to express ideas in writing causes difficulty in all academic areas. The impulsivity and lack of attention to detail, common to students with ADHD, affects their ability to put thoughts on paper, frequently causing omission of words and punctuation. These omissions (in addition to lack of attention to penmanship) make the work difficult to read and understand for both the teacher and the writer. As the student stops writing to edit his work, he becomes more frustrated as ideas and thought drift away. After making numerous scratch-throughs a student may crumple the paper in frustration, refusing to continue. The adolescent with ADHD must learn strategies for organization of thoughts and ideas and for editing written work. The strategies listed in Figure 8–14 involve the student in active writing and editing procedures.

Many of the students who show characteristics of ADHD without hyperactivity demonstrate these handwriting behaviors. However, some—particularly those who are lethargic and underactive—often have extremely neat handwriting in which the individual letters appear to be drawn rather than written with a fluid stroke. These students have an extremely slow handwriting rate, and their work appears methodical and laborious. They will frequently overstrike existing letters or erase and rewrite letters or words that already appear to be adequately legible, sometimes to the degree that their behavior takes on an almost compulsive tone. The pencil grip of

- Remove the fear of writing.
- Have students use journals daily, in all subject areas.
- Teach students to brainstorm (anything goes).
- Have students write without interruption; they shouldn't stop to edit.
- Establish rules of writing (e.g., always write at a table or desk, write on every other line, write on one side of the paper, (which allows for "cut and paste" corrections).
- Provide time to correct/edit.
- Provide an editing checklist each time there is a written assignment, and teach how to use it.
- Encourage students to read their work aloud to listen for corrections (in syntax errors, word omissions, meaning, etc.).
- Provide graphic organizers for sequencing, cause and effect, etc.
- Use movement or "noises" (caps, snaps, shrugs, fist in the air, etc.) to delineate punctuation needed. Have students proofread work aloud to a partner. The partner will clap, stomp, etc., at each point where punctuation may be needed.
- Provide colored pencils for editing. Label each color as follows:

  period—red

  comma—yellow

  exclamation point—purple

  question mark—blue

  capital letter—green

FIGURE 8–14
Teaching Strategies for Improving Written Expression Skills

such students is usually cramped, with excessive muscular tension present in the hand and lower arm. Efforts to increase the speed of their writing may be fruitless. Figure 8–15 offers suggestions for remediation of these difficulties if it is necessary for the student to write with pen and pencil.

Work Rate

An obviously closely related academic problem to that of handwriting is that of work rate, an issue that plagues classroom teachers and disrupts classroom structure to an inordinate degree. Students with ADHD often do little or no independent work and must be continually reminded by the teacher to begin or return to task. They may procrastinate on academic tasks

- Reduce the need for handwriting.
- Do not have the child recopy material. It will get progressively worse rather than better.
- Allow student to copy a peer's notes or teacher's notes, or give an able student a piece of carbon (or NCR) paper so that as he or she takes notes, a second copy is made for the student who has difficulty taking notes.
- Reduce standards on some assignments, and make relevant standards clearer on important assignments.
- Have students use a Hoyle gripper (triangular-shaped pencil gripper) or soft "sponge" grip to ease pressure and strain from holding a pencil or pen too tightly.
- Have students use pens or mechanical pencils with a slightly larger diameter.
- Have students use notebook paper that has lines of alternating color (available through Narcam).
- Teach word processing skills.
- Have students leave every other line blank.
- Have sample organized paper laminated for students to keep in appropriate subject section of notebook (include heading, name, date, sample paragraph form, etc.). This sheet could be color-coded by subject (e.g., red is English; blue is math) which enables the child to find the appropriate heading for each class easily and quickly.
- Accept tape-recorded assignments.
- Accept typed assignments.

FIGURE 8–15
Teaching Strategies for Remediation of Difficulties with Handwriting

to a remarkable degree. When they are actually on-task, however, their work is usually done extremely rapidly with poor legibility, little attention to directions, and numerous attentionless errors. Some students with ADHD with neurologic preference for this work style are able to slow their work rate and produce high-quality, cautious work, but only for limited periods of time and with extreme effort. This pattern may lead to teacher comments such as, "This student could do better work if he tried." The teacher may never recognize that the problem is not one of lack of effort but one of excessive degree of cognitive effort necessary to produce good work.

In contrast, the lethargic student with ADHD usually works fairly carefully, sometimes even meticulously. However, the work rate is so slow that written tasks are rarely completed within classroom time constraints. This work style often leads to students being graded down for incomplete assignments or tests or to their having to complete work during break periods, during physical education periods, or at home. Figure 8–16 presents a number of individual suggestions for these students.

Math

Adolescents with ADHD may have difficulty in math due to conceptual difficulties or difficulties with computational accuracy (Nolting, 1995). Conceptual difficulties should be addressed by using manipulatives when introducing a new concept. Development of mathematical concepts and use of vocabulary and symbols may be impeded by problems similar to those that interfere with the student's acquisition of reading and spelling skills (Tomey, 1995). See Figure 8–17 for a list of common math difficulties.

In teaching math, therefore, specific areas of difficulty for each student should be known before the lesson begins. The students then must be provided with sequence and structure that will enable them to recognize the patterns into which they must organize larger and more meaningful units. The lesson must recognize that the learner needs to internalize each concept learned as the basis for further study (Tomey, 1995).

Adolescents with ADHD encounter many of these same problems, and a significant percentage of them appear to have visual-motor copy problems as well. Slowness of work rate is often a critical factor in lack of success in math classes, since much math work must be done under fairly considerable time pressure. Figure 8–18 offers suggestions for improving math abilities (Copeland, 1993).

The concrete-to-abstract instruction approach is crucial for many adolescents with ADHD. Students should be led through the following levels when learning a new concept. The enactive level involves direct manipulation of concrete objects. The ikonic level involves manipulation of mental images of objects. And the symbolic level involves the manipulation of symbols without mental images/abstraction. In processing through these levels,

- Practice planning (what is needed, how to break tasks into parts, etc.).
- Practice estimating time needed for activities.
- Teach outlining skills.
- Practice sorting, ordering, and reordering.
- Teach the use of a word processor to reorder ideas.
- Increase the use of lists and assignment organizers (notebooks with dividers, etc.).
- Give both verbal and written directions (write directions/assignments in the same place each day).
- Structure written assignments and tests (e.g., use graph paper for math, state standards of acceptable work, etc.).
- Point out overall structure of tasks (topic sentences, headings, tables of contents, etc.).
- Allow to work with partners or in small groups with quiet talking.
- Color, circle, underline, or rewrite directions, specific problems to complete, etc.
- Establish object-placement routines to retrieve routinely used objects such as books, assignments, and supplies.
- Tape prompt cards in desks, on books, or on assignment folders/dividers.
- Teach self-questioning (e.g., "What supplies do I need before I begin?").
- Use a timer and self-monitoring.
- Give time limits ("By the count of five, have your math book open to page 118").
- Monitor progress throughout assignment by using time prompts (e.g., "If you are attending well, you should be on question three at this time").

Assignment Completion Strategies

Teach self-instruction in the following areas:

- Using daily, weekly, and monthly planning forms
- Recording assignments quickly (e.g., use of abbreviations) and accurately
- Analyzing whether requirements of assignments are understood
- Estimating how much time each assignment will take
- Scheduling where and when to work
- Focusing on quality of work
- Keeping track of finished product

FIGURE 8–16
Work Rate Suggestions for Students with ADHD

- Reversal, transposition, inversion, and substitution of numbers when copying from the board, tests, worksheets, etc.
- Spatial disorganization, as in poor arrangement of number columns and other work on ruled or unruled paper
- Confusion in writing numbers from dictation, especially when there are many digits or the digit 0 is involved
- Memorization difficulties in retaining a series of digits, a series of steps, or multiplication tables
- Confusion of symbols that indicate quantitative or other relationships, such as "greater than," "less than," and "equal to"
- Manipulation of written mathematical symbols involving form perception, memory, sequence, and spatial organization in association with concepts
- Confusion of vocabulary terms such as *commutative, associative, distributive, numerator, denominator, prime number, prime factor, carrying and borrowing,* etc.

FIGURE 8–17
Difficulties in Math

it is very important as a teacher to take the opportunity to listen to your students. No matter how much you have to teach, there should be a time in every lesson when you stop teaching to let the students speak. Some adolescents with ADHD learn only through talking about what they have done. Build time into your lesson for talking about the math lesson. Mathematics is a language and needs to be discussed. It is not pushing numbers around and memorizing facts. Rather, it is problem solving, which involves communicating and reasoning. Instructional time spent on these aspects of math can enhance the quality of life for the adolescent with ADHD (Steves, 1995).

Reading and Spelling

The issue of the overlap between reading and spelling disabilities and ADHD is among the most exciting and hotly debated research topics at this time. Various studies have been conducted indicating that between 9% and 45% of the school-age population with ADHD have a coexisting reading disorder. The extreme variation in these estimates has to do with various research methods, and experience tells us that a significant number of students with ADHD also have substantial reading problems.

There is a significant overlap of dyslexia and ADHD, demonstrated by students who reverse letters, inverse letter order in words, confuse and transpose relatively common words, produce dysgraphic misspellings, and

- Limit the number of problems to be completed.
- Highlight the problems to be completed.
- Teach students how to space between problems. Don't assume that they know how. If necessary, divide paper into sections (boxes) before beginning—one problem per section; gradually fade boxes.
- Teach students how to use a "math chart," finger calculate, use a calculator, etc. (Teach the concept—not the rote facts. If the facts have not been learned by now...).
- Make math relevant. Use a checking account. Deduct a percentage of the total points when a paper is turned in late. Prepare taxes.
- Use "hands-on" problems whenever possible. Always introduce a new concept with manipulatives.
- Allow student to devise mnemonic devices for specific steps in multistep problems ("Dirty, muddy, stinking, boots" for "Divide, multiply, subtract, and bring down"). They will remember them more if they make them up.
- Begin the assignment with easy problems so the student does not become discouraged before getting a good start.
- Play games to overteach concepts, vocabulary, etc.
- Use faint line graph paper for arithmetic computation problems, or use dark line graph paper under a regular sheet of notebook paper.
- Highlight operational signs in computational problems.
- Highlight "clue" words (e.g., *and, how much more*, etc.) in problem-solving problems.
- Provide visual reminders for sequential steps. For example: (1) read the problem, (2) determine what the question is asking, (3) eliminate any nonessential information, (4) look for and highlight clue words, (5) determine appropriate operation(s) to use, (6) compute answer, (7) check to see if answer makes sense.
- Use flip chart for visual reminders.
- Include variety in lesson.
- Move from concrete to abstract.
- Allow student to "talk through" math problems.

FIGURE 8–18
Teaching Strategies for Improving Math Skills

make frequent visual substitutions in oral reading. Many other students with ADHD do not have reading disorders per se but are so inattentive and distracted while reading that their comprehension of the material is significantly impaired. Again, work rate is a factor. Many students with ADHD scan rapidly, missing key passages, in the interest of speed and completion. Some students with ADHD process reading material very slowly, in a similar manner to their writing, and the reading is so labored that they may forget the initial part of a paragraph or even a single sentence before coming to its conclusion, again negatively affecting comprehension.

The ability to spell accurately is generally impaired in students with ADHD except for students who are strong visual learners, since they are unable to display the necessary focusing and concentration to lock the forms of the work into long-term storage. Students may study the words at night and appear to have total command of the list but forget them before

- Make reading fun! Use newspapers or magazines the students like. Let the students choose novels to read. (Skills can be taught using any of these materials!)
- Teach skills (do not assume that middle and high school students have learned the rules for decoding and encoding).
- Use a visual approach to teach phonetic rules (e.g., use a web to show all the different ways an "a" can sound).
- Use colors to break the word into syllables or roots, prefixes, suffixes, etc.
- Teach students to use SQ3R (Survey, Question, Read, 'rite, Review) any time they begin a new chapter, book, etc.
- Teach outlining skills (which helps with topic and details).
- Teach students to highlight important information as they read.
- Teach vocabulary, not spelling.
- Teach how to use a word processor with spell check or a Franklin Spell Check.
- Have students read into a tape recorder and then listen to the playback.
- Have students read to younger children (excellent reward and great for self-esteem, too).
- Allow students to get comfortable.
- Allow movement while reading—many students read better when swaying slightly back and forth, shaking a foot, or walking around the room.

FIGURE 8–19
Reading Decoding, Comprehension, and Spelling

the test is administered the next day. Figure 8–19 offers suggestions for teaching reading decoding, comprehension, and spelling.

Following Directions

Students with ADHD so frequently fail to follow oral directions and instructions that this problem is listed as a diagnostic characteristic of the disorder. A number of factors relate to their difficulties in this area. Inattention and distractibility obviously play a significant role—when instructions are given, students with ADHD are frequently attending to some other aspect of the environment. There is also strong evidence that a significant proportion of students with ADHD experience auditory processing and discrimination difficulties (Dornbush & Pruitt, 1992). Figure 8–20 presents suggestions that should assist the adolescent with ADHD in this regard.

Memory Problems

Memory difficulties can play a significant role in the academic problems of adolescents with ADHD since many secondary tasks require high levels of both auditory and visual memory. Students with ADHD who are inattentive

- Have student develop a strong positive color, then use this color for a colored transparent film over reading material, have glasses tinted to this color, put colored felt on the desktop to frame in study space, or have student visualize this strong color prior to reading.
- Provide books on tape (student may qualify for "Recording for the Blind" tapes and recorder).
- Allow students to underline, circle, or highlight in texts (establish a routine: circle all unfamiliar words in green, highlight topic of paragraph in yellow, etc.).
- Issue the student two textbooks, one for school and one for home.
- Encourage the student to read and reverbalize material in small segments.
- Provide a prewritten outline to help student focus on important material.
- Present material in cloze format (the vocabulary removed from the passage can be carefully selected to highlight certain vocabulary).
- Teach note-taking techniques to be used as the material is read (mapping, outlining, etc.).
- Encourage students to "visualize" the material being read and to associate what they are reading to knowledge they currently know.

FIGURE 8–19, *continued*

- Expect the student to look at your eyes when you are talking.
- Request that the student nod his or her head to show that the request is understood.
- The student should be attentive and display minimal physical movement while listening.
- Expect the student to repeat directions or ask questions when the request is not understood.
- Use short, complete sentences, especially when giving oral directions. Pause after the delivery of each idea.
- Use vocabulary that is familiar.
- Avoid figurative language (idioms, metaphors, etc.).
- Reduce the amount of irrelevant information.
- Have the child repeat directions in his or her own words to see if they are understood.
- Oral discussions or directions should be accompanied by visual stimuli whenever possible.
- Give directions in the correct time sequence (e.g., "Put your books in your locker, then wash up for lunch," rather than, "Wash up for lunch after you put your books in your locker").
- In developing short-term memory, use a preprogrammed assignment card that is reviewed daily and kept at the student's desk.
    a. List each activity separately. If necessary, list specific steps separately.
    b. Require that the child have activities checked off as progress is made.
    c. Set approximate time limits for an activity. It may be helpful to provide a timer.
    d. For maximum retention in short-term memory, use the following steps:
        (1) Tell the students, "Please pay attention. Tell me when you are ready. Very good; listen carefully to (these words)," etc.
        (2) Break the material to be retained into small units.
        (3) Use a multisensory approach to allow rehearsal of the material.
        (4) Have the child repeat orally the material to be committed to long-term memory.
        (5) Provide frequent rehearsals.
        (6) "Chunk" material (combine into meaningful units).
        (7) Strongly reinforce any increment in amount of material remembered.

FIGURE 8–20
Listening Skills/Following Directions

and have problems in auditory memory frequently fail to process oral directions and instructions and often receive negative feedback in the school environment for their inability to perform in accordance with the teacher's directions. Many students with ADHD do not have difficulty with short-term memory and are able to retain information for brief periods of time; nevertheless, they do not process information deeply enough when coded into long-term storage.

Problems of visual memory may also appear in some students with ADHD. For example, their ability to memorize lists of spelling or vocabulary words may be impaired because of their inattention and distractibility. Even when such lists are successfully memorized, the students frequently show problems of long-term retention and forget material that they previously appeared to have learned.

Although auditory and visual-memory problems are fairly common among students with ADHD, motor memory and kinesthetic-tactile problems appear to be relatively rare. As a result, multisensory strategies that emphasize kinesthetic and tactile approaches often seem to enhance the memory skills of these students. Figure 8–21 presents several suggestions for memory difficulties.

- Give a context.
- Teach mnemonic devices.
- Use rhythmic patterns (songs are great).
- Elicit emotional responses when possible.
- Use memory-jarring connections or associations.
- Tell students to create a mental picture or visualize what is to be remembered.
- Reduce the amount of information.
- Organize information by categories.
- Pace rote items 8 to 10 seconds apart.
- Present information in a variety of ways.
- Use a multisensory approach.
- Teach for overlearning.

FIGURE 8–21
Memory Skills

Cooperative Learning

The supportive teacher recognizes that many students, particularly those with ADHD, need creative, engaging instruction and classroom activities that provide them with frequent opportunities to interact with their peers and showcase their strengths. It is important to use a variety of strategies and multisensory techniques to teach to the different learning styles present in the classroom. To maintain the attention of the student with ADHD it is important to allow for active participation in the lessons. Techniques that are most effective increase student response opportunities and limit the amount of time the teacher is doing all the talking or calling on students one at a time. Strategies such as asking for unison responses or saying something like, "Turn to your partner and share or write . . . " work well. In addition, the numerous benefits of cooperative learning structures and techniques in the classroom are well recognized and documented. Cooperative learning is particularly beneficial for the student with ADHD in the classroom because it allows for high response opportunities, shorter wait time, and increased structured peer interactions; it is a perfect vehicle for teaching social skills in an authentic setting and context (Lazear, 1991).

Key ingredients for success in cooperative learning include bringing higher-order thinking and reasoning to a lesson, using a variety of strategies to unify the teams, structuring the lesson to ensure individual learning, providing enough time for the students to look over and discuss both the lesson content and their cooperative behavior, and carefully and explicitly developing the social skills necessary for effective cooperation and collaboration with others (Lazear, 1991).

SUMMARY

Teachers must be willing to accommodate the extreme difficulty many students with ADHD have by accepting alternative methods of assessing their skills and mastery of concepts. It is critical to modify assignments and the written workload for these students and to teach them organizational and study skills. With the modifications specified throughout this text, most adolescents with ADHD will successfully complete their high school academic tasks.

REFERENCES

Abikoff, H. (1987). An evaluation of cognitive behavior therapy for hyperactive children. In B. B. Lahey & A. E. Kazdin (Eds.), *Advances in clinical child psychology* (Vol. 10, pp. 171–216). New York: Plenum.

Abikoff, H. (1992). Attention deficit hyperactivity and conduct disorder: Comorbidity and implications for treatment. *Journal of Consulting and Clinical Psychology, 60*(6), 881–892.

Abikoff, H., & Gittelman, R. (1984). Does behavior therapy normalize the classroom behavior of hyperactive children? *Archives of General Psychiatry, 41*, 440–454.

Anderson, J. C., Williams, S., McGee, R., Silva, P. A. (1987). DSM-III disorders in preadolescent children: Prevalence in a large sample from the general population. *Archives of General Psychiatry, 44*, 69–76.

Barkley, R. (1994). Prolonging the events in our mind. *ADHD Report*, 2(2).

Barkley, R., Anastopoulos, A., Guevremont, D., & Fletcher, D. (1992). Adolescents with attention deficit hyperactivity disorder: Mother-adolescent interactions, family beliefs and conflicts, and maternal psychopathology. *Journal of Abnormal Child Psychology*, 20(3), 263–288.

Barkley, R. A. (1990). *Attention deficit hyperactivity disorder: A handbook for diagnosis and treatment.* New York: Guilford Press.

Barkley, R. A., DuPaul, G. J., & McMurray, M. B. (1991). Attention deficit disorder with and without hyperactivity: Clinical response to three dose levels of methylphenidate. *Pediatrics.*

Barkley, R. A., Fischer, M., Edlebrock, C. S., & Smallish, L. (1990). The adolescent outcome of hyperactive children diagnosed by research criteria: An 8 year prospective follow-up study. *Journal of the American Academy of Child and Adolescent Psychiatry.*

Biederman, J., Newcorn, J., & Sprich, S. (1991). Comorbidity of attention deficit hyperactivity disorder with conduct, depressive, anxiety, and other disorders. *American Journal of Psychiatry*, 148, 564–577.

Bloomquist, M. L., August, G. J., & Ostrander, R. (1991). Effects of a school-based cognitive-behavioral intervention for ADHD children. *Journal of Abnormal Child Psychology*, 591–605.

Bradley, C. (1957). Characteristics and management of children with behavior problems associated with oganicin damage. *Pediatrics Clinics of North America, 4*, 1049–1060.

Brown, R. T., & Borden, K. A. (1986). Hyperactivity at adolescence: Some misconceptions and new directions. *Journal of Clinical Child Psychology, 15*, 194–209.

Brown, R. T., Wynne, M. E., & Medenis, R. (1985). Methylphenidate and cognitive therapy: A comparison of treatment approaches with hyperactive boys. *Journal of Abnormal Child Psychology, 13*, 69–88.

Canter, L. (1993). *Succeeding with difficult students.* Santa Monica, CA: Lew Canter & Associates.

Copeland, E. D., & Love, V. (1990). *Attention without tension: A teacher's handbook on attention disorders.* SPI Press.

Copeland, E. (1993). *ADHD/ADD 2000 training program: Educator Institute on Attention Deficit Disorders.* Atlanta: Resurgens Press.

Copeland, E. D., & Walker, R. A. (1989). *Understanding attention deficit disorders: The school's critical role in ADD.* Atlanta: 3C's of Childhood, Inc.

Douglas, V. I. (1972). Stop, look, and listen: The problem of sustained attention and impulse control in hyperactive and normal children, *Canadian Journal of Behavioral Science, 4,* 259–282.

Douglas, V. I., Parry, P., Marton, P., & Garson, C. (1976). Assessment of a cognitive training program for hyperactive children. *Journal of Abnormal Psychology, 4,* 389–410.

DuPaul, G. J., & Barkley, R. A. (1990). Medication therapy. In R. A. Barkley, *Attention-deficit hyperactivity disorder* (pp. 573–612). New York: Guilford Press.

Eisenberg, L. (1966). The management of the hyperkinetic child. *Developmental Medicine and Child Neurology, 8,* 593–598.

Falkenstein, E. (1994). *Speech and language: An overview.* Atlanta: Parkaire Consultants, Inc.

Fister, S., & Kemp, K. (1994). *Social skills survival kit.* Sopris West, P. O. Box 1809, 1140 Boston Avenue, Longmont, CO; 800-547-6747, Fax: (303) 776-5934.

Fowler, M. (1992). *CH.A.D.D. educators' manual: An in-depth look at attention deficit disorders from an educational perspective.* Fairfax, VA: CASET Associates, Ltd.

Fowler, M. C. (1990). *Maybe you know my kid: A parent's guide to identifying, understanding, and helping your child with attention deficit hyperactive disorder.* New York: Berch Lane Press.

Goldstein, S., & Ingersoll, B. (1992). Controversial treatments for children with ADHD. *Chadder, 6*(2), 19–22.

Goldstein, S., & Goldstein, M. (1988). *The multi-disciplinary evaluation and treatment of children with attentional deficit disorders.* Neurology, Learning and Behavior Center, 670 East 3900 South, Suite 100, Salt Lake City, UT 84107.

Goldstein, S., & Goldstein, M. (1990). *Managing attention disorders in children: A guide for practitioners.* New York: John Wiley and Sons.

Gordon, M., Thomason, D., Cooper, S., & Ivers, C. (1991). Nonmedical treatment of ADHD/hyperactivity: The attention training system. *Journal of School Psychology, 29,* 154–159.

Goor, M. (1995, March). *Snap shot IEP and accompanying manual.* Presentation at annual International Conference of Learning Disabilities Association, Orlando, FL.

Guevremont, D. (1990). Social skills and peer relationship training. In R. Barkley, *Attention-deficit hyperactivity disorder* (pp. 540–572). New York: Guilford Press.

Hagerman, R. J. (1983, March 8). *Developmental pediatrics.* Paper presented at the New Frontiers Symposium, Steamboat Springs, CO.

Hallowell, E., & Ratey, J. (1994). *Driven to distraction: Recognizing and coping with ADHD.* New York: Pantheon Books.

Hamlett, K. W., Pelligrini, D. S., & Conners, C. K. (1987). An investigation of executive processes in the problem-solving of attention deficit disorder hyperactive children. *Journal of Pediatric Psychology, 12,* 227–240.

Hartman, T. (1993). *Attention deficit disorder: A different perception.* Lancaster: Underwood-Miller.

Higgins, P. (1993). *ASSIST program.* Sopris West, P. O. Box 1809, 1140 Boston Avenue, Longmont, CO; 800-547-6747, Fax: (303) 776-5934.

Hinshaw, S. P., & Erhardt, D. (1991). Attention deficit-hyperactivity disorder. In P. C. Kendall (Ed.), *Child and adolescent therapy: Cognitive-behavioral procedures* (pp. 98–128). New York: Guilford Press.

Hinshaw, S. P., Henker, B. N., & Whalen, C. K. (1984). Self-control in hyperactive boys in anger-inducing situations: Comparative and combined effects. *Journal of Consulting and Clinical Psychology, 52,* 739–749.

Hinshaw, S. P., & Melnick, S. (1992). Self-management therapies and attention-deficit hyperactivity disorder: Reinforced self-evaluation and anger control interventions. *Behavior Modification, 16*(2).

Jordan, D. R. (1988). *Jordan prescriptive/tutorial reading program.* Austin, TX: PRO-ED.

Jordan, D. R. (1989). *Overcoming dyslexia in children, adolescents, and adults.* Austin, TX: PRO-ED.

Jordan, D. (1992). *Attention deficit disorder: ADHD and ADD syndromes.* Austin, TX: PRO-ED, Inc.

Kendall, P. C., & Braswell, L. (1982). *Cognitive-behavioral therapy for impulsive children.* New York: Guilford Press.

Kukic, S. (1995, March 14). Inclusion options as one choice. In W. Bender (Chair), *Including students with ADHD in regular education.* ITN telecast conducted at UGA, Athens.

Laufer, M., & Denhoff, E. (1957). Hyperkinetic behavior in children. *Journal of Pediatrics, 50,* 463–474.

Lazear, D. (1991). *Seven ways of teaching: The artistry of teaching with multiple intelligences.* Palatine, IL: IRI/Skylight Publishing.

Levine, M. (1994). *Educational care: A system for understanding and managing observable phenomena that impede performance in school.* Cambridge, MA: Educator Publishing Service.

Loney, J., & Milich, R. (1982). Hyperactivity, inattention, and aggression in clinical practice. In D. Routh & M. Wolraich (Eds.), *Advances in developmental and behavioral pediatrics* (Vol. 3, pp. 113–147). Greenwich, CT: JAI Press.

Loper, S. (1989). *Increasing spelling performance with learning disabled students by teaching metacognitive strategies.* (ED. 330140). Nova University.

Luria, A. R. (1966). *Higher cortical function in man.* New York: Basic Books.

Meichenbaum, D. H. (1977). *Cognitive behavior modification: An integrative approach.* New York: Plenum Press.

Meichenbaum, D. H., & Goodman, J. (1971). Training impulsive children to talk to themselves: A means of developing self-control. *Journal of Abnormal Psychology, 77,* 115–126.

Mendelson, W., Johnson, N., & Stewart, M. A. (1971). Hyperactive children as teenagers: A follow-up study. *Journal of Nervous and Mental Disease, 153,* 273–279.

McInerney, M. (1994). *Effective practices for educating children with attention deficit disorder.* Presentation at 6th annual conference of Children and Adults with Attention Deficit Disorders.

Minde, K., Lewin, D., Weiss, G., Lavigueru, H., Donglass, V., & Sybes, E. (1971). The hyperactive child in elementary school: A 5-year, controlled follow-up. *Exceptional Children, 38,* 215–221.

Nolting. (1995, March). *Using manipulatives in middle school math.* Presentation at annual conference of Learning Disabilities Association, Orlando, FL.

Parker, H. (1992). *The ADD hyperactivity handbook for schools.* Plantation, FL: Impact Publications.

Parker, H. (1990). *The hyperactivity workbook for parents, teachers, and kids.* Plantation, FL: Impact Publications.

Pfinner, L. J., & Barkley, R. A. (1990). Educational placement and classroom management. In R. A. Barkley, *Attention-deficit hyperactivity disorder* (pp. 498–539). New York: Guilford Press.

Quinn, P. (1994). *ADD and the college student.* New York: MAGINATION Press.

Robin, A. L. (1990). Training families with ADHD adolescents. In R. A. Barkley, *Attention-deficit hyperactivity disorder* (pp. 462–497). New York: Guilford Press.

Ross, D. M., & Ross, S. A. (1976). *Hyperactivity: Research, theory, and action.* New York: Wiley.

Schachar, R., & Logan, G. (1990). Impulsivity and inhibitory control in normal development and childhood psychopathology. *Developmental Psychology, 26,* 710–720.

Schlichter, C. L., & Hobbs, D. (1983, April). Extending talents unlimited to secondary school. *Educational Leadership, 45,* 736–740.

Suid, M. (1991). *Demonic mnemonics.* Carthage, IL: Fearon Teachers Aid.

Sullivan, M. A., & O'Leary, S. G. (1990). Maintenance following reward cost and token programs. *Behavior Therapy, 21,* 139–149.

Tant, J. L., & Douglas, V. I. (1982). Problem solving in hyperactive, normal, and reading-disabled boys. *Journal of Abnormal Child Psychology, 10,* 285–306.

Taylor, J. F. (1990). *Helping your hyperactive child.* New York: Prima.

Tomey, (1995, March). *Improving reading and language arts skills.* Presentation at annual conference of Learning Disabilities Association, Orlando, FL.

Voelker, S. L., Carter, R. A., Sprague, D. J., Gdowski, D. L., & Lachar, D. (1989). Developmental trends in memory and metamemory in children with attention deficit disorder. *Journal of Pediatric Psychology, 14,* 75–88.

Weiss, G., & Hechtman, L. (1986). *Hyperactive children grown up: ADHD in children, adolescents, and adults: Empirical findings and theoretical considerations.* New York: Guilford Press.

Wender, P. (1987). *The hyperactive child, adolescent, and adult: Attention deficit disorder through the lifespan.*

Zentall, S. (1988). Production deficiencies in elicited language but not in the spontaneous verbalizations of hyperactive children. *Journal of Educational Psychology, 78,* 159–165.

Zentall, S. (1993). Research of the educational implications of attention deficit hyperactivity disorder. *Exceptional Children, 60*(2), 143–153.

CHAPTER 9

The Adult with ADHD

Laura M. Franklin, M.Ed.
University of Georgia

William N. Bender, Ph.D.
University of Georgia

CHANGES AND CHALLENGES IN ROLES AND EXPECTATIONS

The transition into adulthood denotes the onset of many changes. Changes in physiology, emotions, and familial and societal expectations are all indicators of the arrival of adulthood. While the physiological changes that often accompany the cessation of puberty may have a calming effect and therefore be beneficial to the adult with ADHD (Barkley, 1990; Weiss & Hechtman, 1993), emotional changes and new societal and familial expectations seem to have the most profound impact on the lives of adults with ADHD.

Upon graduation from high school, the young adult is faced with many important decisions. He or she must decide whether college, technical school, or work is the most appropriate course to take to achieve success. Furthermore, parents often expect that the young adult will become more independent and begin assisting with a greater number of the household responsibilities, including financial obligations. The young adult is also plagued by the decision of whether to leave home, either for dorm life or as an assertion of independence. Soon the young adult will begin to feel the pressure of deciding whether to settle down with a prospective mate or at least to become seriously involved in a romantic relationship. With each of these decisions come heavy obligations and responsibilities quite different from those previously encountered in adolescence.

While practically every young adult feels at least some anxiety concerning the transition into adulthood, one can well imagine how terrifying this may seem to the young adult with ADHD. Prior to adulthood, the adolescent with ADHD may have done all that he or she could possibly do to downplay the symptoms of ADHD to be a good son or daughter, a good student, a good friend, or a good worker. Now he or she is part of the adult world and is expected to be a mature, responsible, productive member of society. The young adult is no longer a member of the subculture "children." Sailing into these previously uncharted waters of adulthood will undoubtedly cause difficulties for these individuals. The changes in expectations and roles may cause the emergence of symptoms formerly undetected in childhood or adolescence or the reemergence of symptoms that were successfully managed in adolescence.

In this chapter we will discuss the manifestations of the most common symptoms observed in the various aspects of the adult's life with ADHD and offer some strategies for mastering these problems.

RISK AND RESILIENCY IN ADULTS WITH ADHD

The concept of risk and resiliency (Garmezy, Masten, & Tellegen, 1984) has recently received a great deal of attention from experts in several fields of study (Garmezy, 1983; Maag, Irvin, Reid, & Vasa, 1994). Simply stated, risk refers to the presence of one or more of the factors that increase the probability of behavioral difficulties in the future (Ramey, Trohanis, & Hostler, 1982). The term *risk* can be applied to just about anything. For example, most people would probably agree that buying retread tires in lieu of new tires increases the risk of a flat tire and that smoking increases the risk of developing heart disease. Regarding ADHD, however, risk refers to congenital factors and environmental conditions that would likely increase the probability that a person will develop ADHD and/or the degree to which the problematic symptoms associated with ADHD will manifest themselves throughout life. Risk factors vary from person to person but typically include socioeconomic status, intelligence of the subject, and numerous other factors (Garmezy, 1991). Figure 9–1 is a partial list of risk factors typically cited in the literature concerning risk and resilience.

Resiliency refers to elements of a person's physiological and psychosocial constitution—whether intrinsic, environmental, or biological in nature—that would positively affect the outcome of the problem for which the person is at risk (Garmezy & Masten, 1986). In other words, if the conditions (e.g., hyperactivity, low intelligence, chronic poverty) are right for a person to develop particular problems (risk), other aspects of the person or the person's environment (e.g., good maternal parenting skills, mentally healthy family members) might help the individual manage the problems during later stages of life (resiliency). Thus, resiliency factors tend to reduce somewhat the degree to which the behavioral problem manifests itself.

Many experts on ADHD concur that several factors contribute to how well the adult with ADHD adjusts to the adult world (Weiss & Hechtman, 1993; Barkley, 1990; DuPaul & Stoner, 1994; Garmezy & Masten, 1986). Some of the contributing resiliency factors (such as the subject's intelligence and the degree of hyperactivity) may at least be partially genetically predetermined. Other factors that may affect emanation of the problem (such as the parenting skills of guardians or parents, socioeconomic status, emotional

Intelligence of subject	Socioeconomic status of family
Maternal education level	Temperament as a child
Degree of hyperactivity	Educational intervention
Mental health of family members	Parental absence
Parenting skills	Prenatal and perinatal problems
Low birth weight	Maternal drug abuse
Relationships with siblings	Central nervous system insult or injury

FIGURE 9–1
Selected Risk and Resiliency Factors Affecting Adults with ADHD

stability of the home, and the mental health of the family members) are contingent solely on the environment in which the subject is raised. Obviously, any child, disabled or otherwise, would benefit optimally when raised in a happy, stable home with two mentally and physically healthy parents with excellent parenting skills. Combine this with sufficient income to expose the subject to a variety of cognitive enriching experiences and you have optimal conditions in which to successfully nurture a child. Unfortunately, this is rarely the circumstance.

It also stands to reason that the higher the degree of intelligence of the child, the greater the likelihood the child will develop coping strategies to combat the symptoms of ADHD (Hartmann, 1993). Furthermore, since a more intelligent subject learns more rapidly, teachers and parents may be less likely to become frustrated or upset with inappropriate behaviors, especially if learning is commensurate with that of the subject's peers, regardless of the subject's hyperactivity, distractibility, and inattentiveness. Teachers and parents may simply say something like, "He's all boy," as an excuse for a young boy's aggressiveness, impulsivity, or hyperactivity or, "She's just bored with the curriculum," as an excuse for a young girl's incomplete assignments, disorganization, or underachievement. However, researchers have determined that the presence or absence of one or more of the aforementioned resilience conditions can lessen the effects of ADHD on the adult (Barkley, 1990).

Almost any single element described as a resilience factor could also be considered a risk factor. For example, intelligence is considered a resiliency factor, whereas the lack of intelligence is a definite risk factor. Additionally, both the quantity and the quality of the resilience factors associated with a particular subject are important. Since some resilience factors may not be sufficient in strength to outweigh the effects of the risk factors manifested within a particular individual, they may have little or no effect on the indication of the disorder. Yet, awareness of the risk and of the resilience factors associated with a particular subject may be beneficial in designing treatment and predicting outcomes for adults with ADHD.

Furthermore, Weiss and Hechtman (1993) contend that there are specific risk/resilience predictors that indicate how well the adult with ADHD will adjust relative to particular areas. For instance, the ability to develop and maintain friendships is predominantly affected by the emotional stability of the home, whereas a combination of factors such as childhood intelligence, degree of hyperactivity, parenting skills, socioeconomic status, and the emotional climate of the home is related to educational achievement. Relationships with adults and intelligence are both indicators of employability. Barkley (1990) contends that the combination of the emotional climate of the home, the mental health of the family members during the subject's childhood, and the subject's cognitive level and degree of emotionality is predictive of the subject's emotional adjustment in adulthood. The symptoms of ADHD detected in adulthood and the degree to which they are manifested seem to correspond to specific childhood risk/resiliency factors (Barkley, 1990).

CHARACTERISTICS OF THE ADULT WITH ADHD

Only in the past two decades has any attention been given to the consideration that ADHD continues into adulthood (Weiss, 1992; Hallowell & Ratey, 1994; Wender, 1987). Previously considered a temporary problem that would dissipate with adulthood, ADHD is now recognized by clinicians and researchers to have possible lifelong repercussions (Weiss & Hechtman, 1993; Barkley, 1990; Hallowell, 1993; Nadeau, 1995). However, there are scant data about adults with ADHD from which practitioners might be able to draw conclusions, make predictions, and design effective treatment programs.

Weiss (1992) reports that approximately 35% of children diagnosed with ADHD between the ages of 6 and 12 will display symptoms of ADHD in adulthood. She further contends that these symptoms may sometimes diminish further in later adulthood (Weiss, 1992). Others contend that as many as 50% of children diagnosed with ADHD continue to experience behavioral problems (Barkley, 1990).

While empirical research on adults with ADHD is rather limited, there is some evidence of adulthood ADHD based on the clinical experiences of many experts in the field. Most concur with the findings of Weiss and Hechtman (1993) that indicate that many of the problems encountered in childhood and adolescence still plague the adult with ADHD (Weiss, 1992; Barkley, 1990; Hallowell & Ratey, 1994; Wender, 1987; Jordan, 1992). Clinicians who specialize in the field of ADHD report that the symptoms detected in adults with ADHD differ in severity and combination from person to person (Nadeau, 1995; Jordan, 1992; Shakim, 1992). It is not surprising that the most prevalent overt symptoms manifested by the adult with ADHD are the same ones most frequently displayed in children and adolescents with ADHD: inattentiveness, impulsivity, and some excessive motor activity. These problems can, in turn, cause problems in marriage, mental health, employment, and daily functionality (Murphy, 1992; Nadeau, 1995; Weiss & Hechtman, 1993).

While many of the symptoms of ADHD seem to be exacerbated by the additional risk factors encountered in adulthood, others may decrease or become less problematic. Still, evidence based on clinical studies indicates that the degree of the symptoms manifested during childhood is a strong indicator of how well an adolescent will adjust to adult life (Weiss & Hechtman, 1993). Generally speaking, gross motor hyperactivity (e.g., jumping out of one's seat) is usually not as evident in adults with ADHD, though adults with ADHD tend to present an inordinate amount of motor activity; this may appear as fine motor activity, such as finger tapping, excessive talking, shifting in the seat, or foot tapping. The adult with ADHD appears to be "always on the go" (Weiss, 1992). The decline in gross motor activity may be due to the leveling off of growth hormones or some other physiological change, combined with the tendency to "mellow" somewhat as we get older.

Weiss and Hechtman have published a series of studies on a 15-year follow-up of adults with ADHD (Weiss & Hechtman, 1993, 1986; Weiss, Hechtman, & Perlman, 1978). This represents one of the most extensive long-term studies to date on the outcomes of adults with ADHD. Additionally, these studies provide both the clinician and the teacher with vital information on which to base treatment or make predictions regarding the outcome of adults with ADHD. The studies, which began in 1960, initially involved 106 hyperactive children between the ages of 6 and 12 years. The subjects were selected from patients seen at Montreal Children's Hospital. Subjects selected for the study were required to meet the following criteria:

- ❑ The main problems must have been the presence of restlessness and poor concentration since the subject's early years.
- ❑ The restlessness and poor concentration must have been problematic both at home and at school.
- ❑ The subject must have had at least average intelligence.
- ❑ The subject must have been free of psychoses, borderline psychoses, epilepsy, and cerebral palsy.
- ❑ The subject must have lived at home with at least one parent (Weiss & Hechtman, 1993).

The subjects were traced for a 5-year follow-up (91 subjects remained), a 10-year follow-up (76 subjects remained), and a 15-year follow-up (63 subjects remained) (Weiss, Hechtman, & Perlman, 1978; Weiss & Hechtman, 1993). Subjects were matched with controls on intelligence, socioeconomic status, and sex (Weiss, Hechtman, & Perlman, 1978; Weiss & Hechtman, 1993). The children involved in the study were representative of a wide variety of personality characteristics, socioeconomic status, family functioning, degrees and types of learning disabilities, and degrees of associated conduct disorders.

The researchers conducted a 15-year follow-up because they believed that the average age at the 10-year follow-up study (19 years old) was too young to determine the risk for development of psychiatric disorders in adulthood. For our purposes, we present the data that were obtained from the 15-year follow-up. For this follow-up, both the controls and the subjects were evaluated using an interview with a psychiatrist, a test of affective disorders and schizophrenia (administered by a qualified psychiatrist different from the one who administered the initial interview; this psychiatrist was not told which subjects were hyperactive), and two self-rating psychiatric scales. Other information regarding drug abuse, antisocial behaviors, court and police records, and work records was obtained through other interviews. Tests were administered in the same order, as much as possible, to both groups. Subjects were evaluated with respect to the following parameters: psychiatric status; antisocial behaviors; drug and alcohol use and abuse; values and beliefs; work history; life-style; physiological matters; familial aspects; self-esteem; and social skills. Because of the heterogeneous nature of the disorder, Weiss and Hechtman found it beneficial to group the subjects into three categories, with severity of the symptoms providing the basis for the categories. Other experts in the field of ADHD have also used such categories (Jordan, 1992; Shakim, 1992; Nadeau, 1995). The groups are described as mild (i.e., having no major repercussions from the syndrome); moderate (i.e., having symptoms that may noticeably affect normal day-to-day functioning); and severe (i.e., having symptoms that interfere significantly in all aspects of the adult's life; also possibly having antisocial or psychiatric disorders) (Weiss & Hechtman, 1993). Figure 9–2 gives a more detailed description of the functionality of each of the aforementioned groups as described by Weiss and Hechtman (1993).

Academic Skills

Academic difficulties for the person with ADHD have a tendency to worsen with the subject's passage into adulthood (DuPaul & Stoner, 1994; Barkley, 1990). Adults with ADHD often have achieved less academically and have less academic ability than adults without ADHD. In their 15-year follow-up study, Weiss and Hechtman (1993) concluded that at a mean age of 21 years, 53% of the controls were continuing their education on a full-time basis, whereas this was true for only 20% of the adults with ADHD. Most of the subjects who fell within the mild range of symptoms had pursued either a formal postsecondary education or technical training. Some of these subjects were attending evening courses while working full-time. The mild group even included a medical student who got along well with others.

As adolescents, these subjects may have had a higher incidence of suspensions, expulsions, and grade retentions during the later school years than did adolescents without ADHD. The dropout rate also increases in later schooling. Over 30% of adolescents or young adults with ADHD will drop out and never complete high school (Weiss & Hechtman, 1993). Only 5% of the adults with ADHD earn a degree from a university (Weiss &

Mild

Roughly 30%–40% of adults with ADHD fall within the mild range of symptoms. Moreover, approximately one-third of adults who display symptoms of ADHD are virtually indistinguishable from the normal adult population. While these subjects still exhibit some of the symptoms of ADHD, these symptoms do not interfere significantly with everyday living.

The functionality of this group ranged from excellent to fair, but these subjects had no major complaints or psychiatric difficulties. The work records of the subjects in this group were stable. Most were working full-time or were working on eductional degrees (some even postgraduate degrees). Some had received technical training rather than a formal education. The living arrangements of this group are rather consistent. These subjects may live either at home or with friends. They generally have well-established relationships with both sexes. They get along well with their co-workers and bosses, and familial relationships are satisfactory. The members of this group are generally not depressed or anxious. Mood lability is appropriate for respective circumstances and subjects enjoy the positive aspects of their lives. Most are social drinkers and have tried marijuana. There is no indication of antisocial behavior. Subjects' self-esteem is good, and they have set realistic goals for themselves.

Moderate

Approximately 40%–50% of adults with ADHD fall within the moderate range of symptoms. These subjects reported that one or more of the symptoms of the disorder affected their day-to-day functioning.

Although these subjects usually have jobs, their job histories are incon stant; frequently change jobs as a result of problems with a peer or supervisor. The subjects in this group wish to advance along a career ladder but lack the know-how to do so. Moves are more frequent and impulsive among this group. Interpersonal problems continue into adulthood for these individuals.

FIGURE 9–2
Functional Groupings of Adults with ADHD

Hechtman, 1993). It appears that most adults with ADHD are simply not equipped with the strategies necessary to handle the rigorous academic requirements and responsibilities of a college or technical school.

Self-esteem

One of the most prevalent characteristics found in the adult with ADHD is poor self-esteem (Weiss, 1992; Nadeau, 1995). In fact, most researchers contend that a low self-concept can be quite problematic in adulthood and may tremendously affect the lives of these adults (Wender, 1987; Weiss, 1992).

Subjects rarely have enduring friendships or other types of relationships. Some reported feelings of loneliness. These individuals are disposed to a greater number of emotional problems than are present in the general adult population. They are more likely to be depressed, to abuse alcohol and/or drugs, and to demonstrate antisocial personality characteristics. This group, generally speaking, has lower self-esteem and is not particularly happy with life as it presently exists; subjects are not particularly optimistic about improving their lot.

Severe

This group is divided into two subgroups, those with psychiatric disturbances and those who are antisocial. Members of this group are frequently unemployed and drift from job to job. The antisocial subjects have problems with law enforcement agencies, and those with psychiatric problems have a greater number of psychiatric hospitalizations than in the general adult population. These individuals are usually living alone, they also move frequently and impulsively. They experience serious interpersonal problems and tend to be socially isolated. Friendships are based on need. That is, if someone had something the subject needed, he or she struck up a friendship. Needless to say, these friendships lasted only until the "friend" no longer had what the subject needed.

Members of the severe group have serious emotional problems, with several subjects bordering on psychosis. These subjects abuse drugs and alcohol, a vast array of drug usage. Suicide attempts are more common in this group. Subjects have increased incidences of crime (assault, armed robbery, breaking and entering, and drug dealing). Self-esteem is very poor. Subjects live for the present, with no consideration of the future.

FIGURE 9–2, *continued*

Weiss and Hechtman (1993) assert that adults with ADHD scored significantly lower than the controls on two of the three measures administered to determine self-esteem. Further, self-esteem may be worse in adults whose ADHD has gone undiagnosed (Hale & Hale, 1993). This low self-esteem can, in turn, become a risk factor and intensify the other symptoms of ADHD. The adult with ADHD may begin to feel stupid and frustrated. These feelings of inferiority are often due to a seemingly endless series of failures, unfinished projects, and battles with parents, siblings, spouses, and bosses. The adult with ADHD begins to believe the negative things that others may have said about his or her competence (Weiss, 1992); thus begins a self-fulfilling prophecy.

Social Interaction Problems

Researchers suggest that adults with ADHD frequently experience greater difficulties in the areas of social skills and social interactions than do their peers (Weiss & Hechtman, 1993). As many as 75% of the adults with ADHD complain of interpersonal difficulties, especially in the area of heterosexual relationships (Weiss & Hechtman, 1993). While very little is known about the repercussions of ADHD on sexual relations, a common complaint of both males and females with ADHD is the inability to sufficiently focus enough to enjoy sex (Hallowell & Ratey, 1994). Partners and spouses also complain that the moment the adult with ADHD sits down in the evening, he or she is asleep. This would make it difficult to find an appropriate time for intimacy (Hallowell & Ratey, 1994). Therefore, it follows that marital discord may also be a problem for these adults; numerous clinicians assert that adults with ADHD do experience a higher level of marital difficulties than do adults without ADHD (Weiss, 1992; Nadeau, 1995). It is quite difficult to identify which specific risk factors correlate with this particular problem. Still, a variety of problems—such as low self-concept, moodiness, substance abuse, hyperactivity, hot temper, and inattentiveness—may combine to create interpersonal difficulties for these adults (Weiss, 1992; Barkley, 1990; Hallowell & Ratey, 1994). For example, distractibility and inattentiveness interfere considerably with communication between sexual partners and cause roadblocks in intimate relationships. Also, certain traits could create complications in a relationship; these traits include stress intolerance, unrecognized potential, a short temper, the need for "a high" (or stimulation), the constant changing of jobs or losing of jobs, inability to follow through with projects, poor listening skills, disorganization, antisocial personality, and social immaturity. Often, several of these risk factors destroy the very fibers that bind a relationship. From this perspective, it is easily understood why the adult with ADHD frequently experiences problems with relationships.

Psychiatric Disorders

The presence of ADHD in childhood may increase the risk for psychiatric diagnoses in adulthood (Weiss & Hechtman, 1993). Antisocial behaviors can be found in 20%–25% of adults with ADHD, and as many as 50% of adults with ADHD may develop other symptoms of psychopathology (Weiss & Hechtman, 1993); however, Weiss and Hechtman do attest that few end up in jail or psychiatric institutions. In their 15-year follow-up, Weiss and Hechtman (1993) found no higher incidence of somatic symptoms, psychotic symptoms, and symptoms related to autonomy in adults with ADHD than in the controls. It has been theorized that many people diagnosed with antisocial personality disorder may actually suffer from ADHD (Hallowell &

Ratey, 1994). These individuals may display all the characteristic behaviors of the antisocial personality, such as lying, cheating, and breaking the law (Hallowell & Ratey, 1994). Acts of violence and possession of weapons may occur more often in adults with ADHD (Weiss & Hechtman, 1993). The adult with ADHD is occasionally misdiagnosed with manic-depressive illness since both syndromes display elevated energy levels. Adults with ADHD sometimes become manic for short periods of time, and periods of depression may follow the periods of mania (Hallowell & Ratey, 1994).

The adult with ADHD is more likely to have a higher incidence of contacts with law enforcement officials than the non-ADHD adult (Barkley, 1990). While most of these instances have to do with traffic violations, there is also evidence that a greater number of adults with ADHD are involved in the selling of illegal substances (Weiss & Hechtman, 1993). Jails and mental institutions often contain numerous adult patients, usually male, with undiagnosed ADHD labeled sociopathic, psychopathic, or behavior disordered (Hallowell & Ratey, 1994). Although the rate of occurrence of antisocial behaviors in adults with ADHD is relatively low (Weiss & Hechtman, 1993), one should not ignore that these behaviors may persevere into adulthood.

Substance Abuse

Substance abuse and addictive behaviors also seem to be more prevalent among adults with ADHD than in the normal population (Weiss & Hechtman, 1993; Hartmann, 1993; Hallowell & Ratey, 1994). While Weiss and Hechtman (1993) found no statistical difference between the controls and the adults with ADHD, they do report a slightly higher use of drugs and possibly alcohol by the adults with ADHD. Addictive behaviors are commonly seen in adults with ADHD. The addiction may be to either a substance or an activity. For instance, some of the substances to which the adult with ADHD may become addicted are caffeine, alcohol, food, and illegal drugs. Addictions to activities might include excessive gambling, compulsive shopping, or overworking (Wender, 1987).

The adult with ADHD who uses illegal drugs or abuses prescription drugs may be attempting to escape from the emotional pain and frustration caused by the continual onslaught of problems that accompany ADHD (Wender, 1987; Hallowell & Ratey, 1994). It has been reported by some that cocaine and other stimulants often assuage the symptoms of ADHD (Hallowell & Ratey, 1994). Adult patients with ADHD who have used cocaine report that it does not give them a high but helps them to become more focused (Hallowell & Ratey, 1994). Addictive behaviors, a poor self-concept, depressive tendencies, attempts to self-medicate, and several other factors associated with ADHD combine to increase the vulnerability to substance abuse in adults with ADHD.

An Alternative View

Some researchers argue that, in contrast to the negative manifestations of ADHD in adults, certain positive aspects to ADHD may benefit certain individuals in some situations. For instance, Hartmann (1993) has taken a remarkably different and insightful approach to ADHD. Hartmann asserts that ADHD is neither a disorder nor a genetic defect but rather results from the manifestation of the genetically based "hunt" code. Hartmann maintains that the symptoms exhibited by those labeled ADHD are a practically perfect match to those skills critical to being a successful hunter in early preagrarian societies (Hartmann, 1993). Thus, the adaptive capabilities of the person with ADHD represent a type of primitive survival mechanism. "Hunters" are always watching, waiting, ready for action. They are independent, restless, adventurous, risk-taking, and always on the move.

Hartmann (1993) further contends that the problem with being a "hunter" is that our society is organized primarily to benefit and fit the needs of "farmers." Hartmann refers to "farmers" as capable of sustaining attention to a particular task for an extended period of time, not easily distracted, able to follow tasks through to completion, and able to think things through prior to taking action. Figure 9–3 contrasts the characteristics of hunters and farmers.

While there is no medical evidence to support Hartmann's theory, this perspective seems to give a more positive view of behaviors previously considered undesirable and detrimental. In one sense, Hartmann considers many characteristics of ADHD as resilience factors from the days when survival was contingent on successful hunting. Hartmann (1993) points out that there are numerous jobs that a hunter would perform much better than a farmer, such as private detective, police officer, reporter, military combat personnel, pilot, spy, and entrepreneur, to name a few. This approach may give those affected with ADHD and people who play an integral part in their lives an alternate, more positive, view of the disorder.

Case Study

The following vignette is a case study of Terry, a typical adult male with undiagnosed ADHD. He is plagued by many of the common symptoms found in the adult with ADHD: impulsivity, disorganization, immaturity, irresponsibility, and some compulsivity. He exhibits symptoms of an addictive disorder and engages in risky behaviors. Interpersonal relationships are weak. He feels frustrated with himself and cannot understand his behavior. Terry's mother is now also beginning to question why her son has not matured, has never been able to maintain a long-lasting relationship with a female, and is experiencing so many difficulties in sustaining a job.

Hunters
- Constantly monitor their environment
- Can totally throw themselves into the hunt; time is elastic
- Are flexible, capable of changing strategy on a moment's notice
- Can throw an incredible burst of energy into the hunt
- Think visually
- Love the hunt, but are easily bored by mundane tasks
- Will face danger that so-called normal individuals would avoid
- Are hard on themselves and those around them

Farmers
- Are not easily distracted by their environment
- Sustain a slow-and-steady effort
- See the long-range picture
- Are not easily bored
- Are team players
- Attend to details
- Are cautious
- Are patient with others

FIGURE 9–3
Hartmann's Hunters and Farmers

Terry: An Adult with ADHD

Terry is a 25-year-old male. He currently lives at home with his mother and has since his graduation from high school. His father died when Terry was six years old. The death of his father was very difficult for his mother and for Terry. Terry and his mother moved soon after the death of his father to be close to his maternal grandparents because his mother was somewhat depressed and Terry was beginning to have some difficulty in school. Terry and his mother moved again just prior to his entrance into high school. Terry's father, a college business major, had been an insurance salesman for a rather large medical insurance firm. Fortunately, Terry's father had obtained a life insurance policy that has enabled Terry and his mother to live comfortably. Terry's mother, who also has a college degree, works as a branch manager at a local bank.

During Terry's childhood, his mother was contacted by his school on many occasions regarding his poor academic performance and his behavior. It seemed that he was not interested in doing well in school, and his short temper seemed to result in frequent fist fights with other boys at school. Terry's mother believed that Terry's problems stemmed from losing his father at such a young age and not having a male role model. She further reported that she was not much of disciplinarian and had traveled a good deal because her job required her to do so.

Although Terry's intelligence is above normal, his high school career was somewhat less than spectacular. His grades were generally C's, D's, and several F's. Most of the failures were a result of too many incomplete homework assignments. His high school football career started off well because he was quick and loved the physical contact. However, after the first year he no longer met eligibility requirements because of failure in his school courses. Needless to say, Terry was not on target for graduation early in his high school years. He finally graduated just shy of his 20th birthday.

Upon graduation, he worked at a nearby fast-food restaurant. He had hoped to attend a technical school, but he did not complete the application in time for admission, even though the counselor at his high school offered to assist him. Terry never bothered to reapply. The fast-food job was short lived because of a "personal problem" with the manager of the restaurant. He has since been employed by a grocery store and by a number of stores in the two malls nearby. Terry reports that he usually gets bored with these jobs and quits. The bosses, however, maintain that he was fired because of tardiness, forgetfulness, frequently missing store meetings, and not showing up for work. One boss reported that Terry did not show up for his six-month evaluation appointment and did not call to explain why he would not be there. Terry reports that on the days he was late he had legitimate excuses. He says that on a couple of occasions he ran out of gas. He does not see this as something he should have planned for in advance but rather as something that "happened to him." Terry has had six different jobs since graduation from high school and has held none of them for longer than six months.

Terry has plenty of dates. He usually meets girls at the local bars. However, he has never had a lengthy relationship. He reports that he would like to have a girlfriend but that things just don't seem to work out. He says that he often forgets about dates or shows up late, and they get upset with him. The girls often tell him that he is thoughtless and immature. After a while, they get fed up with his irresponsible behavior and sever the relationship.

Terry loves cars. He races practically every Friday night at a nearby raceway for amateurs and frequently wins. He has a couple of old cars that he and a partner work on and use for racing. The partner does most of the engine and maintenance work, which Terry finds boring, and Terry drives the cars. This is where most of Terry's money goes, and he identifies this as his one success in life.

Terry also likes to frequent the local nightclubs. He particularly enjoys country music and country western dancing. He says that lately he has been drinking more than usual but that it is probably because he is between jobs. He says that he might drink 8–12 beers every Friday and Saturday night. He further reports that he generally drinks about a six-pack on week nights.

Terry spends his money irresponsibly. Often, he cannot pay his debts, such as car insurance and telephone bills. He is still very much dependent on his mother for financial support. He is supposed to be giving his mother money each month for rent and groceries but usually spends it on cars and beer. She has also had to bail him out of jail for fighting a couple of times. Terry's mother gave him several thousand dollars once when he ran up some very large credit card bills. Terry says that he feels like a loser except when he is racing. He doesn't understand why he can't "get his act together."

For Terry, the absence of a high degree of hyperactivity combined with his above-average intelligence probably prevented his teachers and his mother from considering the possibility of a more serious problem than just the result of the lack of a proper role model. The few risk factors associated with this case (absence of a male parent, lack of educational intervention, and poor parental involvement) may have been, in part, offset by the resiliency factors. In Terry's case, the resilience factors include above-average intelligence, an educated mother, a middle to upper socioeconomic status, no prenatal or perinatal problems, and the absence of substance abuse by the mother.

The many variations of the disorders make identification of the problem by teachers and parents difficult unless a high degree of hyperactivity or inattentiveness is observed. Additionally, the relative newness of the idea that ADHD continues into adulthood indicates that there may be many unidentified adults with ADHD.

INDICATORS OF ADHD IN ADULTS

There are several assessments, or screening devices, available to assist in determining the existence of ADHD in adults (Hallowell & Ratey, 1994; Wender, 1995). Though research support for these criteria is lacking, they are beneficial in a screening capacity and may provide some guidelines for practitioners.

Figure 9–4 shows one diagnostic tool that bears the criteria for determining ADHD in adults. The Utah Criteria, designed by Paul Wender, were published in *Attention-Deficit Hyperactivity Disorder in Adults* (Wender, 1995). These criteria were the first to summarize the disorder in adults and focus more on the major symptoms without discussing the related symptoms.

Wender's Utah Criteria are intentionally broad to include the characteristics of the conduct disordered and the oppositional-defiant disordered because of the frequency of comorbidity of these disorders and ADHD in adulthood (Wender, 1995). While there are some criticisms of the Utah Criteria (lack of field trials, lack of normative data), these criteria give a good description of the disorder as seen in adults with ADHD (Nadeau, 1995).

PATIENT'S INITIALS ________	PATIENT'S NUMBER ____________	DATE ____________	M.D.'s INITIALS _____		
AS A CHILD I WAS (OR HAD)	Not at all or very slightly	Mildly	Moder-ately	Quite a bit	Very much
1. Active, restless, always on the go					
2. Afraid of things					
3. Concentration problems, easily distracted					
4. Anxious, worrying					
5. Nervous fidgety					
6. Inattentive, daydreaming					
7. Hot or short tempered, low boiling point					
8. Shy, sensitive					
9. Temper outbursts, tantrums					
10. Trouble with stick-to-it-tiveness, not following through, failing to finish things started					
11. Stubborn, strong willed					
12. Sad or blue, depressed, unhappy					
13. Uncautious, dare-devilish, involved in pranks					
14. Not getting a kick out of things, dissatisfied with life					
15. Disobedient with parents, rebellious, sassy					
16. Low opinion of myself					
17. Irritable					
18. Outgoing, friendly, enjoy company of people					
19. Sloppy, disorganized					
20. Moody, have ups and downs					
21. Feel angry					
22. Have friends, popular					
23. Well organized, tidy, neat					
24. Acting without thinking, impulsive					

FIGURE 9–4

Wender Utah Rating Scale

Scoring: Not at all or very slightly = 0; mildly = 1; moderately = 2; quite a bit = 3; very much = 4.

AS A CHILD I WAS (OR HAD)	Not at all or very slightly	Mildly	Moder-ately	Quite a bit	Very much
25. Tend to be immature					
26. Feel guilty, regretful					
27. Lose control of myself					
28. Tend to be or act irrational					
29. Unpopular with other children, didn't keep friends for long, didn't get along with other children					
30. Poorly coordinated, did not participate in sports					
31. Afraid of losing control of self					
32. Well coordinated, picked first in games					
33. (for women only) Tomboyish					
34. Ran away from home					
35. Got in fights					
36. Teased other children					
37. Leader, bossy					
38. Difficulty getting awake					
39. Follower, lead around too much					
40. Trouble seeing things from someone else's point of view					
41. Trouble with authorities, trouble with school, visits to principal's office					
42. Trouble with the police, booked, convicted					
Medical Problems as a Child: 43. Headaches					
44. Stomachaches					
45. Constipation					
46. Diarrhea					
47. Food allergies					
48. Other allergies					
49. Bedwetting					

AS A CHILD I WAS (OR HAD)	Not at all or very slightly	Mildly	Moder- ately	Quite a bit	Very much
As a Child in School: 50. Overall a good student, fast					
51. Overall a poor student, low learner					
52. Slow reader					
53. Slow in learning to read					
54. Trouble with mathematics or numbers					
57. Bad handwriting					
58. Though I could read pretty well, I never really enjoyed reading					
59. Did not achieve up to potential					
60. Repeated grades (which grades?)					
61. Suspended or expelled (which grades?)					

FIGURE 9–4, *continued*

These criteria also minimize the problem of confounded diagnoses, with the exclusion of persons suffering from mood disorder, psychosis, or borderline personality disorders (Shaffer, 1994).

Although these screening devices are by no means exhaustive and the symptoms displayed will vary from person to person, it is apparent that experts in the field have observed many similarities in the behaviors exhibited by the adult with ADHD. It is not surprising that these are essentially the same symptoms previously denoted in children and adolescents. ADHD does not disappear with the onset of adulthood but merely acquires a new facsimile in adulthood (Weiss, 1992). Within this framework of characteristics and diagnostic criteria, the remainder of this chapter will be devoted to a discussion of the adult with ADHD in several main facets of life: familial relations, the workplace, and postsecondary education.

FAMILY RELATIONSHIPS OF THE ADULT WITH ADHD

There is an increasing demand for information concerning the effect of ADHD on the family (Nadeau, 1995), yet presently there is very little empirical data. The lack of empirical data has forced clinicians to base their treatment on their own experience. Since the symptoms of ADHD continue into adulthood, the need for empirical data to assist in the treatment of familial relations is clearly evident.

Prior to entering adulthood, the closest relationships of the adult with ADHD have probably been with the members of the immediate family, specifically the parents and siblings. Hence, the family members are usually the first to feel the repercussions of the anxieties that result from the additional stressors associated with adulthood. Later, perhaps, the spouse and others who enter the affected adult's life in mid- and late adulthood will be privy to these difficulties.

It is becoming increasingly clear that the severity of ADHD symptoms significantly affects familial relations (Nadeau, 1995; Jordan, 1992; Weiss & Hechtman, 1993). Several other risk/resilience factors that have been identified in clinical settings to indicate how well a family will function include intellectual ability of the subject, the ability of the subject to deal with stress, the functionality and support of the parents and the spouse, the presence of additional stressors, the number of children the subject has, and whether the subject has been treated for ADHD (Nadeau, 1995).

Parental Relations

When considering the familial relations of the adult with ADHD, it is important to understand the interplay between the family and the child with ADHD (Weiss & Hechtman, 1993; Jordan, 1992). It is evident that the relationship between the child with ADHD and other family members is a good predictor of either positive or negative outcomes in adulthood. A variety of family parameters affects the outcome of the child with ADHD, such as parenting skills, mental health of the family members, parent–child relations, emotional climate of the home, and overall family functioning (Weiss & Hechtman, 1993).

Conversely, studies suggest that the functionality of the home seems to be affected somewhat by the person with ADHD (Jordan, 1992). The impact of a child with ADHD on a family can be extremely disruptive. Having a child with severe ADHD in the home may result in poorer mental health of the family members, anger, frustration, marital strife, feelings of resentment, and a generally higher degree of family dysfunctionality (Nadeau, 1995; Jordan, 1992). For example, parents often become frustrated with the child who has ADHD, and this frustration all too often can lead to abuse of the child (Jordan, 1992). It is clear that the presence of a child with ADHD in the home creates stress and disorder within the family. However, the cumulative effect of the severity of the ADHD and the particular family parameters determine the extent to which the problems associated with the disorder affect the familial relationships.

For adults with ADHD, there is a lack of sufficient empirical data on which to base an effective treatment. Additionally, once the adolescent with ADHD leaves the public school system, collecting data becomes even more difficult. For this reason, much of the information regarding the familial relationships of adults with ADHD is based solely on clinical experiences. There is, however, Weiss and Hechtman's (1993) long-term follow-up study of adults with ADHD, mentioned previously, which categorizes ADHD in adults as either mild, moderate, or severe.

Research indicates that the majority of young adults with mild symptoms of ADHD live either at home or with a friend (Weiss & Hechtman, 1993; Nadeau, 1995). Living situations for these individuals are fairly constant. Moves tend to be less frequent and less impulsive than moves of adults with more severe ADHD (Weiss & Hechtman, 1993). This group tends to function normally within the family infrastructure (Weiss & Hechtman, 1993; Nadeau, 1995).

Subjects in the moderate group continue to experience significant difficulties with parents or other family members (Nadeau, 1995; Weiss & Hechtman, 1993). Impulsivity often leads to rash reactions to disagreement and frequent moves. The familial relationships within this group are less stable and more problematic than in the mild group (Weiss & Hechtman, 1993). Most adults seen in clinical situations fall into the moderate range of symptoms (Nadeau, 1995).

The more severe the symptoms that permeate into adulthood, the more seriously the familial relations are affected (Nadeau, 1995). Those in the severely affected group, who demonstrate more serious psychiatric disturbances or antisocial behaviors, tend to live alone (Weiss & Hechtman, 1993). The inclination of this group is to develop acquaintances with persons who have something the adult with ADHD wants. They tend to sever relationships whenever there is a dispute. This results in frequent and impulsive moves. This group has few or no familial ties. However, a small faction of this group is completely dominated by one or more of the family members with very little outside contact (Weiss & Hechtman, 1993). The presence of other risk factors sometimes noted in adults with severe ADHD (e.g., drug abuse, obsessive/compulsive behaviors, anxiety, learning disabilities, poor socioeconomic status, dispositional attributes) may also affect familial relations (Weiss & Hechtman, 1993).

Parents' Views of Adult Offspring with ADHD

Parents of adults with ADHD report that they recognize both the positive and the negative changes in the various aspects of their offspring's life. These parents generally do not have a negative outlook regarding their child's future (Weiss & Hechtman, 1993). While the parents of adults with ADHD see their children as having more problems than non-ADHD individuals, they generally do not feel doubtful about their child's ability to function successfully in society (Weiss & Hechtman, 1993).

Furthermore, there is some indication that parents of adults with ADHD feel optimistic about their offspring's future (Weiss & Hechtman, 1993). The parents of adults with ADHD believed that the plans being made by their adult sons and daughters were realistic (Weiss & Hechtman, 1993). Parents of adults with ADHD do not see their children as having more psychiatric problems than the normal population (Weiss & Hechtman, 1993).

Sibling Relations

The information available from the current literature concerning the relationships between the adult with ADHD and his or her siblings is meager at best. However, based on collective clinical experience, there are a few areas of concern in relation to sibling difficulties and the adult with ADHD (Weiss, 1992). Clinicians have frequently reported that the siblings of a person with ADHD maintain that their brother or sister is a nuisance (Weiss, 1992). They do not understand the continual upheaval this individual causes and feel that too much of their parents' time is spent with the ADHD sibling. Non-ADHD siblings also report that the individual with ADHD will occasionally pick a fight for absolutely no reason (Weiss, 1992). This may be due to hypersensitivity or poor communication skills of the individual with ADHD. Subjects with ADHD will often pursue a particular course of action heedless of the consequences (Weiss, 1992). For example, if a discussion becomes a heated argument and threatens to flare into a fight but is terminated before a punch can be thrown, the individual with ADHD may be so set on fighting that he or she thinks of little else and may strike out even hours or days later.

It must be assumed that problems exist between adults with ADHD and their siblings, as they do in many other aspects in the life of the ADHD adult. Figure 9–5 lists a few suggestions made by Weiss (1992) for when diagnoses do not take place until the individual with ADHD has entered adulthood.

Since the emotionality of the home and of the individual affect the adult outcome for the person with ADHD, it is apparent that there is a need for positive sibling relations. Thus, further study into the relationships of the person with ADHD and his or her siblings is undoubtedly needed.

The Adult with ADHD as a Spouse

Developing and fostering a healthy intimate relationship requires much hard work and dedication even without the confounding effects of ADHD. The pres-

- Each sibling may want to share his or her feelings, even grieve together, because both may feel as if they lost a "normal" sibling relationship to ADHD.
- Each sibling can share what he or she likes about the other's skills (e.g., what is admired, what is respected).
- Both can agree on cues to be used when either sibling is becoming frustrated or angry.
- Siblings should realize that ADHD will continue to be a factor in the relationship and that it may still be difficult for them to work together.
- Reconciliation over the ADHD can bring about understanding and empathy.

FIGURE 9–5
Suggestions for ADHD Adults and Their Siblings

ence of ADHD in an intimate relationship is an obstacle with which both persons must learn to cope effectively if the relationship is to be a healthy and happy one. It is important that both of the partners understand the disorder, its manifestations, and elements that either work well or exacerbate the condition.

Codependency

Far too often the intimate partnership between an individual with ADHD and a non-ADHD individual results in failure. People who suffer with ADHD are often attracted to non-ADHD people because of needing help with the problems and chaos that may come with the disorder (Nadeau, 1995). However, it is quite easy for a codependent relationship to develop under these circumstances. Each partner begins to concern himself or herself with the needs and wants of the other instead of assuming responsibility for himself or herself. The non-ADHD partner may begin to assume all the responsibility for the problems and make the necessary corrections. The partner with ADHD may begin to blame everyone and everything for his or her problems (Weiss, 1992; Nadeau, 1995). The codependent relationship is extremely unhealthy because it forces the couple to remain together not out of love for one another but because of the feelings of inadequacy that bind them (Weiss, 1992; Nadeau, 1995). Additionally, a codependent relationship discourages the learning and use of strategies to help manage the disorder (Nadeau, 1995).

Hallowell (1993) states that the tendency of couples to divide tasks to fit the strengths and weaknesses of each person sets the stage for the development of a codependent relationship that nurtures the negative aspects of the disorder. Therapy helps the couple to recognize a codependent relationship. It can also help with the setting of clearer, more concise boundaries for the couple, thus warding off the development of a codependent relationship (Hallowell, 1993).

Intimacy

Often, intimacy is difficult for the ADHD adult (Weiss, 1992). This is true for several reasons. The adult with ADHD is overly sensitive not only emotionally but physically as well. Physical stimulation can sometimes be painful for the person with ADHD (Weiss, 1992). Touching, stroking, even putting an arm around the shoulder can become physically painful to the person with ADHD. In addition to the hypersensitivity, the person with ADHD seems to know only two speeds: full speed ahead and stop. After a full day at work or school, the individual is often physically, mentally, and emotionally exhausted. He or she will often fall asleep, almost immediately, leaving little opportunity for intimacy. This can lead to feelings of resentment, anger, and inadequacy in the non-ADHD partner (Weiss, 1992).

Sex with an ADHD adult may also involve frustration and dissatisfaction (Weiss, 1992; Hallowell & Ratey, 1994). The combination of hypersensitivity to touch, inability to focus sufficiently to receive pleasure from the sexual act itself, and "feast or famine" energy levels makes sex with an ADHD adult quite challenging. Alternately, sexual stimulation sometimes enables the person with ADHD to actually become focused; so the partner with ADHD can derive benefits from the sexual experience as well as from the feeling of being focused (Hallowell & Ratey, 1994; Weiss, 1992). The adult with ADHD may even become obsessed with sex and frequently seek it out because it enables him or her to focus (Weiss, 1992).

During intimate moments, both of the parties involved must be understanding and make every effort to verbally communicate their wants and needs (Weiss, 1992). While it is fine to be concerned with satisfying the needs of your partner, it is also important that the needs of both partners are met. If the couple is unable to develop a mutually beneficial intimate relationship, they may want to consider counseling (Weiss, 1992).

The presence of ADHD can cause tremendous difficulties in relationships with members of the opposite sex, just as it can within the family infrastructure. It is important that both partners maintain an open mind and open lines of communication and find workable solutions to problems. The relationship can benefit when both partners educate themselves regarding the disorder and its manifestations in adulthood and when both stay abreast of current findings and treatments. Nadeau (1995) contends that the adult with ADHD may need to be confronted with the defenses and maladaptive coping strategies employed as survival mechanisms but that are harmful to the relationship. She further maintains that a combination of strategies and treatments may help reduce blame and guilt, thereby encouraging a more positive relationship. If problems persist to a detrimental level, it would be wise to seek outside assistance.

Both Partners with ADHD

If both partners in an intimate relationship have ADHD, the difficulties are multiplied and intensified. In this instance, the disorder may lead to mutual blaming because of the increased disorganization and confusion (Nadeau, 1995). Furthermore, it is highly possible that neither spouse will be able to attend to the responsibilities of running a household. This combination will certainly increase the risk of dysfunctionality in the family. Alternately, neither is likely to have high expectations of the other, and both are likely to be more tolerant of the other's difficulties (Nadeau, 1995).

Other Factors Affecting Spousal Relations

Interpersonal problems may also plague the relationship (Weiss, 1992). With the abrasive personality sometimes found in people with ADHD, a playful gesture can result in an out-and-out fight. The adult with ADHD may also become obsessed with blaming other people or things for his or her inappropriate behaviors. The person with ADHD often places blame on those with whom he or she resides.

The lack of organizational skills and the distractibility combine to hinder the ability of the adult with ADHD to complete home projects. As mentioned earlier, the adult with ADHD is frequently exhausted when he or she arrives home from work or school. He or she has used all available energy to "hold it together" so far during the day. Adults with ADHD have nothing left for those at home (Weiss, 1992). This leaves practically all the responsibilities of organizing and managing the household in the hands of the non-ADHD spouse. He or she will soon begin to feel that the spouse with ADHD is taking advantage. It is obvious that resentment and anger can build when the one spouse feels unloved, unappreciated, and used.

The combined effect of the elements of an ADHD adult's behavior creates a tremendous amount of strain on the relationship; these elements include poor financial management, obsessive/compulsive behaviors, addictive disorders, risk-taking behaviors, explosive temper, lack of effective communication skills, disorganization, imbalance in responsibilities, impulsivity, immaturity, sexual difficulties, irresponsibility, and low self-esteem. This is especially true when the person with ADHD has received no treatment for the disorder. Ignorance of the disorder can lead to feelings of hurt and resentment and marital discord because the person without ADHD frequently views the adult with ADHD as being able to control these problems (Nadeau, 1995). Figure 9–6 lists selected concerns frequently held by partners of adults with ADHD (Myers, 1993).

- Determining which problems are a result of ADHD and which are problems found in normal relationships
- Being made to feel at fault themselves as a result of a long-standing relationship with an individual with ADHD
- Harboring feelings of anger
- Realizing the intent of the partner with ADHD instead of the behavior exhibited
- Knowing how to encourage the person with ADHD to accept help
- Handling the denial often associated with the illness (frequently seen in both the person with ADHD and the partner)

FIGURE 9–6
Concerns of Partners of ADHD Adults

Parenting Skills

When a parent is afflicted with ADHD, the family dynamics are strongly affected. The presence of ADHD in a parent makes it difficult for a strong, healthy, cohesive bond to develop between the parent and the children (Nadeau, 1995). The main concern regarding the parent with ADHD is not the day-to-day requirements of heading a household but the inability of the parent to apply child management principles with the necessary consistency to foster a healthy, stable environment (Nadeau, 1995). Such activities as establishing and enforcing limits for the children, disciplining the children, and meeting the emotional needs of the children (as well as of the spouse) are frequently problematic for parents with ADHD (Nadeau, 1995). Particular risk factors that may affect the ability of the parent to successfully do his or her part in child-rearing are the number of children in the household, the degree to which the parent suffers from ADHD, and whether any of the children have ADHD (Barkley, 1990; Nadeau, 1995). When conflicts arise between the parent with ADHD and the children, it is important for the parent to recognize when he or she is approaching his or her "danger zone" to avoid losing control (Nadeau, 1995). Kelly and Ramundo (1993) stress the need for quiet areas in the house with established boundaries, respected by all to guarantee that at least a certain portion of the day is free from conflict. Most experts in the field of ADHD stress that the parent with ADHD should seek the assistance of a clinician or another outside source for help in parenting skills if needed (Nadeau, 1995; Kelly & Ramundo, 1993).

ADHD in a Parent and a Child

When both a parent and a child suffer from ADHD, the problems of parenting are compounded considerably. As one might speculate, the parent and the child "butt heads" on numerous occasions. The environment of the household often approaches one of anarchy (Nadeau, 1995), and there is a sort of "feeding frenzy" where the parent and the child feed off of each other's problems. The difficulties and confrontations that arise between these individuals seem to be endless. Feelings of frustration and anger can, and often do, potentiate abuse, either verbal or physical (Nadeau, 1995). It is important that the parent and the child spend some quiet time away from each other. They may also require the assistance or support of the other spouse during conflicts or stressful times.

It is all too obvious that the parent with ADHD is subject to more stress and difficulties associated with the raising of children than is a parent without ADHD (Nadeau, 1995). While there is little empirical evidence to verify this statement, it would seem that having a parent with ADHD would definitely be considered a risk factor and increase the likelihood of a negative outcome for a child with ADHD. There is no question that further research is needed in the area of ADHD parenting and when both a parent and a child have ADHD; effective treatment plans need to be developed, and more accurate predictions regarding outcomes need to be made.

THE ADULT WITH ADHD IN THE WORKPLACE

The Modern Working World

Securing a job is becoming increasingly more difficult, especially for the adult with ADHD, for several reasons. First, the increased use of automation and mechanization within the workplace has meant the elimination of many jobs previously suited to the adult with ADHD, such as gas station attendant, short-order cook, and cargo loader (Jordan, 1992). Today's workplace requires higher-level skills, more education, and the ability to perform well under stress (Jordan, 1992). For example, an automotive technician must be adept at conducting and evaluating computerized diagnostic analyses on automobiles (Jordan, 1992).

Given these job requirements, the adult with ADHD may find that the skills required to perform successfully in the workplace are in direct conflict with the deficits associated with ADHD (Barkley, 1990). Since the specific symptoms associated with ADHD and their severity vary from person to person, the effects of ADHD on a particular individual's ability to function on the job will also vary from person to person (Nadeau, 1995). Weiss and Hechtman (1993), in their 15-year follow-up study, report that subjects with mild ADHD symptoms have fairly consistent work records, which indicates the potential for career advancement within their particular field or company. Many of these subjects' training was of a technical or mechanical nature rather than a formal higher education. Some were even attending school on a part-time basis while maintaining a full-time job.

Subjects who fall into the moderate ADHD group are generally employed, but their work history is less stable (Weiss & Hechtman, 1993). Job changes occur more frequently and are more often the result of interpersonal problems. This group tends to hold more jobs involving manual labor where there are few opportunities for career advancement. Subjects in this group seem to be unable to develop a plan for improving their career situation. Adults with severe ADHD are often chronically unemployed or have inconsistent unemployment (Weiss & Hechtman, 1993). These subjects may drift aimlessly from one job to the next.

The experience of clinicians regarding adults with ADHD may not be reflective of all adults with ADHD (Nadeau, 1995). The lack of recent empirical data regarding adults in the workplace is one reason clinicians may not have a complete picture of the adult with ADHD in the workplace. Additionally, the fact that most ADHD adults who seek assistance from a clinician are generally a higher-functioning and more educated group may also give clinicians a skewed notion of how the adult with ADHD performs in the workplace (Nadeau, 1995). It seems that the adults who exhibit less hyperactivity or less impulsivity seek out career counseling (Nadeau, 1995). Many who seek career counseling have recently been promoted to a managerial or administrative position, and some realize that they lack organizational and/or managerial skills (Nadeau, 1995).

Characteristics of the Adult with ADHD in the Workplace

Based on reports from employers and clinicians, adults with ADHD often exhibit numerous characteristics associated with the disability that may negatively affect job performance (Nadeau, 1995; Hartmann, 1993; Jordan, 1992). These include inattentiveness in staff meetings, impulsive decision making, and poor communication with peers (Barkley, 1990; Jordan, 1992; Nadeau, 1995; Hartmann, 1993). Other difficulties encountered by the adult with ADHD in the workplace are listed in Figure 9–7.

Additionally, employers report that the emotional immaturity of some adults with ADHD renders them incapable of handling job stress (Jordan, 1992). The adult with ADHD may need help but is often unwilling to accept assistance and is frequently self-centered (Jordan, 1992). Adults with ADHD are more likely than adults without ADHD to quit jobs, hold part-time jobs in conjunction with their full-time jobs, and lack interviewing skills (Barkley, 1990). The adult with ADHD tends to have a lower socioeconomic status

- Poor organizational and planning skills
- Lack of self-control
- Inadequacy in fulfilling job demands
- Poor communication skills
- Difficulty following through on paperwork
- Impulsive decision making
- Fluctuations in motivation
- Poor peer/supervisor relations
- Easily bored with mundane tasks
- Elevated activity level
- Attention difficulties
- Procrastination
- Frequently late to work
- Poor task completion
- Missed appointments
- Self-centeredness
- Missed deadlines

FIGURE 9–7
Characteristics Commonly Found in ADHD Adults That May Impede Job Performance

than his or her peers or siblings (Barkley, 1990). Nadeau (1995) contends that the adult with ADHD may be a chronic underachiever with the talent and cognitive capacity to handle a job that is more intellectually demanding.

Many researchers and clinicians believe that the reason the adult with ADHD does poorly in the workplace is because there is a poor match between the skills of the individual and the skills required to do the job (Nadeau, 1995). Some of these adults, with the help of luck or intuition or the assistance of others, find their way into jobs well suited to their abilities (Nadeau, 1995).

Positive Traits Associated with ADHD in Adulthood

On a more positive note, certain characteristics of ADHD can be beneficial to the adult in the workplace. Because of the variable nature of the disorder, the adult with ADHD may display one or more of these characteristics or none of these traits (Nadeau, 1995; Hartmann, 1993). Some of the characteristics often considered positive or beneficial to the adult with ADHD in the workplace are listed in Figure 9–8.

- Boundless energy
- Creativity
- Immediate problem-solving skills
- Crisis intervention skills
- Great business ideas
- Creative consultant abilities
- Leadership ability
- Decisiveness

FIGURE 9–8
Traits Potentially Beneficial for Adults with ADHD in the Workplace

There is some indication in the available literature that adults with ADHD are more successful in certain jobs than in others (Nadeau, 1995; Hartmann, 1993). For example, Hartmann (1993) suggests that adults with ADHD often make successful entrepreneurs because of their creativity, boundless energy, and ability to become intensely focused on one idea.

Some researchers recommend a "mentor–mentee" program to tap this creative potential and to assist the adult with ADHD with work adjustment or other difficulties that might arise (Nadeau, 1995). Since the adult with ADHD is weak in the areas of organization and finances, an adult without ADHD should be given these tasks in the relationship (Hartmann, 1993). Often a husband and wife, in which one spouse has ADHD, team up quite successfully in the business world (Hartmann, 1993). As you recall from the earlier case study, Terry's success in car racing resulted from teaming with a mechanically inclined person.

Help for the ADHD Adult in the Workplace

While most experts would readily agree that ADHD can significantly hinder job performance, most would also agree that there are many strategies available to assist the adult with ADHD in the workplace (Nadeau, 1995; Murphy, 1992; Hartmann, 1993; Barkley, 1990; Hallowell & Ratey, 1994; Jordan, 1992). Some suggestions for compensating for ADHD in the workplace are listed in Figure 9–9. Although this list is quite lengthy, it is by no means exhaustive. It is crucial that the strategies chosen best meet the individual needs of the adult with ADHD (Murphy, 1992; Hallowell, 1992). The strategies must be employed systematically until they become routine (Murphy, 1992).

As mentioned earlier in this chapter, education is paramount to understanding and coping with ADHD. Furthermore, family members, spouses, bosses, and friends should educate themselves as well (Murphy, 1992). Education helps all who are closely involved with the individual to make sense of the difficulties associated with ADHD; it also helps with realistic goal setting and behavioral management strategies (Murphy, 1992). The individual with ADHD should also explore various behavior and management strategies to help ameliorate deficit areas (Murphy, 1992).

The range of difficulties experienced by the adult with ADHD in the workplace is wide (Nadeau, 1995; Murphy, 1992; Weiss & Hechtman, 1993). As in the area of familial relations, it is evident that further research in this area is sorely needed (Nadeau, 1995). The lack of empirical data regarding the effect of ADHD on the adult at work and the effectiveness of particular treatments and strategies leaves clinicians and career counselors to speculate how to best assist the adult with ADHD in the workplace.

- **Utilize a master planner calendar.** This is your lifeline. Keep it with you at all times. There are several different types available. Shop around; find the one that best suits your needs and job requirements. Be sure to have a month-to-month calendar (at the very least) in the master planner. A day-to-day calendar is preferable if your day is extremely busy. Some are available with a twelve-hour day broken down hour by hour. Put both personal and business obligations in the master planner to avoid scheduling conflicts. Check with your master planner throughout the day at set times (e.g., as soon as you get up, during lunch break, before leaving work); this helps to break the day into smaller, more workable time periods. Add sections that aid in your organization. For instance, sections entitled "Projects" or "Memos" or an address section may be beneficial. A master planner with three binding rings is more easily utilized than are other types.
- **Break big jobs into small ones.** Breaking a large job into several small ones helps to alleviate anxiety associated with monumental tasks. This also helps to prevent procrastination.
- **Organize your time around these jobs.** Take frequent breaks. Individuals with ADHD give short bursts of high-quality energy.
- **Reward yourself for accomplishing each goal.** Buy yourself something or treat yourself to something special for each goal accomplished.
- **Get organized.** The external environment is an important element in achieving success. Be sure that you have a distraction-free area in which to work. Keep an ample supply of materials on hand so that you can work without having to stop and secure materials. Be sure that you have sufficient drawer space, file cabinets, and closet space to organize your workspace. Use color coding as an organizational tool.

FIGURE 9–9
Suggestions for the Adult with ADHD in the Workplace

THE ADULT WITH ADHD IN A POSTSECONDARY SETTING

Because of the widespread attention recently given to ADHD, and as a result of the memo of clarification from the U.S. Department of Education—Office of Special Education regarding Section 504 of the Rehabilitation Act of 1973 (Davila, Williams, & MacDonald, 1991), postsecondary institutions are required to offer academic assistance to students with ADHD (Richard, 1995). While colleges may make modifications so as not to discriminate against students with ADHD based on their disability, they will typically not modify required courses and academic requirements (Richard, 1995).

First-year postsecondary students who were previously enrolled in a public school system are used to having school personnel who were responsible for meeting their special needs. However, in the postsecondary setting

- **Set your own deadlines.** Setting deadlines for yourself ahead of the actual deadline will also help combat procrastination. Put "your" deadline as well as the actual deadline in the master planner calendar.
- **Practice paying attention.** Your family, friends, and co-workers can help you with this. Teach them the things to do or say that help remind you to tune in to what they are saying.
- **Know what you do well and stick to it.** Find the job that matches you and your unique strengths and interests.
- **Consider enrolling in a time management course.** These are often available through colleges, community schools, and sometimes businesses.
- **Consider stress management training.** Alleviating the effects of stress may help to improve performance.
- **Seek outside assistance.** The resources available through a career counselor, medical professional, therapist, or job coach may be beneficial to you in such areas as resolving the problems at work and finding a more suitable career.
- **Utilize behavior modification techniques.** One of the more recently heralded techniques, metacognition (self-monitoring), is discussed in depth in Chapter 8. Additionally, hundreds of books and journal articles are available on behavior modification techniques.
- **Train your attention span.** Hartmann (1993) maintains that there is a type of meditation that helps bring back the wandering mind. Metacognition strategies will help with training a person to attend longer to a task.

it is the responsibility of the student to self-identify and self-advocate (Richard, 1995). Usually, counselors or support personnel at the college or university will assist the student in developing strategies for self-advocacy rather than doing the actual advocating (Richard, 1995).

As mentioned at the beginning of the chapter, the transitions associated with adulthood are quite stressful, and the decision to attend college or to pursue postsecondary training or education may also be stressful. Many first-year students with ADHD are not equipped to suddenly handle such a tremendous amount of responsibility. Frequently, postsecondary students with ADHD do not have a good understanding of their disability and of the rigorous requirements associated with postsecondary education (Richard, 1995).

ADHD can cause a variety of difficulties for the young adult in the postsecondary situation. Some problems that have been observed are listed in Figure 9–10 (Richard, 1995).

• Distractibility	• Disorganization	• Forgetfulness
• Boredom	• Procrastination	• Restlessness
• Test anxiety	• Low self-esteem	• Depression
• Mood swings	• Chronic tardiness	• Absenteeism
• Substance abuse	• Academic failures	• Relationship problems

FIGURE 9–10
Common Symptoms of Students with ADHD in the Postsecondary Setting

Margaret Stolowitz (1995), who attended college as a nontraditional student, was not diagnosed as having a learning disability and ADHD until well into her adult life. She divulges some of the difficulties she has faced in postsecondary education and gives some suggestions for students with ADHD (Figure 9–11) (Stolowitz, 1995).

The student with ADHD can take various steps to help ensure success in the postsecondary setting. First, students should give careful consideration to their choice of a postsecondary institution. They should consider only those institutions that provide specialized services for students with learning problems such as ADHD (Richard, 1995). Figure 9–12 includes a list of services typically offered (Richard, 1995).

While empirical data concerning the postsecondary student with ADHD is lacking, Richard's (1995) work as an educator has enabled her to

- Be honest and realistic about your goals.
- Discover your learning style.
- Allow for your differences and find the good aspects associated with them.
- Never believe that one person has all of the answers.
- Do not permit someone else to decide what you need.
- Use the services available. Seek assistance from many sources: teachers (high school or postsecondary), friends, others with ADHD, doctors, or counselors.
- Never stay in a class where you are made to feel stupid.
- Buy only second-hand textbooks of "A" students. They are great highlighters.
- Do not use ADHD as a crutch.
- Find someone who loves you and will support whatever you do.
- Let go of old hurts and emotional scars. They only get in the way.

FIGURE 9–11
Suggestions for Students with ADHD in the Postsecondary Setting

- Support service
- Suitable programs of study
- A variety of modifications (such as alternative testing environments, note-taking services, taped texts, etc.)
- Assistance in finding other support personnel, such as psychologists, counselors, and support groups

FIGURE 9–12
Services Typically Offered to Students with Special Needs

realize how imperative it is that the student with ADHD receive adequate support and become his or her own best advocate. Effective interventions will only serve to improve the chance of achieving academic success (Richard, 1995).

CONCLUSION

Based on the evidence presented in this chapter, we conclude that ADHD is not an ephemeral disorder but rather a condition that persists past adolescence and well into adulthood. Although some of the symptoms may abate with physical maturation, most will continue to manifest themselves to a sufficient degree as to cause frustration and problems in one aspect or more of the adult's life.

Research concerning the effects of ADHD on the adult, and even on the prevalence of the disorder, is lacking. Physicians, parents, teachers, employers, spouses, clinicians, and sufferers of ADHD need current and reliable information regarding ADHD. Without empirical research on which to base diagnoses, treatments, and strategies, clinicians and practitioners must speculate about what works best in the battle against ADHD.

REFERENCES

Barkley, R. A. (1990). *Attention deficit hyperactivity disorder.* New York: Guilford Press.

Davila, R. R., Williams, M. L., & MacDonald, J. T. (1991). Memorandum to chief state school officers re: Clarification of policy to address the needs of children with attention deficit disorders with general and/or special education. Washington, DC: U.S. Department of Education.

DuPaul, G. J., & Stoner, G. (1994). *ADHD in the schools: Assessment and intervention strategies.* New York: Guilford Press.

Garmezy, N. (Ed.). (1983). *Stressors of childhood.* Minneapolis: McGraw-Hill.
Garmezy, N. (1991). Resiliency and vulnerability to adverse developmental outcomes associated with poverty. *American Behavioral Scientist, 34,* 416–430.
Garmezy, N., & Masten, A. S. (1986). Stress, competence, and resilience: Common frontiers for therapist and psychopathologist. *Behavior Therapy, 17,* 500–521.
Garmezy, N., Masten, A. S., & Tellegen, A. (1984). The study of stress and competence in children: A building block for developmental psychopathy. *Child Development, 55,* 97–111.
Hale, D., & Hale, R. (1993). Pay attention: Hyperactivity isn't just for children anymore. *American Health,* 62–65.
Hallowell, E. M. (1992). The emotional experience of attention deficit disorder [Special issue]. *CH.A.D.D.ER,* 9–12.
Hallowell, E. M. (1993). Living and loving with attention deficit disorder: Couples where one partner has ADD. *CH.A.D.D.ER, 7,* 13–15.
Hallowell, E. M., & Ratey, J. (1993). 50 tips on the management of adult attention deficit disorder. *CH.A.D.D.ER Box, 6,* 5–8.
Hallowell, E. M., & Ratey, J. (1994). *Driven to distraction: Recognizing and coping with ADHD.* New York: Random House.
Hartmann, T. (1993). *Attention deficit disorder: A different perception.* Lancaster: Underwood-Miller.
Jordan, D. (1992). *Attention deficit disorder.* Austin: Pro-Ed.
Kelly, K., & Ramundo, P. (1993). *You mean I'm not lazy, stupid or crazy?!* Cincinnati: Tyrell & Jerem Press.
Maag, J., Irvin, D., Reid, R., & Vasa, S. (1994). Revalence and predictors of substance use: A comparison between adolescents with and without learning disabilities. *Journal of Learning Disabilities, 27,* 223–234.
Myers, R. (1993). Spouses' premier meeting review. *ADD-Vantage, 2,* 6.
Murphy, K. R. (1992). Coping strategies for ADHD adults. *CH.A.D.D.ER, 6,* 10.
Nadeau, K. G. (1995). *A comprehensive guide to attention deficit disorder in adults.* New York: Brunner/Mazel Publishers.
Ramey, C., Trohanis, P. L., & Hostler, C. (1982). An introduction. In C. Ramey & P. L. Trohanis (Eds.), *Risk in infancy and early childhood.* Baltimore: University Press Park.
Richard, M. M. (1995). Students with attention deficit disorders in postsecondary education: Issues in identification and accommodation. In K. G. Nadeau, *A comprehensive guide to attention deficit disorder in adults* (pp. 284–307). New York: Brunner/Mazel Publishers.
Shaffer, D. (1994). Attention deficit hyperactivity disorder in adults. *American Journal of Psychology, 151,* 633–638.
Shakim, W. (1992). Adult attention deficit hyperactivity disorder, residual state (ADHD,RS) [Special issue]. *CH.A.D.D.ER, 7.*

Stolowitz, M. (1995). How to achieve academic and creative success in spite of the inflexible, unresponsive, higher education system. *Journal of Learning Disabilities, 28,* 4–6.

Weiss, G., & Hechtman, L. T. (1986). *Hyperactive children grown up.* New York: Guilford Press.

Weiss, G., & Hechtman, L. T. (1993). *Hyperactive children grown up* (2nd ed.). New York: Guilford Press.

Weiss, G., Hechtman, L. T., & Perlman, T. (1978). Hyperactives as young adults: School, employer, and self-rating scales obtained during ten-year follow-up evaluation. *American Journal of Orthopsychiatry, 48,* 438–445.

Weiss, L. (1992). *Attention deficit disorder in adults: Practical help for sufferers and their spouses.* Dallas: Taylor.

Wender, Paul H. (1987). *The hyperactive child, adolescent and adult: Attention-deficit disorder through the life span.* New York: Oxford University Press.

Wender, Paul H. (1995). *Attention-deficit hyperactivity disorder in adults.* New York: Oxford University Press.

Index